Aunt Hattie's Cookbook

Southern Comfort Food Favorites

Dr. Hattie N. Washington

Wonderful Reviews About Aunt Hattie's Southern Comfort Cookbook...

"Simple recipes that are easy to prepare and are full of flavor. Each recipe tells a very unique story in its own way. I have prepared 20 of the recipes in this book and 100% endorse the products to be tasteful and user friendly for the simplest cooks. Homestyle cooking with a twist: Simple foods, easy preparation, great stories."

-Chef Charles Warner, Jr.
Executive Chef, Blues on The Water
Co-Chef, La Fontaine Bleue Caterers

"Great comfort food that will become staples in your home. A must have cookbook for all skill levels."

- Daniel Quick, Culinary Institute of America '01

"This is an awesome cookbook. Total cookbook: Great pictures, great food, food that's detailed in recipes. Food that you want to make for your family. Great gift for your family also."

- Chris Loucks, CSC, Sales for Feesers Food Distributor

"Hattie's Red Beans recipe was the best I have ever tasted! I had to ask her what did she put in those red beans to make them sooooo delicious. She shared with me what she put in them and I tried to duplicate cooking them the way she did. But, they just did not have that something loving from the oven that she put in them. The cookbook will help me follow the instructions to the tee, and I look forward to eating them again and her many other delectable dishes from her cookbook."

- Melody Jackson, M.D.

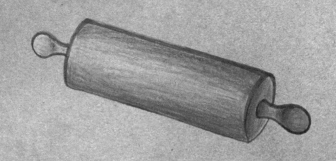

Aunt Hattie's Cookbook

Southern Comfort Food Favorites

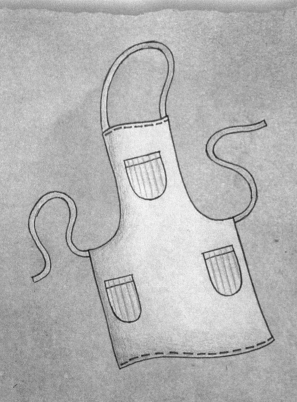

COOKLOOK
PUBLISHING

Aunt Hattie's Cookbook
Southern Comfort Food Favorites
Dr. Hattie N. Washington

COOKLOOK PUBLISHING
Hanover, Maryland

Aunt Hattie can conduct cooking demonstrations at your live event. To book an event or for more information about special discounts for bulk purchases, contact her at info@drhnwashington.com or visit her website www.cooklookpub.com or www.drhnwashington.com.

Cover and Book Interior Designed by Bruce Smallwood | Mt. Vernon Marketing
Illustrations by Cecilia "CiCi" Brooks

Library Of Congress Number: 2019907688

Library Of Congress Cataloging-in-Publication Data: Washington, Dr. Hattie N.
Aunt Hattie's Cookbook: Southern Comfort Food Favorites/Dr. Hattie Washington
p. cm

Paperback: ISBN: 13: 978-1-950707-00-3
Hardcover: ISBN: 13: 978-1-950707-01-0
E-Book: ISBN: 13: 978-1-950707-02-7

Printed in the United States of America
10 9 8 7 6 5 4 3 2 1

Publisher's Note

Dedication

Dedicated to my late stepmother, Hilda Lee Neal, who lovingly taught me many of the recipes in this cookbook. Until the age of 11, I lived in the country, thus we used many fresh ingredients directly from her garden, orchard, barnyard and pasture.

I also dedicate this cookbook to my two precious granddaughters, Cameron and Reagan. It is my hope that these recipes will serve as a resource as they carry on the tradition of cooking these southern dishes and further continue the legacy as they pass them on to generations to come.

Recipe For A Happy Life

A Pinch of Prayer for a Purpose;
A Dash of Dedication To A Cause;
A Handful of Hugs For The Heart;
A Spoonful of Smiles For The Soul;
And A Forkful of Faith For God's Favor.

Marinade them all together with Patience and Persistence;
Bake Until Golden; and
Served With TLC--Tender Loving Care.

-By Aunt Hattie (Dr. Hattie N. Washington)

Credits

Bruce Smallwood, Photography | Graphic Design

Charles Warner, Jr., Professional Chef | Kitchen Tester

Cecilia "CiCi" Brooks, Illustrations

Diane Pruitt, Research | Additional Graphics

CookLook Publishing/An Imprint of Washington Publishing Enterprises

Acknowledgements

Kellie Johnson, Typist
Julie Haskins-Turner, Proofer

Sean Thomas, Charrell W. Thomas, M.D., Reagan Thomas, Cameron Thomas, Vivian Mallory,
Cheryl Y. Washington, Esq., Marilyn Massey-Ball, Brenita Young, Courtney Wiggins-Lloyd,
Rebecca Lee Randolph, Patricia Lee Adams, Shaunda Eppes, June W. Lee, Lottie Miller,
Peggy Morris, Monica Chestnut, Jackie Turner, Debbie Ambush, Tony Ambush,
Ruby Burrell, Clifford Burrell, Sharon McCullough, Rev. Samuel Williams Jr.,
Wayne Saunders, Beverly Thomas, Rev. Steve Thomas, Barbara Munden,
Bettie Goganious, Lorenzo Goganious, Jackie G. Owens,
Audrey Meredith, Estelle McCormick, Joyce Madison,
Leona Davis, Joy Cabarrus Speakes, Phyllis Lee,
Betty Baldwin

Table of Contents

Introduction

This cookbook is a companion book to my first book: an award-winning memoir, **"Driven To Succeed: An Inspirational Memoir of Lessons Learned Through Faith, Family and Favor"**, that mentioned many of the down-home dishes from my early childhood living in the country my stepmother and other relatives cooked fresh from the gardens, orchards, barnyard and pasture. Many readers of my memoir remarked how hungry they had gotten after reading about the homemade dishes I mentioned when I lived in Meherrin, Virginia. They essentially pleaded that I simply MUST write a cookbook soon to share some of those southern-comfort food recipes with my readers and others.

My stepmother and two aunts, Aunt Hattie and Aunt Sadie, had given me a wonderful lifelong gift: the ability to cook. I loved my stepmother's delicious old-fashioned Christmas fruitcake, and my Aunt Hattie's big pots of tasty kidney beans and hot flapjacks. Aunt Sadie owned three restaurants that stayed packed with people all day from early mornings. She sold her delicious complete breakfasts, from scrapple or Smithfield® Ham or Bacon and cheese eggs and hash brown potatoes with onion to hot buttermilk pancakes. For lunch people came from miles around for Aunt Sadie's mouth-watering chilidogs, juicy hamburgers and cheeseburgers, homemade barbecue sandwiches with homemade coleslaw and hot sauce, and hand-cut French fries. Her dinners were just as popular. She sold southern fried chicken, pork chops, pigs' feet, homemade barbecue ribs, fried crabs, spicy steamed crabs, and slices of Aunt Sadie's homemade apple, cherry and coconut custard pies.

The two restaurants were called, Sadie's & Buddie's. The atmosphere was filled with hunger inducing aromas and popular music to eat and sway to. The jukebox in the corner had the old hits and popular songs of the 50's and 60's—Sam Cook, Fats Domino, The Platters, The Drifters, Jackie Wilson, James Brown, Nate King Cole, and others. There was also room for couples to dance some of the popular dances at that time like the Stroll, the Twist, and slow dancing with that special someone, especially on Friday and Saturday nights. Not only did the restaurants provide good clean fun, but they were also places where people loved to get together and eat my aunt's delicious food. The customers' hardest problem was deciding which of the dishes they would select to eat. Some of the customers were such regulars that they thought their name was on a certain seat.

Faith and prayer are the vitamins of the soul;
Man cannot live in health without them.
—Mahalia Jackson

Her restaurants had a friendly tone as everyone seemed to be in a great mood. I liked meeting new people and I loved serving folks meals that I had learned to cook. In lieu of money, my pay was seeing the happy expressions on their faces as they bit into the various tasty dishes.

Many of my recipes have been perfected to replicate those renowned comfort food recipes and that have remained in the family and are revived every chance we take advantage to get together. There is always some great food, good music, and close friends whenever we get together, regardless to where we may be in various parts of the country. I am pleased to bring these great recipes to you so that you can experience that ecstasy of all three sensations together (fantastic food, melodious music and faithful family and friends) and make them available in this cookbook to share with lovers of good old-fashioned comfort dishes.

Throughout my expansive fifty-year professional career as an educator and administrator, I will never forget my humble beginnings as a country girl living in the South, who, to this day, still loves to cook. I've included in this wonderful cookbook such delicious recipes, such as my fried apples, homemade hot buttermilk biscuits dripping with butter, collard greens, kale, cabbages, butter beans, cracklin' buttermilk cornbread, fried golden brown chicken, beef stew, scrumptious fruit cobblers, butter pound cakes, and many more southern dishes.

I also share more of my inspirational life story about the love of family and friends, some unique special anecdotes that a dish invoked while growing up in the country, and other recipes from family and friends whose dishes I have loved over the years.

The cookbook has recipes not only from my living in the south, but also some favorite recipes when I lived abroad in Greece and Scotland. I refer to these additional recipes from family and friends and my recipes from living abroad, under a section called, "**And Beyond**". **ENJOY!**

Blessings,

Aunt Hattie

"I want to reiterate to my readers who wish to enjoy these southern cuisine dishes of yesteryear that country southern comfort food meant--and can still mean "healthy eating."

--Aunt Hattie (Dr. Hattie N. Washington)

APPETIZERS

Every celebration deserves great food. Need food ideas to start the party off right? My quick and easy-to-prepare appetizers have you covered. From the seafood to the carb and veggie lover, you are sure to satisfy all your guests.

Bacon Wrapped Chicken Livers
Bacon Wrapped Brussels Sprout
Bacon Wrapped Mushrooms
Celery Sticks with Homemade Fillings
Crusty Crab Balls
Deviled Eggs

Chicken Lettuce Wraps
Hot Cheesy Spinach Dip
Shish Kebobs
Sweet Potato Puffs
Crescent & Hot Dog Cheese Roll
Seafood Casserole Dip*

*Family & Friends recipes in the "And Beyond" Chapter.

BACON-WRAPPED CHICKEN LIVERS | SERVES 6-8

Ingredients:

8 slices of bacon

16 chicken livers

½ teaspoon garlic powder

2 tablespoon olive oil, divided

1 teaspoon sea salt; divided

½ teaspoon pepper

½ teaspoon sage

½ teaspoon poultry seasoning

½ teaspoon smoked paprika

Preparation:

1. Preheat oven to 300°F
2. Cut bacon slices in half making 2 equal size pieces, about 4 inches each.
3. Place bacon on a cookie sheet and bake for 5 to 8 minutes. Bacon slices should be flexible, not crisp. Drain on paper towels.
4. Rinse the chicken livers.

Instructions:

1. Place chicken livers in a medium saucepan with ½ teaspoon sea salt, 1 tablespoon olive oil and 4 cups of water. Bring to a boil for 5 minutes or until chicken livers are halfway done. Turn off heat.
2. Remove the chicken livers from saucepan and place in colander. Run cold water over chicken livers for 30 seconds. Drain well.
3. In a medium sized bowl. Add 2 tablespoons olive oil, ½ teaspoon of each: sea salt, pepper, garlic powder, paprika, sage and maple syrup. Place chicken livers in the marinade and toss thoroughly.
4. Wrap drained bacon slice around the chicken liver, and insert a toothpick in the bacon and through the center of the chicken liver to keep both together.
5. Follow procedure for each chicken liver.
6. Place chicken livers on a cookie sheet and bake for 10 to15 minutes. Turn each bacon wrapped chicken liver and bake an additional 7 to 10 minutes (may be baked longer depending on desired bacon crispness).
7. Drain on paper towels and serve warm on a decorative platter.

BACON-WRAPPED BRUSSELS SPROUTS | SERVING: 8-10

Ingredients:

5 slices of bacon

1 (12oz.) bag of frozen Brussels sprouts

2 cups water

½ teaspoon garlic powder

2 tablespoons olive oil, divided

1 teaspoon sea salt

½ teaspoon pepper

½ teaspoon sage

½ teaspoon paprika

Preparation:

1. Preheat oven to 275°F
2. Cut bacon slices in half making 2 equal size pieces, about 4 inches each.
3. Place bacon on a cookie sheet and bake for 5 to 8 minutes. Bacon slices should be flexible, not crisp. Drain on paper towels.
4. Cut Brussels sprouts in half (depending on the size, if larger than the size of a quarter)

Instructions:

1. Place Brussels sprouts in a medium saucepan and 2 cups of water with ½ teaspoon sea salt and 1 teaspoon of olive oil. Bring to a boil. Cook for 2 minutes. Remove Brussels sprouts from the saucepan and run cold water over them for 1 minute. Drain well.
2. Place Brussels sprouts in a medium bowl. Add 2 tablespoons olive oil, ½ teaspoon of each: sea salt, pepper, garlic powder, paprika, sage and maple syrup. Toss mushrooms in the marinade thoroughly.
3. Wrap the bacon slice around the Brussels sprouts and then insert a toothpick in the bacon and through the center of each Brussels sprout to keep both together.
4. Follow procedure for each bacon-wrapped Brussels sprout.
5. Place each bacon-wrapped Brussels sprout on a cookie sheet and bake for 10 to 15 minutes. Turn each bacon-wrapped Brussels sprout and cook an additional 5 to 10 minutes (may keep in longer depending on desired bacon crispness). Turn off oven, let sit for 5 minutes.
6. Turn off oven and leave wrapped Brussels sprouts in oven for another 5 minutes. Drain on paper towels and serve warm on a decorative platter.

BACON-WRAPPED MUSHROOMS | SERVES 8-10

Ingredients:

5   slices of bacon

10 medium fresh mushrooms (1 pound)

½ teaspoon garlic powder

2   tablespoon olive oil

1   tablespoon olive oil

½ teaspoon sea salt

½ teaspoon pepper

½ teaspoon sage

½ teaspoon smoked paprika

Preparation:

1. Preheat oven to 300°F
2. Cut bacon slices in half making 2 equal size pieces, about 4 inches each.
3. Place bacon half slices on a cookie sheet and bake for 5 to 8 minutes. Bacon pieces should be flexible, not crisp. Drain bacon on paper towels.
4. Rinse mushrooms, drain (leave on mushroom's stems).

Instructions:

1. Place mushrooms in a medium bowl. Add 2 tablespoons olive oil, ½ teaspoon of each: sea salt, pepper, garlic powder, paprika sage and maple syrup. Toss mushrooms in the marinade thoroughly.
2. Wrap bacon slice around mushroom, and then insert a toothpick through the center to keep the mushroom and bacon together.
3. Follow procedure for each bacon-wrapped mushroom.
4. Place bacon-wrapped mushrooms on a cookie sheet and bake for 10 to 15 minutes. Turn each mushroom and bake an additional 5 minutes (longer depending on desired bacon crispness).
5. Turn off oven, let sit for 5 minutes.
6. Drain on paper towels and serve warm on a decorative platter.

CELERY STICKS & GARLIC CREAM CHEESE DIP | SERVES 6-8

This recipe's crabmeat can be replaced with smoked or baked salmon, sliced cooked beef or cooked shrimp.
Cut celery sticks short, about the length of a baby carrot, to prevent re-dipping.

Ingredients:

12 Celery sticks
2 (8 oz.) container of cream cheese, softened
½ cup of sour cream
1   teaspoon garlic powder
½ teaspoon sea salt

1 tablespoon maple syrup
1 tablespoon fresh lemon juice
½ teaspoon smoked paprika
a few sprigs of fresh chives
1 (8 oz.) container crabmeat

Hattie's Garlic Cream Cheese Dip:

1. Mix cream cheese, sour cream, salt, garlic powder, maple syrup and lemon juice in a medium bowl.
2. Spread cheese dip on each celery stick and add a small piece of crabmeat, along with chives, on top or use the celery sticks for dipping in the cream cheese dip and persons can add crabmeat from a small dish on top of their garlic cream cheese-filled celery stick.

CELERY STICKS WITH PEANUT BUTTER

This is a great choice when you're expecting guests or you're just in the mood for a light snack.
Or, if you have a hankering for something that's sweet & salty *(This recipe's peanut butter can be replaced with Almond Butter or Cashew Butter).*
Cut celery sticks short, about the length of a baby carrot, to prevent re-dipping.

Ingredients:

6 celery sticks (cut approximately two inches long)
½ cup peanut butter
1 tablespoon maple syrup
1 tablespoon honey

Hattie's Nut Butter Mixture:

1. Mix 2 tablespoons peanut butter, ½ teaspoon of each: maple syrup and honey in a small bowl.
2. Spread the nut butter mixture on the celery sticks or use the celery sticks for one-time dipping into the nut mixture.

This is a great choice when you're expecting guests or if you're just in the mood for a light snack.

CRUSTY CRAB BALLS | SERVES 10-12

This same recipe can also be used as an "Entrée" by making the Appetizer Crab Balls double the size and baking them in a muffin pan for 20-25 minutes, rather than on a cookie sheet. Makes 12 Entrée sized muffin-pan crab balls.

Ingredients:

2   cups lump crabmeat (tightly packed), real or imitation
1   medium sweet onion, chopped
1   cup herb and garlic seasoned bread crumbs, divided, to use later in the recipe for coating balls.
½   green bell pepper, diced finely
½   red bell pepper, diced finely
2   eggs
½   teaspoon Old Bay® seasoning
¼   teaspoon garlic powder
½   teaspoon sea salt
¼   teaspoon cayenne pepper
2   tablespoons mayonnaise
2   tablespoons fresh lemon juice
1   teaspoon olive oil

Instructions:

1. Preheat oven to 375°F. Grease the cookie sheet with olive oil.
2. In a medium bowl, combine all the ingredients, except the crabmeat (eggs, onion, green bell pepper, red bell pepper, Old Bay® seasoning, garlic powder, sea salt and cayenne pepper, mayonnaise and lemon juice).
3. Add ⅓ cup of crushed bread crumbs and stir. Fold in the crabmeat and mix gently, to keep some of the lumps intact, making sure mixture is not too loose.
4. Shape crab balls into balls 2-inch balls, the size of a meatball, then roll crab balls evenly covered in remaining ⅔ cup bread crumbs (Optional, may prepare some crab balls with crust (bread crumbs) and some crab balls without crust).
5. Place crab balls on a greased cookie sheet, 4 across and 6 down = 24. Bake for 10 minutes.
6. Turn crab balls and bake 5 additional minutes. Watch for browning.
7. Turn off oven and allow crab balls to sit in oven for 10 minutes.

Variation: *Crusty Salmon Balls* -The same Appetizer or Entrée recipe can be used for Crusty Salmon Balls—Just use 1 (16 oz.) can of salmon, instead of crab meat. Like the Crab Ball recipe, this Salmon Ball recipe can also be prepared as an "Entrée".

Serve with tartar sauce, cocktail sauce or Hattie's Special Seafood Sauce

HATTIE'S SPECIAL DEVILED EGGS | SERVES 6

My family and friends love my special deviled eggs. I think it's my special devilish yolk mixture! These deviled eggs can be used as an "Appetizer" or as a "Side Dish". Enjoy!

Ingredients:

6 eggs
½ cup mayonnaise (non-fat, optional)
2 tablespoon yellow mustard
2 tablespoon brown mustard
1 teaspoon apple cider vinegar (raw)
1 tablespoon plain Greek yogurt
1 tablespoon sour cream
1 tablespoon sweet relish
½ teaspoon sea salt
¼ teaspoon cayenne pepper
½ teaspoon garlic powder
½ teaspoon horseradish
1 tablespoon honey
1 teaspoon smoked paprika, divided
2 pickled red peppers, chopped (optional garnish)

Instructions:

1. Gently crack the cool egg shell all the way around the egg and peel each egg .
2. Cut eggs in half using a sharp knife, remove yolks and place all yolks in a small mixing bowl.
3. Mash the yolks with a fork (or with a potato masher) until there are no lumps.
4. Add all ingredients to the mashed yolks except (pickled slice red pepper optional) smoked paprika.
5. Mix together ingredients thoroughly. Taste for desired salt, sweetness and vinegar.
6. Using a tablespoon, dip the egg yolk mixture into each egg white halve. Smooth the tops of the deviled eggs with the curve of the tablespoon.
7. Sprinkle a dash of smoked paprika on top of each deviled egg.
8. Garnish with a tiny piece of pickled red pepper (optional). Enjoy!!

Chicken Lettuce Wrap w/Garlic Spread & Diced Tomatoes
Serves 6

This recipe's chicken can be replaced with smoked or bake salmon, sliced cooked beef or cooked shrimp.

Ingredients:

12 Lettuce leaves (Butter, Green Leafy or Iceberg)

½ teaspoon chives

1 (8 ounce) package of cream cheese, softened

½ cup sour cream

1 cup fresh tomatoes, diced small

¾ cup onions, diced small

4 cups of cooked pulled chicken breasts
 or canned chicken

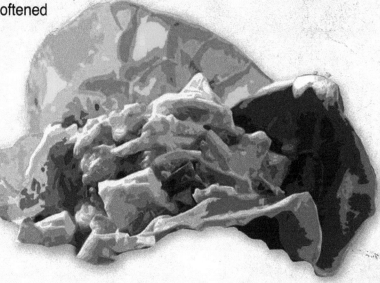

Instructions: (makes 12 wraps)

1. Mix chives, cream cheese, sour cream, and onions together in a medium size bowl.
2. Gently, fold in the diced tomatoes
3. Add pulled chicken breasts to spread and stir (or lay pulled chicken on top of the cream cheese mixture once spread on the lettuce leaf).
4. Spread each lettuce leaf with the cream cheese mixture and wrap the lettuce around the cream cheese filling. Stick a toothpick through each leaf to keep together. Serve!

Optional: Use other meats and/or vegetables on top of the cream cheese before lettuce wrapping. Experiment with various types of lettuce for different effects, sizes and looks even with spinach leaves.

HOT CHEESY SPINACH DIP | SERVES 6-8

Ingredients:

1 (8 oz.) package of cream cheese, softened

1 (16 oz.) frozen spinach, thawed

1 teaspoon olive oil

½ teaspoon hot sauce

1 cup shredded mozzarella cheese, divided

1 cup shredded sharp cheese, divided

1 cup milk (whole or lactaid-free)

1 teaspoon smoked paprika, divided

¼ teaspoon black or cayenne pepper

¼ teaspoon sea salt

2 tablespoons honey or maple syrup

1 teaspoon soy sauce

Instructions:

1. Preheat oven to 275°F

2. Pour milk inside saucepan on low heat, until milk becomes hot (do not let milk boil).

3. Add cream cheese to milk and stir until cheese melts.

4. Add spinach in cream cheese mixture. Stir for 2 minutes.

5. Add ½ cup mozzarella and ½ cup sharp cheese into mixture. Stir for an additional 2 minutes.

6. Add ½ teaspoon smoked paprika, soy sauce, pepper, sea salt, hot sauce and honey (or maple syrup). Stir for 5 minutes.

7. Pour the cream cheese and spinach mixture into a greased casserole dish. Sprinkle remaining ½ cup sharp cheese and ½ cup mozzarella cheese on top of the dip mixture.

8. Sprinkle with remaining ½ teaspoon smoked paprika on top of the cheeses. Bake for 20 to 25 minutes. Turn off oven and let stay in oven for 5 minutes.

Serve hot as a dip with bruschetta bread, chips or soft bread chunks with tongs for dipping.

HATTIE'S SHISH KEBOBS
CHICKEN | STEAK | SALMON | SHRIMP | VEGETABLES | FRUITS
SERVES 6 - 8

24 to 32 cubed pieces	½ cup apple cider vinegar	¼ cup brown sugar
1 teaspoon sea salt	¼ cup wine vinegar	¼ cup maple syrup
1 teaspoon cayenne pepper	¼ cup balsamic vinegar	¼ cup olive oil
1 tablespoon mustard	½ cup ketchup	1 tablespoon butter

Assorted vegetables (large onions, green, red and yellow peppers, cherry tomatoes or tomato chunks, zucchini, broccoli, cauliflower, pineapple, mangos and grapes). Skewers (8 to 12, depending on the number of desired meat cubes per skewer).

Preparation:

1. Cut desired meat in 1 to 1½-chunks. Place prepared meats in separate bowls and place in refrigerator, until ready to cook.
2. Cut desired assorted vegetables and fruits, optional in 1" chunks (think of color, taste and cooking time of the meat as you select skewer combinations of vegetables and/or fruits per skewer).

Instruction:

1. MAKE HATTIE'S SPECIAL KEBOB SAUCE
   A. In a large mixing bowl, mix the vinegars (apple cider, wine and balsamic).
   B. Add brown sugar and maple syrup. Stir until sugar dissolved.
   C. Add Ketchup, mustard, sea salt and cayenne pepper. Stir sauce thoroughly.
   D. Mix in the olive oil. Set sauce aside (sauce can also be prepared ahead of time and stored in the refrigerator).
2. Marinade your meats while in the separate bowl with ½ cup of the sauce;
3. Brush Olive oil on each skewer and thread meat first and alternate with vegetables ending with meat;
4. Lay the skewers on a cookie sheet and brush more sauce on the meats and vegetables.

HATTIE'S KEBOBS: ON THE GRILL

A. Heat Grill to medium-high.

B. Brush olive oil on grill or put foil on the Grill and cook Kabobs on the foil.

C. Lay kebobs on the heated grill and cook 10 minutes.

D. Turn kebob as the meat and vegetables began to cook.

E. Dab a little more sauce, if desired.

F. Cook another 10 minutes to desired doneness.

G. Remove from heat and place on a large platter. Cover with aluminum foil. Allow grilled kebobs to cool for 10 minutes allowing meat to tenderize and the flavor from the onions and vegetables to seep through the meats.

Serve with a salad, over rice, couscous or as a meal itself since you have your meat, vegetables and fruit.

HATTIE'S KEBOBS: OVEN BROILED

A. Heat the oven to 375° F.

B. Cover a large cookie sheet with aluminum foil and brush olive oil on top of the sheet.

C. Lay kebobs on the covered cookie sheet and cook 10 minutes.

D. Turn kebobs in the oven as the meat and vegetables begin to cook.

E. Turn on the Broiler to brown the meats, vegetables and fruit.

F. Brush kebobs with sauce, if desired.

G. Turn off oven. Cover kebobs with aluminum foil. Place back in oven for approximately 10 minutes, allowing the meat to further tenderize and flavors from the onions and vegetables to seep through the meats.

Growing up in the country, our fresh vegetable and/or meat Kebobs were skewered with sticks whittled from local trees. The only sauce we used for our Kebobs was fresh sweet cream butter, salt and pepper.

SWEET POTATO PUFFS

Ingredients:

4 medium sweet potatoes, boiled
2 teaspoon nutmeg, divided
½ cup brown sugar
½ teaspoon sea salt
4 tablespoons maple syrup
1 teaspoon cinnamon
¼ stick melted butter, divided
½ cup condense milk (or heavy cream)
1 teaspoon vanilla extract
½ cup confectioners' sugar, optional

Instructions:

1. Preheat oven to 275° F.
2. Roll out crust the size of a saucer (see instructions under *Crusts for Pies & Cobblers**)

3. Make Sweet Potato Mixture For Filling:
   A. Boil sweet potatoes until done (fork can stick through), remove from hot water, run cold water over potatoes just to cool enough to peel, and then mash sweet potatoes in mixing bowl until smooth (use potato masher or mixer).

   B. Mix all ingredients, except the milk/cream, into the mashed potatoes mixture until the filling is thick and smooth. Add in half of the milk/cream and stir thoroughly (should be a thicker consistency for the filling). Ad d additional milk/cream, if too thick.
4. Place sweet potato filling mixture on one half of crust. Fold crust over filling so edges meet, press fork around edges to seal crust.
5. Brush 2 tablespoons melted butter on the tops and sides of all puffs; Place puffs on a greased cookie sheet and into the preheated oven.
6. Bake for 10 to 15 minutes, turn over and allow puffs to brown on other side for another 5 to 10 minutes.
7. Once brown, sprinkle nutmeg and/or confectionary sugar on top of each puff. Serve warm. Enjoy!

Note: Sweet Potato Puffs can also be served as a "Dessert" (For Desserts, the Puffs can be made larger by the size of the crust dough, still using the same process of filling and fastening the edges. Usually, larger puffs are called "Turnovers" when used as a "Dessert".)

(*See recipe for 'Crust' under 'Crust for Pies & Cobblers' on Pg. 138).

CRESCENT AND HOT DOG CHEESE ROLL | SERVES 6-8

Ingredients:

Eight 5" Flaky Dough Crescent Squares (See "Hattie's Homemade Crust Recipe"--*Pg. 138*)
8 Hotdogs
8 Slices of Applegate® sharp cheese
¼ stick butter, melted
¼ cup olive oil

Instructions:

1. Preheat oven to 275°F

2. Use same dough recipe for the crescents triangles as the crusts recipe for casserole dishes.

3. In a skillet, over medium-high, sear hot sausage links in olive oil, until lightly brown on both sides.

4. Layer each crescent triangle roll with a cheese slice and a hotdog. Fold triangle roll & cheese slice around the seared hot dog.

5. Press the ends together with a fork to fasten and insert a toothpick through the crust and hot dog.

6. Place on a baking sheet. Brush crescents with butter. Bake for 10 to 15 minutes on one side. Turn and cook an additional 10 minutes.

7. Turn off oven and let Crescent hotdogs with cheese set for another 5 minutes.

Use this same crescent triangle idea for any number of other meats and vegetables (for "Appetizers" or "Side Dishes") and fruits (for "Desserts", similar to the turnover recipes under "Turnovers").

BREAKFAST

My stepmom always had a delicious breakfast prepared for us children before we started the day. Whether it was her fried apples, buttermilk biscuits, or scrambled eggs, she always made her meals with plenty of love.

Mama's Hot Buttermilk Biscuits
Hattie's Honey Butter Sauce
Breakfast Hash with Crust
Cheesy Breakfast Hash
Hot Cheesy Balls
Scrambled Cheese & Eggs
Cheese-Egg Frittata
Southern Fried Apples
Fried Fresh Shaved Corn
Fried Sweet Potatoes
Liver Pudding & Grits
Southern Fried Potatoes & Onions
Omelets
Buttermilk Pancakes & Special Syrup
Quiche
Scrapple

MAMA'S SOUTHERN HOT BUTTERMILK BISCUITS

SERVES 6 - 8

Ingredients:
½ cup buttermilk
4 cups of self-rising flour
1 cup lard, divided
¾ cup milk, divided

HATTIE'S HONEY BUTTER SAUCE

Ingredients:
1 tablespoon honey
¼ stick butter, melted
1 tablespoon sour cream
¼ cup confectioners sugar
¼ cup milk

Instructions:

1. Preheat the oven 375°F
2. Grease pan with some of the lard. In a large bowl, knead flour and lard together for about 10 minutes. Make a hole in center of dough mixture. Pour in buttermilk. Knead for another 10 minutes.
3. Place wax paper on counter. Add loose flour on wax paper. Coat your hand and rolling pin with flour.
4. Lightly flatten dough on wax paper and roll dough straight across from you for 4 minutes. Turn wax paper counter-clockwise and roll dough straight across from you again for 4 minutes.
5. Using a biscuit cutter or glass, cut the biscuits. Place the biscuits in prepared pan. Bake for 15 to 20 minutes. Serve biscuits warm with **Hattie's Honey Butter Sauce:** 1 tablespoon honey, ½ stick butter, melted and 1 tablespoon sour cream. Mix until smooth. Drizzle on hot biscuit.

Hattie's Honey Butter Sauce:

1. Mix together the honey, butter and sour cream.
2. Mix until smooth. Drizzle on hot biscuit.

Serve hot biscuits with other breakfast foods, such as my fried apples or fried potatoes with onions, scrambled eggs, country sausage, bacon or Smithfield Ham.

Breakfast Hash with Crust | Serves 8-10

Ingredients:

1 package hot sausage

1 package mild sausage

2 cups sweet onions, diced, divided

1 teaspoon garlic powder

2 tablespoons butter, melted

12 large eggs

½ yellow bell pepper, diced

½ orange bell pepper, diced

1 (8 oz.) bag of sharp shredded cheese

1 teaspoon sea salt

1 teaspoon black pepper

1 teaspoon crushed red pepper (optional)

¼ cup milk

¼ cup water

2 tablespoons cornstarch

½ cup bread crumbs

Preparations:

1. Preheat the oven to 350°F.
2. Make Crust--See Recipe under **"Hattie's Homemade Crust"** *(Pg. 138 & 139).*

Instructions:

1. Place 1 cup sweet onion, yellow bell pepper, orange bell pepper in a bowl.
2. In a large skillet, over medium-high, sauté sausage for 3 minutes or until brown. Add the 1 cup sweet onion and sauté with sausage for an additional 2 minutes. Remove from heat.
3. Line casserole dish with crust and bake for 20 minutes. Brush melted butter on crust and bake for 5 minutes.
4. In a medium bowl, using a mixer, beat eggs, sea salt, garlic, milk, and black pepper. While mixing, add flour (bread crumbs, optional).
5. Transfer sautéed sausage and sweet onions mixture from large skillet to a medium bowl. Add yellow bell pepper, orange bell pepper and remaining 1 cup sweet onion, crushed red pepper (optional) and half a cup of shredded cheese. Stir to combine.
6. Pour all the ingredients into a 9 x 13 casserole dish.
7. Place in the oven for about 1 hour. Use a toothpick to check for doneness. If toothpick comes out clean, sprinkle rest of shredded cheese on top and a dash of Paprika for aesthetic appeal. Turn on broiler for 10 minutes for cheese to melt and brown.
8. Turn off oven and leave breakfast hash in for about 20 to 30 minutes, so the flavors have melded.

Cheesy Breakfast Hash without Crust | Serves 8-10

Ingredients:

1 package hot sausage

1 package regular sausage

2 medium sweet onions

1 teaspoon garlic powder

2 tablespoons butter, melted

12 large eggs

½ yellow bell pepper, diced

½ orange bell pepper, diced

1 (8 oz.) bag of sharp shredded cheese

1 teaspoon sea salt

1 teaspoon black pepper

1 teaspoon crushed red pepper (optional)

¾ cup heavy cream or evaporated milk

¼ cup water

2 tablespoons cornstarch

½ cup bread crumbs or ½ cup self-rising flour

Preparation:

1. Preheat the oven to 350°F.

Instructions:

1. In a large skillet, sauté sausage for 3 minutes or until brown. Add 1 sweet onion and sauté with sausage for an additional 2 minutes. Remove from heat.
2. Brush melted butter all around casserole dish.
3. In a medium bowl, using a mixer, beat eggs, sea salt, garlic powder, milk, and black pepper. While mixing, add flour (bread crumbs are optional).
4. Transfer sautéed sausage and sweet onions mixture from large skillet to a medium bowl. Add yellow bell pepper, orange bell pepper and 1 sweet onion, crushed red pepper (optional) and half a cup of shredded cheese. Stir to combine.
5. Pour all the ingredients into a casserole dish.
6. Place in the oven for about 1 hour. Use a toothpick to check for doneness. If toothpick comes out clean, sprinkle rest of shredded cheese on top and a dash of Paprika for aesthetic appeal.
7. Turn off oven and leave breakfast hash in for about 20 to 30 minutes, so the flavors have melded.
8. Turn on broiler for 10 minutes for cheese to melt and brown.

Please see the Recipe for Hattie's Flaky Homemade Crust under "Casseroles", "Cobblers", "Pies" and other Crust uses in the back of this book in the section on making crusts. Serve as the Entrée for breakfast or for any meal. If you are like me, I like breakfast food sometimes for lunch or dinner.

HOT CHEESY BALLS | SERVES 6-8

Ingredients:

1 cup sharp shredded cheese

4 cups self-rising flour

1 package hot sausage (turkey or pork)

1 sweet onion

2 eggs

½ cup low-fat buttermilk

4 tablespoons butter, melted

1 teaspoon sage

1 teaspoon garlic powder

Preparation:

1. Preheat oven to 375°F
2. Beat eggs in a bowl.
3. Melt butter in microwave in a small bowl.
4. Use a muffin pan for cheese balls (if you want to make more than 12 at a time use a cookie sheet).
5. Grease muffin pan with virgin coconut oil or melted butter.

Instructions:

1. In a large skillet, sauté sausage until partially brown. Add sage and garlic powder and mix thoroughly. Remove from heat and let cool for 5 minutes.
2. Pour sausage in a medium mixing bowl. Add self-rising flour and mix thoroughly—making sure there are no lumps. Add eggs and continue to stir. Add butter and continue to stir thoroughly, using your hands or a fork. Dough should be a thick consistency. If mixture is too thick, add buttermilk.
3. Pour ¾ shredded cheese in the mixture and fold shredded cheese into dough (depends on your preference of cheesiness).
4. Make dough balls about the size of a meatball and place each dough ball in muffin pan. Bake for about 10 minutes. Turn and cook for an additional 10 minutes.
5. Turn and take a few pieces of shredded cheese and lay on top of each ball. Turn off oven.
6. Return cheese balls to oven to allow cheese to melt.

CHEESE & EGGS | SERVES 3-4

Ingredients:

½ cup shredded cheese of your choice, divided

1 tablespoon room-temperature water, optional

1 teaspoon butter or olive oil (or spray oil)

1 Cast iron frying pan or omelet skillet

½ teaspoon smoked paprika, divided

¼ teaspoon garlic powder

¼ teaspoon sea salt

¼ teaspoon pepper

4 eggs, beaten

¼ stick butter

1 tablespoon water

Instructions:

1. In a bowl, mix eggs, seasonings, ¼ teaspoon smoked paprika, and water.

2. In a cast iron frying pan or omelet skillet, over medium-high heat, melt butter.
   Pour egg mixture in hot frying pan and stir until eggs are almost done.

3. Stir in ¼ cup cheese in eggs in the frying pan and cook until eggs are to desired doneness.

4. Turn off stove and sprinkle the remaining ¼ cup cheese on top of eggs; Allow cheese to finish melting for about 5 minutes (Put shredded cheese on top of scrambled egg after almost done and allow to melt as egg finish cooking).

5. Sprinkle the remaining ¼ smoke paprika on top of melted cheese.

Serve with your favorite breakfast meat or alone for a great protein dish.

CHEESE-EGG FRITTATA | SERVES 6-8

Ingredients:

4 medium potatoes
½ cup onion, diced
½ cup sweet onion, diced
8 eggs, beaten
4 egg whites
¾ cup shredded cheddar cheese, divided
¾ cup shredded sharp cheese, divided
1 cup fresh spinach, chopped
1 teaspoon garlic powder
1 teaspoon sea salt
1 teaspoon sugar
¼ cup milk
8 oz. cream cheese, softened
¼ stick butter, melted
¼ cup of olive oil
1 teaspoon smoked paprika

Preparation:

1. Preheat oven to 300°F
2. Peel potatoes and dice in very small pieces or shred
3. Dice onion in small pieces
4. Chop spinach into 1-inch pieces
5. Beat eggs in large mixing bowl; Add in 4 egg whites, all seasonings and beat together.
6. Brush bottom of casserole dish with melted butter.

Instructions:

1. In a skillet, over medium-high, heat olive oil. Add potatoes and onions in hot skillet. Sauté for 5 to 7 minutes. Stir constantly until both are semi-brown and almost done.
2. Turn off stove and pour sautéed potato and onion mixture in a bowl and cool for about 5 minutes.
3. Pour the cooled potatoes and onion mixture into the bowl with your beaten eggs. Stir thoroughly.
4. Pour ½ cup of both of your shredded cheeses into your egg, potato & onion mixture (Leave ¼ cup of cheeses for toping later).
5. Pour frittata mixture into your buttered casserole dish and put in the pre-heated oven and bake; After about 25 min, sprinkle the remaining ½ cup of both cheeses on top; and sprinkle a little smoked paprika on top of the cheese.
6. Turn on broiler for about 2 to 5 minutes to let the cheeses melt and brown.
7. Turn off the oven and let frittata remain in oven for another 5 to 10 minutes (be careful not to let frittata get too brown). Remove from oven and let set for 5 minutes. Serve hot as an entrée alone or as a side dish.

Serve hot as an entrée alone or with a side dish.

HATTIE'S SOUTHERN FRIED APPLES | SERVES 6-8

Ingredients:

12 Granny Smith apples

1 package of bacon

¼ cup bacon drippings

1 ½ cup sugar

1 teaspoon cinnamon

1 teaspoon nutmeg

½ teaspoon ginger

¼ cup water

¼ cup maple syrup

Preparation:

1. Wash apples thoroughly.
2. Cook bacon and pour bacon drippings into small bowl. Set aside.
3. Combine sugar, cinnamon, nutmeg, and ginger in another small bowl.

Instructions:

1. Do not peel the apples. Slice one side of the apple as closely as possible to the core. Repeat with remaining 3 sides. For every piece of apple, hold it cut-side down and slice evenly ¼-inch thick.
2. Follow the same cutting process for all apples. Place sliced apples in a large bowl.
3. In a large skillet, over medium-high heat, heat bacon drippings for 1 minute or until drippings are hot.
4. Add ⅓ of slice apples (listen for a popping sound) to hot skillet. Fry apples for 5 minutes, uncovered or until the bottom starts to brown. Using a spatula, turn apples from the bottom.
5. Add another ⅓ of apple slices. Fry for 3 minutes. Turn apples from the bottom. Add the remaining apples, spreading apples evenly in skillet. Increase to high heat and cook apples for 3 to 5 minutes or until the last bottom of apples are brown.
6. Using a spatula, starting from the bottom, turn apples. Cook approximately 5 more minutes (all the apples should be brown on the bottom, looking rubbery-translucent).
7. Turn apples again from the bottom. Apples should be a nice brown look and consistency. Add butter. Sprinkle sugar, add maple syrup, and the cinnamon, nutmeg, and ginger mixture over apples. Stir.
8. Pour water over apples. Immediately cover skillet and turn off heat (covering apples will create a bubbly effect and bring out the full flavor of the apples).
9. Allow apples to sit for 5 minutes. Stir and check for doneness (fried apples will have a caramelized apple look with brown apple sauce and fried brown peelings). Taste for desired sweetness.

SERVE AS A SIDE OR AS A DESSERT w/WHIPPED CREAM (OPTIONAL).

Fresh Fried Shaved Corn | Serves 4-6

Ingredients:

12 ears of corn

½ cup bacon drippings

½ stick butter

1 teaspoon sea salt

1 tablespoon sugar

1 tablespoon maple syrup

¼ cup water (4 tablespoons, divided)

½ teaspoon crushed red pepper, optional

Preparation:

1. Shuck and clean corn.
2. Cut the corn from the husk using a sharp knife. Continue this process all around the ear of corn.
3. Scrape the sides of the cob. The corn's sweet juice milk will fall into the plate with the kernels.
4. Continue this cutting process for the remaining corn.

Instructions:

1. In a large skillet, heat bacon or turkey drippings over medium-high. Add ½ corn and spread out the corn on the bottom of the skillet. Cook, uncovered, for 5 to 6 minutes or until corn is brown at the bottom.
2. Using a spatula, turn corn. Pour the other half of corn in skillet and mix with half-brown corn in the skillet. Cook for 5 to 6 minutes or until second layer of corn is brown on the bottom.
3. Add sea salt, pepper, (crushed red pepper optional), maple syrup, and sugar. Using a spatula, turn corn over again. Cook for another 5 to 6 minutes or until most of the corn is brown.
4. Turn corn again. Add 3 tablespoons water and cover. Reduce heat to low. Simmer for 5 minutes. If corn is too thick, add 1 tablespoon butter and remaining 1 tablespoon water, depending on desired thickness, and stir. Let corn set covered for 5 minutes. Serve with other vegetables.

Although this recipe calls for bacon or turkey dripping, you may substitute both with butter or other desired oils.

FRIED SWEET POTATOES | SERVES 6-8

Ingredients:

8 medium sweet potatoes (Mama preferred more orangey colored sweet potatoes for frying rather
than the yellowish sweet potato)
¼ cup bacon drippings (or ghee)
¼ stick butter (4 tablespoons)
1 ½ cup regular sugar
1 ½ cup brown sugar
1 teaspoon cinnamon
1 teaspoon nutmeg
1 teaspoon ginger
¼ cup water

Preparation:

1. Wash sweet potatoes thoroughly.
2. Cook bacon first and pour drippings into a small bowl. Set aside.
3. In a small bowl, combine regular sugar, brown sugar, cinnamon, nutmeg, and ginger. Set aside.
4. Using a sharp knife and potato peeler, peel and cut the sweet potatoes into ¼-inch thick slices.
    Place the sweet potato slices in a bowl of cold water and drain.

Instructions:

1. In a large skillet, heat bacon drippings on medium-high until hot; Place ⅓ of sweet potatoes in
    the hot oil at a time, spreading the sweet potatoes out in the skillet; Cook for 5 minute on one side;
    Using a large spatula, turn sweet potatoes over.
2. Add another ⅓ of the sliced sweet potatoes in the skillet. Cook for 3 to 5 minutes; Turn them over
    from the bottom of the skillet to allow the new potatoes to get to the bottom of the skillet to brown;
3. Add the last ⅓ of the sweet potatoes; Cook for 2 to 5 minutes. Turn over again and continue to fry
    until potatoes are brown and almost done. Add butter to the skillet. After butter melts, sprinkle the
    regular sugar, brown sugar, nutmeg, cinnamon, and ginger mixture and stir with the spatula—
    stirring from the bottom;
4. Pour water in skillet. Cover and reduce. Simmer for 5 minutes. Stir again from the bottom, making
    sure all of the water, potatoes and other ingredients are thoroughly mixed. Check for doneness
    and desired sweetness.
5. If done, Turn heat off; let skillet sit for 5 additional minutes.

Serve as a "Side Dish" for Breakfast or for any other meal.

AN ANECDOTE
CHERYL'S FUNNY STORY:
My younger Daughter, Cheryl, & her Girlfriend from her "Black Girls Run" Group, Make A Big Meal Decision When Visiting the South

CHERYL'S "IRON GIRL" REGIMENT VS. THE COUNTRY BREAKFAST?

I wanted to share this comical and cute story about my younger daughter, Cheryl, who was supposed to be on a strict health food, healthy living regimen last summer in Virginia Beach when we had the occasion to go down for Norfolk State University's (our Alma Mater's) Homecoming. Cheryl invited one of her girlfriends to come down with us. This girlfriend ran with her in a group call "Black Girls Run". They were training for the "Iron Girl" Triathlon, and they were "supposedly" strictly adhering to their healthy eating regiment; running every day; and drinking plenty of water, getting prepared for the triathlon. I said "supposedly" because on this particular Saturday morning, my cousin's wife, Bettie, and I were relaxing on the back deck overlooking the water having a cup of coffee. We had not bothered to make our usual big country breakfast that morning because my cousin, Lorenzo, had to go to the office for a meeting, and it was just us in the house; and, of course, Cheryl and her girlfriend.

It was about 10:45 am and Cheryl came downstairs with this quizzical look on her face and said, "Where is breakfast?" Bettie & I looked puzzled to see what breakfast she was referring; because we thought that they were going to drink their "Iron girl" smoothie with spinach and kale and all of those good healthy vegetables in it. But, Oh no, nothing doing on this morning! Cheryl said that she was use to our big country breakfast of fried potatoes with onions and/or my fried apples, grits, scrambled cheese eggs, and hot buttered biscuits that I would cook whenever we came down to Virginia Beach. I said, "I thought you all were on your special "Iron Girl" triathlon diet and that you didn't want the usual big country breakfast? Plus, since Lorenzo left early for a meeting; we were not cooking breakfast this morning". To which she indicated disappointedly that she had told her girlfriend, "My Mom and Aunt Bettie will be 'throwing down' for breakfast when we get there. Watch!" She remarked that she and her girlfriend were looking forward to our usual big country breakfast while they were down here, and that they came prepared to get off of their triathlon diet that weekend. It would be mightily worth it for great southern cooking, and that they would resume their regiment on that Monday. **What a surprise! How were we to know?!**

Bettie & I laughed loudly and got moving to prepare our usual country breakfast for these Iron Girl Triathlon trainees and runners of the Black Girls Run Group. We peeled potatoes and onions for our fried potatoes & onions; sliced apples for the fried apples; cooked some Smithfield bacon, homemade country sausage, buttered grits, scrambled eggs with cheddar cheese, and hot buttered biscuits. The dishes were coordinated and the entire breakfast was ready in less than 45 minutes. We all dined sufficiently, and they indicated how much they thoroughly enjoyed that lovely country breakfast and how it was well worth the wait. They rationalize that because they don't eat this way every day, but coming down south, they felt basically that was their duty to eat the traditional big country breakfast. Then, they would go back on their iron-girl diet when you return home. Needless to say, they had a story to tell my cousin when he returned home about the "Almost No Country-Breakfast Morning". We all chuckled at the incident and knew that we always had to keep up our tradition of our country breakfast regardless to whatever else is happening. In other words, we have spoiled our family with great food; great cooking and fantastic memories.

Liver Pudding & Grits | Serves 4-6
(A Wilmington, N.C. Dish)

Ingredients:
1 package of Neese's Liver Pudding®
8 slices bacon
1 cup onion, diced
¼ cup bacon drippings

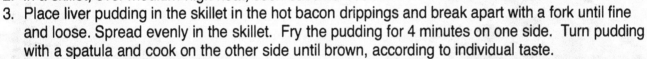

Preparation:
1. Cut off liver pudding casing.
2. In a skillet, over medium-high heat, cook bacon slices.
3. Place liver pudding in the skillet in the hot bacon drippings and break apart with a fork until fine and loose. Spread evenly in the skillet. Fry the pudding for 4 minutes on one side. Turn pudding with a spatula and cook on the other side until brown, according to individual taste.
4. Break apart into fine pieces, add 4 tablespoons water, cover, and turn off heat. Let simmer and set. Stir again and serve over grits.

Southern Fried White Potatoes | Serves 4-6

Ingredients:
12 medium-size regular white potatoes
1 whole medium sweet onion, sliced
⅓ cup cooking oil
1 teaspoon sea salt

1 teaspoon black pepper
⅓ cup water
½ teaspoon crush red peppers (optional)

Preparations:
1. Wash potatoes. Peel potatoes and place potatoes in a colander.
2. Wash potatoes again and let drain.
3. Slice potatoes into ¼-inch thick slices. Place the potato slices in a bowl of cold water. Drain.
4. Cut onion in half & slice the onion across the halves; Place sliced onions in a small separate bowl.
5. Cook bacon and pour bacon drippings into a small bowl. Set aside.

Instructions:
1. In a large skillet, over medium-high, heat bacon drippings. Evenly spread sliced potatoes in the skillet and fry for 5 minutes on one side until brown on the bottom.
2. Turn potatoes over and sprinkle sea salt, black pepper, and sliced onions on top of the potatoes. Fry potatoes on the other side for 5 to 6 minutes or until brown (Turn again for browner potatoes).
3. Add water to skillet and cover. Turn off heat and let potatoes stand covered for 5 minutes.
4. Then, Turn potatoes over gently–from the bottom with a wide spatula.
5. Remove from heat and let stand for 5 minutes. Serve with your other favorite breakfast sides.

Omelets | Serves 2-4

Ingredients:

½ cup green, red, and yellow bell peppers
1 cup loosely packed fresh or frozen spinach
⅓ cup sharp cheese, shredded
⅓ cup ham, diced
3 eggs
½ cup sweet onion, diced
¼ teaspoon sea salt
¼ teaspoon black pepper
1 teaspoon olive oil
¼ teaspoon garlic powder
1 tablespoon lukewarm water

Instructions:

1. Beat three eggs in a bowl. Add sea salt, black pepper and garlic powder. Set egg mixture aside.
2. In a medium skillet, heat olive oil or butter on medium heat for about 1 minute or until hot. Place onions, red peppers and green peppers and ham pieces in skillet and sauté until the edge of the diced onions and other ingredients turn slightly brown.
3. Place other chopped vegetables and continue to sauté for 1 minute.
4. Pour egg mixture into the skillet, stirring frequently until eggs are almost done.
5. Spread eggs out in skillet. Evenly, sprinkle shredded cheese on top of almost-done eggs. Do not stir. Fold eggs in half over the cheese; After 1 minute, Turn omelet over, and turn off stove and let omelet sit on the other side for another 1 minute until the cheese melts.

Broccoli, Onions & Cheese Omelet

Same instructions and ingredients as above, except add 1 cup loosely-packed chopped broccoli.

Spinach & Cheese Omelet

Same instructions and ingredients as above, except add 1 cup chopped spinach.

I sometimes garnish my omelet with shredded carrots, whole snow pea, a couple of whole strawberries, a few pieces of broccoli & cauliflower. I serve this spinach and cheese omelet by itself or with other breakfast meat/s and Grits. Excellent dish for vegans.

Buttermilk Pancakes | Serves 6-8

Ingredients:

3 eggs
1 cup of Wheat flour
1 cup of almond flour
1 tablespoon of baking powder
1 tablespoon of baking soda
1 ½ cup of buttermilk, divided
Olive oil or spray
¼ cup of Maple syrup or honey
¼ stick of butter, melted
½ cup confectioners sugar, divided
¼ cup sour cream or Greek yogurt
Fruit of choice: optional

Preparations:

Beat 3 eggs
Mix 1 cup buttermilk and other ingredients to make pancake batter (Add buttermilk for desired consistency).
Heat pancake pan or griddle.
Fold in fruit or nuts just before putting in hot pan.

Instructions:

1. Spray flat pancake pan with cooking oil.
2. Pour ½ cup batter on preheated pan.
3. Cook 2 to 3 minutes until bubbles form around the edges of the pancake and the edges start to brown; Flip over only once until done.
4. Place pancakes on a cookie sheet in preheated oven (250°F) to keep hot until ready to serve. (Before placing in the warm oven, brush top of pancakes with remaining melted butter, optional).

HATTIE'S SPECIAL SYRUP

Ingredients:

1 cup of Maple syrup

½ cup of honey

½ cup of brown sugar

4 tablespoon of butter, divided

¼ teaspoon of hot sauce (to desired taste)

¼ teaspoon of wine vinegar

¼ cup confectioners sugar

½ teaspoon of cornstarch (If you wish a thicker syrup)

Instructions:

1. Put butter, confectioners sugar and brown sugar in a sauce pan and heat on medium-high until hot (do not boil); Stir until smooth; Add in all of the other ingredients; Stir until all are combined; Turn heat on low (Add a few drops of cornstarch mixed with water, if you wish a thicker syrup). Stir well.
2. Pour warm syrup mixture over the warm and fluffy pancakes.
3. Sprinkle a little confectioners sugar over the pancakes and garnish with blueberries or strawberries. Enjoy!!

TIP: We would also use Mama's homemade preserves or Grandma's Molasses® on top and between the layers of our pancakes.

Spinach, Onion & Cheese Quiche | Serves 6-8
with crust

Ingredients:

8 eggs
1 cup spinach, chopped
½ cup onion, diced
½ cup sharp cheese, divided
½ cup extra sharp cheese, divided
½ cup mild cheese, divided
¼ cup butter, melted
½ cup buttermilk
1 teaspoon cornstarch
1 teaspoon sea salt
¼ teaspoon ground black pepper
¼ teaspoon cayenne pepper
¼ teaspoon smoked paprika
2 tablespoons cornstarch
1 (9-inch) refrigerated pie crust

Preparation:

1. Preheat oven to 375°F
2. Stick holes in the bottom of the crust with a fork and bake for 5 minutes.
3. Remove crust from the oven and allow to cool.
4. Brush sides of crust with butter. Reduce oven to 350°F

Instructions:

1. In a skillet, over medium-high heat, sauté spinach and onions for 5 minutes or until vegetables are half done. Set aside to cool.
2. In a large bowl, whisk eggs, Stir in buttermilk, sea salt, ground black pepper, cayenne pepper and cornstarch mixed with 2 tablespoons of water, sautéed vegetables, and half of the cheeses.
3. Pour Quiche mixture in the buttered crust. Bake at 350°F for 25 to 30 minutes.
4. Sprinkle the remaining cheeses on top and bake 10 minutes more, or until an inserted knife comes out clean.
5. Turn oven off and allow to set for 5 minutes, or until ready to serve. Serve hot alone or with a bowl of fruit.

Broccoli, Onions & Cheese Quiche
Same instructions as above but substitute 1 cup chopped broccoli for spinach.

Mixed Vegetables & Cheese Quiche
Same instructions as above but combine 1 cup chopped spinach and 1 cup broccoli.

Meat & Vegetables Quiche
Same instructions as above but add 1 package of hot or mild sausage. In Step 1, sauté sausage for 5-8 minutes and proceed with original steps.

SCRAPPLE | SERVES 2-4
FRIED OR BAKED

Ingredients:
2 pounds old fashioned southern scrapple
1 cup fine bread crumbs
¼ cup olive oil
1 tablespoon buttermilk
2 eggs

Instructions:
1. Slice scrapple into ¼ of an inch thick.
2. Whisk eggs in a bowl. Stir in buttermilk.
3. On a platter, spread out the bread crumbs.
4. Dip a slice of scrapple in egg mixture; Then, place the scrapple in the bread crumbs and coat evenly on both sides.
5. Place coated scrapple in hot skillet and fry for 5 minutes on both sides and allow to get brown.

BAKED SCRAPPLE
OVEN BAKED OR BROILED

1. Perform steps 1 – 4. Place slice of scrapple on a cookie sheet lined with foil; drizzle with olive oil.
2. Place slices in preheated oven of 275ºF and bake for 10 minutes on each side.
3. Turn slices over again and turn oven off. Let slices remain in oven for another 5 minutes.

BATTER FRIED SCRAPPLE

Ingredients:
Old fashioned southern scrapple
Fine breadcrumbs
Chicken batter
¼ cup of olive oil
1 tablespoon of buttermilk

Instructions:
1. Dip scrapple in egg and dip in batter.
2. Allow to drain and place in frying pan.
3. Once brown, turn over and turn fire down so that batter can cook.

ENTREES

These main course recipes will have you going back for seconds. I have southern classics like Fried Chicken, Ole Fashion Meatloaf, Chicken & Dumplings and casseroles prepared like mom used to make them, but with a twist.

Chicken

Buttermilk Battered Fried Chicken
Southern Fried Chicken
Mama's Old-Fashioned BBQ Chicken
Skillet BBQ Chicken*
Smothered Fried Chicken
Hattie's White Chicken Chili
Chicken & Dumplings
Chicken Pot Pie
Chicken Salad
Chicken Shepherd's Pie **
Chicken & Waffles

Beef

Beef Brisket *
Beef Shepherd's Pie **
Hattie's Famous Homemade Chili
Hamburger Patties & Gravy
Stuffed Green Peppers
Ole Fashioned Meatloaf
Spaghetti & Meatballs
Spaghetti & Meat Sauce
Caramelized Steak & Mixed Vegetables
Stir Fry Beef

Pork

Chitterlings
Chopped Pork Barbecue *
Pigs Feet
Pigs Tails
Fried Pork Chops
Fried Pork Chops & Gravy
Stuffed Pork Chops
Ribs

Seafood

Crabs
Baked Fish
Salmon Loaf
Salmon Cakes *
Baked Salmon & Vegetables
Lobster Pot
Shrimp or Mussel Pot
Fish & Chips Hattie's Style**

Casseroles

Tuna Casserole
Seafood Casserole *
Cheesy Cauliflower & Vegetables
Sweet Potato & Carrot Casserole
Seven Vegetable Chicken Meal
Oxtails *
Zucchini Lasagna *

*Family & Friends recipes in the "And Beyond" Chapter.

**Greek & Scottish recipes In the "And Beyond" Chapter.

BUTTERMILK BATTERED
SOUTHERN FRIED CHICKEN
SERVES 6 - 8

Ingredients:
12 chicken parts (4 breasts,
4 thighs, 4 drumsticks)
4 cups lard
2 cups buttermilk, divided
2 eggs, beaten
5 cups all-purpose flour, divided
2 teaspoons sea salt, divided
2 teaspoons black pepper,divided
2 teaspoons garlic powder
1 teaspoon baking powder
1 teaspoon sugar
1 teaspoon apple cider vinegar
¼ cup water, divided
¼ teaspoon cayenne pepper

Preparation:

Marinade Chicken Pieces:
1. Cut chicken breasts in half; wash all chicken pieces thoroughly and drain.
2. Place chicken in a large bowl and sprinkle 1 teaspoon sea salt, 1 teaspoon pepper, 1 teaspoon garlic powder, and ¼ cup buttermilk. Toss chicken parts in this mixture; marinade for 15 minutes.

Make Batter:
1. In a bowl, combine eggs, water, buttermilk, sugar, remaining salt, black pepper, garlic powder, apple cider vinegar, and (cayenne pepper, optional).
2. Add 4 cups flour; Stir well, be sure consistency of batter is not too thick. Add water and buttermilk alternately to a thinner consistency of pancake batter.

Instructions:

1. Using a deep fryer or a deep sauce pan for a fryer heat lard over medium-high heat, about 4 minutes. Check for ripple effect. Grease should be up to about ¼ of the pan.
2. Drain excess marinade before dipping into batter for immediately placing into hot grease.
3. Start with thighs, dip in batter, drain excess batter. Using tongs, place thigh in the deep fryer of hot grease.

BUTTERMILK BATTERED SOUTHERN FRIED CHICKEN (CONT.)

Instructions (cont):

4. Follow the procedure with the remaining thighs, putting all 4 thighs in the grease together. Cook thighs for 5 to 7 minutes, uncovered. Reduce heat to medium-low. Cook another 5 to 7 minutes. Check for doneness and desired brownness. Remove chicken from deep fryer and drain on paper towels.

5. Follow steps 2 through 4 for breasts and drumsticks. Place drained fried chicken pieces on a cookie sheet, cover tightly with foil and place in a preheated oven 250°F. (For a crispier chicken, move foil after 5 minutes and leave uncovered for a few more minutes).

NOTE: Place the 1st and 2nd batch of chicken parts on same cookie sheet in the oven; but can use a separate cookie sheet for the last batch of chicken parts and keep in oven another six minutes as the other pieces can be removed. Serve with your favorite side dish.

TIPS: Using cayenne pepper in the batter gives the batter a spicy taste. I recommend giving it a try. Feel free to use other desired hot temperature frying oils, instead of lard (see article on the benefits of using Lard for cooking in the Resource Directory); and feel free to use a sugar substitute instead of sugar (see Ingredient Substitution Chart in the Resource Directory).

SOUTHERN FRIED CHICKEN | SERVES 8-10

Ingredients:

12 chicken parts
2 cups lard or desired cooking oil
1 cup buttermilk
1 egg
3 cups all-purpose flour

2 teaspoons sea salt
2 teaspoons ground black pepper
2 teaspoons garlic powder, divided
½ teaspoon paprika

Preparation:

1. Cut chicken breasts in half and then wash chicken thoroughly and drain.
2. In a small bowl, mix buttermilk and egg. Add a pinch of salt and ground black pepper and 1 teaspoon garlic powder to buttermilk solution. Stir and set aside.
3. In a large freezer bag, add flour, remaining 1 teaspoon garlic powder, 1 teaspoon salt, 1 teaspoon black pepper and paprika. Shake bag to mix well. Dip 4 to 6 pieces of chicken in buttermilk solution, first, and place chicken in the bag and shake well. Repeat procedure for remaining chicken. Set aside coated chicken pieces.

Instructions:

1. Using a cast iron skillet, heat lard over medium-high heat, about 4 minutes. Check for ripple effect. Oil should be up to about ¼ of the pan.
2. Starting from the back of the pan, add chicken, working towards the front to avoid grease splashes.
3. Cook chicken for 7 to 10 minutes, covered. Turn and cook for 5 minutes, covered. Check chicken for desired brownness. Turn and reduce heat to medium-low. Simmer for 5 to 10 minutes. Turn again and reduce heat to low heat and cook for 5 minutes.
4. Remove chicken from cast iron skillet and drain on paper towels.
5. Place pieces on a cooking sheet and place in a preheated oven 200 to 250°F. Cook for 6 minutes.
6. Follow steps 1 through 5 for the remaining chicken pieces. In step 5, place the last chicken parts on the same cooking sheet with the other pieces or on a separate sheet and cook for 6 minutes. Serve with your favorite side dish.

Although I recommend lard--lard is what we used in the country, feel free to cook your chicken in your favorite high-temperature oil (clear or almost clear oil is best). See article in Resource Directory on "The Benefits of Cooking with Lard"--considered a "good fat"--a country stable in all households where I grew up.

Mama's Old-Fashioned Barbecue Chicken | Serves 6-8

Ingredients:

12 raw pieces of chicken

1 small red onion, sliced thin

2 medium sweet onions, sliced thin

BBQ Sauce Ingredients:

1 tablespoon sea salt

1 tablespoon red pepper

1 tablespoon poultry seasoning

1 (16 oz.) container of chicken broth

2 (18 oz.) bottles of plain BBQ sauce of choice

2 (14 oz.) containers of ketchup

2 tablespoons regular mustard

1 tablespoon brown mustard or Dijon

¾ cups apple cider vinegar

½ cup brown sugar

1 tablespoons garlic powder

¼ stick butter, melted

4 tablespoon cornstarch, divided

Preparation:

1. Preheat the oven broiler.

Aunt Hattie's Barbecue Sauce Recipe

1. In a saucepan, over medium-high heat, stir in ketchup, BBQ sauce, apple cider vinegar, brown sugar, garlic, salt, pepper, poultry seasoning, and butter. Stir in both mustards. Cook for 2 minutes.
2. Stir in chicken broth and cornstarch mixture. The BBQ sauce will thicken. Let simmer on low heat for 10 minutes. Turn off heat and set aside.

Note: Taste Aunt Hattie's Barbecue Sauce to see if any additional ingredients should be added to suit your taste – I don't mind you making my sauce your very own favorite sauce.

MAMA'S OLD-FASHIONED BARBECUE CHICKEN (CONT.)

Instructions:

1. In a roaster, add chicken and chicken broth over chicken (lay pieces in roaster so that you can see the surface on most pieces).
2. Place uncovered roaster in the oven at the bottom level of the oven. Turn oven light on to check chicken frequently through oven door glass.
3. Monitor chicken for brownness, about 10 minutes, per side. Using long tongs, turn chicken pieces.
4. Turn chicken and add both onions on top of the chicken pieces. Brown under broiler for 10 minutes.
5. Remove roaster from oven and set aside.
6. Turn off broiler and turn on bake, 350°F.
7. Slowly and evenly pour my BBQ sauce over the top of your browned chicken and onions. Cover roaster and bake for 30 minutes.
8. Stick a fork in chicken to test for doneness; for thicker BBQ sauce to be, add I teaspoon cornstarch to two corners of your roaster and hold the pan at an angle to allow cornstarch to run into sauce so that the thickness of the BBQ sauce increases.
9. Cook for about 10 minutes. Turn off oven and let roaster set for about 5 minutes.

I serving this dish over brown rice or my Garlic Mashed Potatoes, Cauliflower Rice or Garlic Mashed Cauliflower recipes, under "Vegetables: or Side Dishes". Enjoy!

SMOTHERED FRIED CHICKEN I SERVES 8-10

Ingredients:

12 raw chicken parts (no wings)
2 cups lard
1 cup buttermilk
2 cups water
1 egg
3 cups all-purpose, divided

2 teaspoons sea salt, divided
2 teaspoon and ground black pepper, divided
2 teaspoons garlic powder, divided
1 large red onion, cut in half
¼ teaspoon of paprika
½ teaspoon sugar

SMOTHERED FRIED CHICKEN (CONT.)

Preparation:

1. Wash chicken and drain. Cut chicken breasts in half.
2. In a bowl, combine buttermilk and egg, 1 teaspoon sea salt, 1 teaspoon pepper, and 1 teaspoon garlic powder to the liquid and set aside.
3. In a large freezer bag, add 2 cups flour, 1 teaspoon garlic powder, 1 teaspoon sea salt, 1 teaspoon Black pepper and paprika. Shake the bag to mix well.
4. Dip 4 to 6 pieces of chicken in buttermilk solution, then, place them in the bag of flour and shake well. Place coated chicken on a plate and set aside. Follow this procedure for the remaining chicken.

Instructions:

1. Using a cast iron skillet, heat lard over medium-high heat, about 4 minutes. Check for ripple effect. Oil should be up to about ¼ of the pan.
2. Starting from the back of the pan, add chicken, working towards the front to avoid grease splashes.
3. Cook chicken for 7 to 10 minutes, covered. Turn and cook for 5 minutes, covered. Check chicken for desired brownness. Turn and reduce heat to medium-low. Simmer for 5 to 10 minutes. Turn and reduce heat to low heat and cook for 5 minutes.
4. Remove chicken from cast iron skillet and drain on paper towels.
5. Place pieces on a cooking sheet and place in a preheated oven 200 to 250°F. Bake for 6 minutes.
6. While chicken is baking, bring water to a boil in a kettle.

Make The Gravy:

1. Using the same cast iron skillet, discard most of the lard, leaving 2 tablespoons of lard in the cast iron skillet. Heat to medium-high. Add the onions and sauté, until the onions are brown and lightly caramelized. Remove onions from pan. Add 2 tablespoons to frying pan and reheat until hot.
2. Add remaining 1 cup flour to the hot grease and stir constantly until flour is absorbed in the grease and desired brownness is reached.
3. Reduce heat to medium. Gradually stir in some of the hot water, stirring constantly until gravy becomes smooth. Repeat with more water until the gravy has the desired thickness and no lumps.
4. Add remaining 1 teaspoon salt, remaining 1 teaspoon ground black pepper, and sugar and stir constantly. Cook for 1 minute.
5. Add the cooked chicken pieces in the gravy and cover. Cook for 5 to 7 minutes. Turn chicken pieces and reduce heat to low. Allow chicken to simmer for an additional 5 to 7 minutes.

HATTIE'S WHITE CHICKEN CHILI | SERVES 6-8

Ingredients:

4 cups chicken (3 breasts and 4 drumsticks), diced

2 large sweet onions, diced

1 (16 oz.) package of frozen corn

1 (14.75 oz.) can of cream corn

2 cups cauliflower, finely chopped

1 teaspoon sea salt

2 teaspoons cornstarch, divided

1 stalk of celery, chopped

1 teaspoon celery seed

1 teaspoon of poultry seasoning

1 tablespoons garlic powder

1 (10 ½ oz.) can cream of chicken

1 (10 ½ oz.) can cream of celery

2 cups chicken broth, divided

¼ cup olive oil

1 tablespoons light brown sugar

1 tablespoons apple cider vinegar

Instructions:

1. Heat olive oil in a medium sized skillet. Add onion and celery, and sauté for about 4 minutes.
2. Add cubed chicken and sauté for 2 minutes. Stir in light brown sugar, vinegar, salt, poultry seasoning, celery seeds and vinegar. Cook for 5 minutes.
3. Stir 1 cup chicken broth and reduce heat. Add cream of chicken, cream of celery, frozen corn and creamed corn, stirring constantly. Add remaining 1 cup chicken broth and cauliflower, and then cover. Cook for 8 minutes.
4. Transfer mixture to a large saucepan, cooking over low heat for 5 to 8 minutes. Periodically, check for thickness. Turn off heat.

CHICKEN & DUMPLINGS | SERVES 6-8

Ingredients:
6 boneless thighs (cut in 4 pieces)
4 breasts (cut in 4 pieces)
4 cups self-rising flour, divided
2 cups lard
2 cups cold water
1 (10 ½ oz.) can cream of celery soup
½ cup of cornstarch, divided
2 sweet onions, thinly sliced
1 onion, diced
1 (10 ½ oz.) can cream of chicken soup
1/3 cup sugar
1 (10 ½ oz.) can cream corn
½ cup butter
1 teaspoon celery seeds
1 teaspoon poultry seasoning
1 teaspoon sea salt
1 teaspoon garlic powder
1 teaspoon paprika
1 (12 oz.) bag of frozen mixed vegetables

How to Make Dumplings
1. In a large bowl, combine lard and 2 cups flour, until smooth and lump free.
2. Form an indenture in the center of dough and add about ¼ cup cold water, mixing constantly with your hands, blending in a little flour at a time from the outer edges of the bowl until consistency is doughy.
3. Lightly flour surface and knead dough thoroughly, until smooth.
4. Divide in half and spread flour on rolling pin. To form dumplings, roll dough about 1/8-inch thick. Take a knife to cut in slits at the top. Slits should be about 1-inch thick. Cut dough into 1" x 2" strips.
5. If you prefer round dumplings roll dough into 1" balls. Set dumplings aside.

Instructions:
1. In a large pot, over high heat, add chicken broth and bring to a boil. Stir in sugar, ¼ cup plain flour, frozen mixed vegetables, 2 cups water, cream corn, cream of celery soup, cream of chicken soup, ½ teaspoon celery seed, poultry seasoning, sea salt, garlic powder. Reduce heat and simmer uncovered for 30 minutes.

CHICKEN & DUMPLINGS (CONT.)

2. When it's almost done, stir in remaining ¼ cup plain flour, until absorbed. Add ¼ cup cornstarch. Constantly stir from the bottom to ensure cornstarch and flour do not stick. If necessary, add remaining ¼ cup cornstarch. Cook for 10 minutes.
3. Increase heat. Gently add dumpling strips by laying 12 across top of chicken broth and 12 diagonally. For round dumplings drop the dough balls down into the hot chicken broth mixture. Sprinkle remaining ½ teaspoon celery seeds and paprika on dumplings.
4. Reduce heat to low and simmer covered for 10 minutes, allowing dumplings to rise. Using a spoon, gently push dumplings down in broth.
5. If broth is not as thick as desired, simmer, covered, for 30 additional minutes and turn off heat. Push dumplings down in broth every 5 minutes.

CHICKEN POT PIE | SERVES 6-8

Ingredients:
Hattie's Homemade Crust (Pg. 138) or 9-inch deep-dish frozen refrigerated pie crust with a top
4 cups self-rising flour
2 cups lard
5 ½ cups water (4 cups to boil chicken and 1 ½ cup for chicken paste)
whole chicken or 12 chicken parts
1 (10 ½ oz.) can cream of celery soup
½ cup cornstarch
2 cups sweet onion, diced
1 cup onion, diced
1 (10 ½ oz.) can cream of chicken soup
1 (10 oz.) bag of shredded carrots
1 (10 oz.) bag of sliced fresh mushrooms
¼ cup sugar or sugar substitute
1 (10 ½ oz.) can cream of corn soup
1 (12 oz.) bag of frozen mixed vegetables
2 (16 oz.) containers of chicken broth
1 teaspoon garlic powder
1 teaspoon sea salt
½ teaspoon pepper
¼ stick butter

CHICKEN POT PIE (CONT.)

Preparation:

1. In a large pot, place 4 cups water, whole chicken or chicken parts in a pot. Allow to boil until done.
2. Grease casserole dish with ½ teaspoon lard. Preheat oven to 350°F.
3. Make crust while chicken is boiling.

MAKE THE CRUST (See Page 138)

Instructions:

MAKE THE POT PIE CHICKEN/VEGGIE MIXTURE:

1. Remove all bones from cooked chicken. Dice chicken, making sure it is ¼ of an inch thick, resulting in 6-8 cups of diced chicken. Set aside.
2. In a large pot, over high heat, add both containers of chicken broth and bring to a boil. Add shredded carrots, mushrooms and chicken and sweet onion.
3. Reduce heat and stir in can cream of celery soup, and cream of chicken soup, salt, pepper, ½ cup of both onions, sugar and garlic powder. Stir together, making sure soup is loose and lump free. Add frozen vegetables and cream corn. Stirring constantly.

PREPARE CASSEROLE DISH AND PRE-BAKE:

1. Line prepared casserole dish bottom with crust and bake 25 minutes at 350°F.
2. In a small bowl, combine ¼ cup flour with 1 ½ cup water to make a paste. Gradually, pour ½ of paste in large pot with other ingredients and stir. Stir in cornstarch and remaining ½ paste.
3. Add 1 cup of diced onion and stir constantly. Cook for 15 minutes. Turn off stove and allow chicken/ veggie mixture to set for 8 minutes.
4. Check crusted dish in oven. Should not be brown, but 1/3 of the way done. Take crust out of oven and wait 10 minutes.
5. Stir chicken/veggie mixture in pot on stove one last time to ensure all ingredients are mixed well. Using gloves, pour chicken/veggie mixture evenly in pre-cooked crusted casserole dish.
6. Sprinkle a dash of paprika on top of mixture before adding top crust. Cut small slits in the top crust and brush top crust with melted butter. Bake for 20 minutes at 350°F or until crust is golden brown. Turn off oven and allow pot pie to set in oven for 10 minutes. Serve hot.

CHICKEN SALAD | SERVES 6-8

Ingredients:

1 large rotisserie chicken
(6 cups chopped breasts and thighs)
¼ cup sweet onion, diced
1 celery stalk, chopped
¼ cup red pepper, diced
½ teaspoon sea salt
½ teaspoon sugar
1 tablespoon vinegar
1 tablespoon mustard
1 tablespoon sweet relish
¼ teaspoon garlic powder
¼ teaspoon celery seeds
½ cup cream cheese
½ cup Greek yogurt
1 tablespoon lemon juice
2 eggs

Preparation:

1. Remove skin from breasts and thigh parts of the cooked chicken and chop. Place chopped chicken in a bowl and set aside.
2. Cut celery stalk into ¼-inch dice and ¼-inch sweet onion.
3. Boil eggs. Remove from hot water, cool, peel and chop.

Instructions:

1. Combine all ingredients in a large bowl and stir until cream cheese and Greek yogurt are mixed well. Chill for at least 30 minutes before serving.

CHICKEN & WAFFLES | SERVES 6-8

Ingredients: Chicken

Deep fryer or deep pot
12 boneless breasts and thighs
4 cups lard
2 cups buttermilk (low-fat, optional)
2 eggs
5 cups plain flour
4 teaspoon sea salt
2 tablespoons pepper
2 tablespoons garlic
1 teaspoon baking powder
1 teaspoon sugar
1 teaspoon raw apple cider vinegar
¼ cup water
¼ teaspoon cayenne pepper (optional)

Preparation:

1. Wash chicken and drain. Cut chicken breasts in half. Sprinkle sea salt, pepper and garlic powder on chicken and place chicken in a bowl to marinate.
2. In a large freezer bag, add flour.

Make The Batter:

1. In a bowl, combine eggs, water, buttermilk, sugar, remaining 1 tablespoon sea salt, remaining 1 tablespoon ground black pepper, remaining 1 teaspoon garlic powder, raw apple cider vinegar, and (cayenne pepper optional).
2. Stir well, making sure consistency of batter is not too thick. Add water, if thinner batter is desired.

Instructions:

1. Using a skillet, heat lard, about 4 minutes. Oil should be up to about ¼ of the pan.
2. Start with thighs. Place 4 to 6 pieces in buttermilk solution and place in bag of flour and shake well. Using tongs, place thighs in oil.
3. After coating chicken pieces, place on a plate and set aside.
4. Cook thighs for 5 to 7 minutes, covered. Turn and cook for 5 minutes. Check chicken for desired brownness. Turn and reduce heat. Simmer for 5 to 10 minutes. Remove chicken from skillet and drain on paper towels.
5. Place pieces on a foil-covered cookie sheet and place in a preheated oven, 350°F. Cook for 6 minutes.

CHICKEN & WAFFLES (CONT.)

Waffles Ingredients:

3 eggs

1 cup of wheat flour

1 cup of almond flour

1 tablespoon of baking powder

1 tablespoon baking soda

1 cup buttermilk

¼ cup of sour cream or Greek yogurt

Olive oil or spray

¼ cup of maple syrup or honey

¼ stick butter, melted

Fruit of choice (optional)

Preparation:

1. Beat 3 eggs.
2. Mix all ingredients to make waffle batter.
3. Make sure waffle pan is hot.

Instructions:

1. Spray waffle pan and pour in ½ cup batter.
2. Put electric fryer on 350°F
3. Should be done after about 5 minutes.
4. Put waffles on a cookie sheet in oven on to keep hot

HATTIE'S SYRUP

1 cup maple syrup

½ cup honey

½ cup brown sugar

3 tablespoons butter

½ teaspoon hot sauce

½ teaspoon wine vinegar

½ teaspoon cornstarch

Instructions:

1. Put everything in a saucepan and stir together.
2. Pour sauce over waffles and put breast or thigh on top and pour syrup again.

HATTIE'S FAMOUS HOMEMADE CHILI | SERVES 6-8

Ingredients:

1 pound ground turkey
1 pound lean ground beef
2 packages sausage (1 regular & 1 hot, optional)
1 (6 oz.) can of tomato paste
1 (4 oz.) box of chili powder
4 tablespoons garlic powder
1 teaspoon of black pepper
2 (28 oz.) cans of whole peeled tomatoes
2 large onions, diced
2 medium sweet onion, diced

4 bell peppers (green, red, yellow and orange)
1 medium can mushroom with stems & pieces
1 can of red beans or kidney beans, optional
4 tablespoons sea salt
⅓ cup of raw brown sugar
¼ cup of maple syrup
⅓ cup apple cider vinegar
2 to 4 cups water
⅓ cup olive oil

Preparation:

1. Place the diced bell peppers (red, green, yellow & orange) in 2 small bowls.
2. In a blender, blend the whole peeled tomatoes for about 2 minutes.
3. Preheat oven to 350°F.

Instructions:

1. In a large pot over medium-high heat, sauté the ground lean beef and ground turkey in olive oil. Cook until the meat is no longer pink.

2. Stir, 1 onion, 1 sweet onion, half of all four of the bell peppers (the other half of these ingredients will be added to the chili later).

3. Stir in the box of chili powder and tomato paste.

4. Stir in sea salt, black pepper, and garlic powder. Cook for 8 minutes, stirring constantly from the bottom.

5. Add the blended whole peeled tomatoes and the can of mushroom with stems and pieces, optional. Stir together thoroughly.

6. Add the ketchup, the apple cider vinegar; brown sugar, maple syrup, the other half of the bell peppers, and 1 large onion and 1 sweet onion.

7. Stir in 2 to 4 cups water, depending on desired thickness. Taste for the addition of ingredients, such as salt, sugar, garlic, vinegar, chili powder.

8. Reduce stove to medium-heat and let chili cook slowly covered for 15 minutes. Stir often. Reduce stove to low heat and let chili simmer covered for another 10 minutes.

9. Turn off the stove and stir. Allow the chili to sit and cool for 30 minutes before serving.

NOTE: *Whether you are making the Hattie's Three Meats Chili (ground beef, ground Turkey and/or regular and hot sausage) or using only one meat, you will use the same other ingredients above and the same Instructions below. Just use double the meat when using only one type of meat.*

HATTIE'S FAMOUS HOMEMADE CHILI I (CONT.)

OTHER VERSIONS OF MY CHILI:

Ground Turkey Version: All Ingredients are the same, except add 1 teaspoon of poultry seasoning and 1/2 teaspoon of celery seeds into the ground turkey as you are sautéing it. Then, follow instructions above.

Hot Sausage Version: All ingredients are the same, except add 1 teaspoon of sage in meat as it is cooking.

Vegetarian Version: All the ingredients are the same, except don't add any meat and double the amount of the onions and green peppers. Place ½ cup of shredded carrots, ½ cup of chopped broccoli, and ½ cup of chopped cauliflower and sauté together. Feel free to add other vegetables you desire, as well in your all-vegetable chili, including various beans.

This chili can be served in a bowl as a meal with a salad and garlic butter toasted bread. Put toppings on the chili (optional). Make enough for freezing or for other uses later.

Other ways my family eats my chili: Over hot dogs to make chili dogs, over spaghetti, Sloppy Joe on buns, on open faced hamburger buns with melted cheese. I usually make a big batch for my family to take some home to eat later or freeze the rest for cold and rainy day.

SERVE CHILI With VARIOUS TOPPINGS:
Shredded Cheeses
Sour Cream
Diced Onions
Scallions
Nachos
Fritos

Other Variations For The Chili Dogs:
Chili Dog w/Onions
Chili Dog w/Sauerkraut
Chili Dog w/Shredded Cheese

HAMBURGER PATTIES & BROWN GRAVY OVER LONG GRAIN BROWN RICE | SERVES 6-8

Ingredients:

1 large package fresh lean hamburger meat

1 onion, diced

2 eggs

½ teaspoon of sugar

1 green bell pepper, chopped

½ cup garlic and herb seasoned bread crumbs

1 teaspoon sea salt, divided

1 teaspoon black pepper, divided

1 teaspoon garlic powder

1 cup virgin olive oil, divided

¼ stick butter (4 Tablespoons, divided)

2 cups plain flour (gluten free)

Preparation:

1. Start cooking the long grain brown rice according to package.
2. In a large mixing bowl, combine hamburger meat, sea salt, garlic powder, bell pepper, onions, eggs, and bread crumbs.
3. Form 12 hamburger balls and place on a plate. Flatten into hamburger patties.

Instructions:

1. In a large skillet, over medium-high heat, heat ½ cup virgin olive oil and 2 tablespoons butter; then place patties in hot skillet starting from the back of the skillet.
2. Cook for 4 minutes on one side. Once brown, turn over gently and allow other side to brown for about 4 minutes.
3. Remove patties from skillet and place on a platter.
4. Add 2 Tablespoons of butter to the olive oil and hamburger drippings in the skillet and heat on medium high until hot. Turn heat to medium and add flour to oils and stir constantly to remove any lumps and until the gravy roux turns to desired brownness (at least 5 minutes to remove the raw taste of the flour).
5. Reduce heat to low and continue to stir constantly.
6. Pour ¼ hot tap water in skillet [pan] and stir rapidly from the bottom of the skillet. Add another ¼ cup water and continue stirring, ensuring gravy has no lumps. Add the salt, pepper and sugar.
7. Once desired consistency is obtained, add hamburgers to gravy, starting from the back of the skillet.
8. Cover skillet and let hamburgers simmer in the gravy for about 10 minutes.
9. Turn off stove. Let sit for 5 minutes and serve hot over brown rice.

HATTIE'S STUFFED PEPPERS
SERVES 6-8

Ingredients:

2 lbs. lean ground beef;

¼ cup olive oil

4 cups of Brown rice;

1 cup beef broth;

½ small red onion;

½ small sweet onion;

½ small regular onion;

4 green bell peppers, plus I for dicing;

2 yellow bell peppers, plus 1 for dicing;

2 red bell peppers, plus I for dicing;

2 teaspoon garlic powder, divided;

1 teaspoon sea salt;

1 teaspoon crushed red peppers;

1 teaspoon of black pepper;

4 tablespoons butter;

1 cup of French onion soup;

2 eggs

2 tablespoon cold water

1 teaspoon Paprika (or seasoned salt)

Preparation:

1. Dice red, yellow, and green bell peppers; the red, sweet, and regular onions and in a bowl.
2. Preheat oven 375°F.

Instructions:

1. Cook rice according to directions; however, instead of using water, use beef broth and French Onion Soup. As rice begins to boil, add 1/3 of the onions mixture the onions.
2. Bring to a second boil. Cover and turn heat down. Cook until almost done.
3. Cut off top of green, yellow and red bell peppers. Cover with aluminum foil and place aside.

HATTIE'S STUFFED GREEN PEPPERS (CONT.)

Instructions

4. In a large skillet, saute ground beef in olive oil with the remaining 2/3 diced onions mixture & diced green, yellow, and red bell pepper mixture. Add sea salt, black pepper, and garlic powder. Stir together until beef is no longer pink.

5. Remove rice from saucepan and with spoon, loosen rice. Add 1/2 of the rice to skillet with the meat. Stir gently. Add remaining rice and again, stir gently. Move skillet from stove, allowing it to cool for 45 minutes.

6. Beat eggs in a small bowl. Add in 2 tablespoons of water. Pour egg mixture into cooled ground beef and rice mixture. Stir for about 1 minute. Spoon ground rice mixture into each bell pepper. Sprinkle garlic powder and seasoned sait or paprika on top to give it color (optional).

7. Place in oven. Bake for about 20 minutes. Turn broiler on for about 1 minute or until top of the bell peppers are brown. Serve Hot!

OLE FASHIONED MEATLOAF | SERVES 6-8

Ingredients:

2 packages lean ground beef
1 medium onion, diced
1 green bell pepper, diced
1 red bell pepper, diced
1 teaspoon garlic powder
1 teaspoon sea salt
½ cup seasoned bread crumbs
¼ cup brown sugar
¼ cup maple syrup
2 cups of BBQ sauce
1 cup of ketchup
1 tablespoon mustard
2 tablespoons apple cider vinegar
1 teaspoon lemon juice
1 teaspoon Worcestershire sauce
¼ cup olive oil
2 tablespoons tomato puree

Instructions:

1. Preheat the oven to 375°F.
2. In a large mixing bowl, combine lean meat and all the ingredients, except olive oil and BBQ Sauce.
3. Grease a 9 x 13 rectangular casserole dish with olive oil. Shape meat mixture into a rectangular loaf in prepared casserole dish. Bake for 30 to 40 minutes.
4. Turn casserole dish around 180 degrees and allow meatloaf to cook for an additional 20 minutes.
5. Pour BBQ sauce over the top of the meatloaf. Bake an additional 4 minutes.
6. Turn off heat and let meatloaf stand for 7 minutes. Serve warm with your favorite vegetables.

Note: Instead of ground beef, try ground turkey. Worcestershire sauce can be replaced with soy sauce.

Spaghetti & Meatballs | Serves 6-8

Spaghetti:
Follow instructions on box to cook spaghetti, or use shredded zucchini steamed for 5 minutes.

Spaghetti Sauce:

1 (20 oz.) bottle of ketchup	1/3 cup brown sugar
1 (6 oz.) can tomato paste	1/3 cup apple cider vinegar
1 (8 oz.) can canned tomatoes	¼ stick butter
1 small onion, diced	2 tablespoon garlic powder
1 small sweet onion, diced	1 teaspoon parsley
1 green bell pepper, diced	1 teaspoon oregano
1 red bell pepper, diced	2 tablespoon cornstarch, divided
1 (4oz.) can sliced mushrooms	2 teaspoons sea salt

Instructions:
1. Combine all ingredients in the sauce pan and stir thoroughly continuing to saute all of the ingredients for 10 to 15 minutes.
2. Turn down heat to medium and let cook slowly for another 10 minutes. Taste for desired sweetness.
3. Reduce to low heat and simmer for 15 minutes, stirring to ensure sauce doesn't stick to saucepan.
4. If sauce is too loose, add 1 teaspoon cornstarch mixed with water. Stir thoroughly. If still not thick enough for your personal preference, add more cornstarch, stir and let sit for 5 minutes.

SPAGHETTI & MEATBALLS (CONT.)

MEATBALLS:

Ingredients:
20 oz package lean ground beef
1 small onion, diced
2 eggs
1 medium green bell pepper, diced
1 cup seasoned bread crumbs
1 teaspoon sea salt
1 teaspoon black pepper
1 teaspoon garlic powder

Preparation:
Preheat the oven to 375°F.

Instructions:
1. In a medium bowl, combine all of ingredients.
2. Shape hamburger into 2-inch (2 oz) balls and place on a cookie sheet.
3. Bake for 15 minutes, turn over and bake for 10 additional minutes.
4. Ladel sauce over meatballs and spaghetti. Enjoy with a salad or favorite vegetable.

SPAGHETTI & MEAT SAUCE | SERVES 6 - 8

Meat Sauce:
Same sauce ingredients as the spaghetti and meatballs, but add:
2 (16 oz.) packages of lean ground beef
2 cans (8 oz.) tomato sauce
1 (2.5 oz.) package of chili powder

Instructions:
1. In a large saucepan, heat olive oil medium to high, sauté the lean meat for about 10 minutes.
2. Combine all other ingredients in the sauce pan and stir thoroughly continuing to saute all the ingredients for 10 to 15 minutes.
3. Turn down heat to medium and let cook slowly for another 10 minutes. Taste for desired sweetness.
4. Reduce heat and simmer for 15 minutes, stirring to ensure sauce does not stick to saucepan.
5. If sauce is too loose, add 1 teaspoon cornstarch mixed with water. Stir thoroughly. If sauce is still not thick enough, add more cornstarch, stir and let sit for 5 minutes.
6. Pour meat sauce over spaghetti or shredded zucchini. **Enjoy with your favorite salad or veggie.**

My Meat Sauce can be prepared meatless. Follow the same instructions and delete the meat.

CARAMELIZED STEAK WITH MIXED VEGETABLES | SERVES 6-12

Ingredients:

10 to 12 thin steak medallions

1 small red onion, chopped

½ cup olive oil

1 teaspoon sage

¼ cup honey

¼ stick butter

1 teaspoon sea salt

½ teaspoon of dry or Dijon mustard

2 tablespoon apple cider vinegar

2 tablespoons cornstarch, divided

1 teaspoon pepper

1 pound bag peeled baby-cut carrots, chopped

1 pound bag cauliflower

1 pound bag Brussel sprouts

1 teaspoon garlic powder

2 teaspoon lemon juice

½ teaspoon nutmeg

½ cup beef broth

Preparation:

Wash steak medallion. Drain.

Beat steak medallions with a mallet until flat. Add salt, pepper and garlic powder and place to the side.

In a bowl, add baby-cut carrots, cauliflower, Brussel sprouts and green bell pepper, lemon juice.

Mix well.

Instructions:

1. In a medium skillet, over medium-high heat, sauté red onion in olive oil. Cook for 2 minutes.

2. Add steak medallion in skillet. Cook medium rare by searing until they are a rich brown color, about 5 minutes per side. Sprinkle with sea salt and ground black pepper. Remove medallions from skillet and place to the side.

3. Add beef broth, honey, apple cider vinegar, sage, garlic powder, dry mustard, 1 tablespoon cornstarch, butter and remaining sea salt and ground black pepper and vegetable mix.

4. Lay medallions over vegetables. Reduce heat to medium. Cover and simmer for 10-15 minutes.

5. Add remaining 1 tablespoon cornstarch, ½ teaspoon on each side. Add ½ teaspoon nutmeg.

6. Once sauce consistency is thick enough, dish is done and ready to serve.

STIR FRY BEEF | SERVES 6-8

Ingredients:

1 green bell pepper, sliced (thick or thin)
1 red bell pepper, sliced (thick or thin)
1 red onion, sliced (thick or thin)
(14 oz.) beef broth
1 pound sirloin or flank sliced thinly across
¼ cup olive oil
1 teaspoon sea salt
1 teaspoon garlic powder

½ teaspoon crushed red peppers (optional)
½ teaspoon ground black pepper
½ teaspoon parsley
2 tablespoons cornstarch, divided
1 tablespoon maple syrup
1 tablespoon wine vinegar
1 teaspoon Dijon mustard

This recipe can be prepared with chicken or shrimp. Follow the same instructions above, except add ¼ cup of chicken broth, instead of beef broth. If using shrimp, add ¼ teaspoon of Old Bay® seasoning. Also, instead of olive oil, use unflavored coconut oil. Enjoy!

Instructions:

1. In a large skillet, heat the olive oil over medium-high heat for about 1 minute. Add sirloin or flank. Stir-fry, stirring constantly until beef is almost done, about 3 to 5 minutes.
2. Stir in green bell pepper, onion, garlic powder, sea salt, and ground black pepper. Stir-fry, stir constantly for 8 to 10 minutes.
3. Add beef broth. Reduce heat to medium and shake pan so that stir-fry can get loose from the bottom (If stir-fry is too loose, to reach desired thickness, stir in 1 tablespoon cornstarch and cook for 1 minute).
4. Add wine vinegar, maple syrup, crushed peppers (optional) and Dijon mustard. Cover and reduce heat to low. Simmer for 5 minutes.
5. Turn off heat and simmer an additional 5 minutes and serve with rice.

CHITTERLINGS | SERVES 6-8

Ingredients:

3 pounds chitterlings, cook & cut in 4 to 5-inch pieces
10 cups water
1 medium onion, peeled & quartered
1 small potato, peeled & quartered
1 teaspoons garlic powder
1 teaspoons sea salt, divided
2 tablespoon baking soda
1 (12 oz.) bottle beer (your choice)
1 tablespoon apple cider vinegar
1 tablespoon sugar
¼ teaspoon cayenne pepper
½ teaspoon hot sauce

Preparation:

1. Split and carefully wash the chitterlings thoroughly with plenty of water, Cut chitterling strips into 4 to 5-inch pieces.
2. Soak in vinegar, 4 cups of water and baking soda for 1 hour. Drain in a large colander. Rinse again with Plenty of water and drain.

Instructions:

1. In a large pot, add the chitterlings, 8 cups water, 6 oz. beer, onion, potato, garlic powder and salt. Cover with water by 2 inches over the top of the chitterlings.
2. Bring to a boil, then reduce the heat to a simmer. Cover and cook until done about 45-60 minutes. Remove from the heat and let set and cool.   Sprinkle with hot sauce and/or vinegar (optional).

Serve with collard greens, potato salad and my corny cornbread. Enjoy!

BEER BATTERED DEEP FRIED CHITTERLINGS | SERVES 8-10

Ingredients:
3 pounds chitterlings, cook & cut in 2-inch pieces
8 cups water, divided
1 medium onion, peeled & quartered
1 small potato, peeled & quartered
2 teaspoons garlic powder, divided
2 teaspoons sea salt, divided
3 cups Lard, melted
6 oz. beer

Batter Ingredients:
3 pounds chitterlings, cook & cut in 2-inch pieces
8 cups water, divided
1 medium onion, peeled & quartered
1 small potato, peeled & quartered
2 teaspoons garlic powder, divided
2 teaspoons sea salt, divided
3 cups Lard, melted
6 oz. beer (your choice)

Instructions:
1. The Preparation would be the same as the Regular Chitterlings above
2. Pre-Cooking the Chitterlings For Deep Frying
   A. In a large pot, add the chitterlings, 7 cups water, 6 oz. beer, onion, potato, garlic powder and salt. Cover with water by 2 inches.
   B. Bring to a boil, then reduce heat to a simmer. Cover and cook until half done about 30 minutes.
   C. Remove from heat and run cold water over chitterlings. Cut chitterling strips into 2-inch pieces.

3. Making The Beer Batter (Same batter recipe can be used for Fried Chitterlings and Fried Crabs —just add 1 teaspoon Old Bay ® Seasoning for the fried crab batter)
4. In a large bowl, mix the eggs, salt, sugar, garlic, cayenne pepper, hot sauce (optional), and vinegar. Slowly whisk in the 6 oz. beer until combined; Add 1 cup water.
5. Add 2 cups flour and mix until batter is smooth. Add more beer or water if too thick.

4. Deep Frying Chitterlings:
   A. Put lard into a deep fryer or deep sauce pan to a depth of at least 3 inches and heat on medium high until hot.
   B. In a shallow bowl, place remaining 1 cup flour; Place chitterling pieces in the flour to pre-coat before placing in batter *(batter sticks to slippery chitterlings better when coating pieces with flour first—a little trick my stepmother taught me).*
   C. Dip a few chitterling pieces (about 10 at a time) into the batter and place into the hot grease and fry until golden brown, about 2 to 4 minutes for each batch. When done, place chitterlings on a paper towel to drain. Repeat the steps 1 and 2 above for the next batch or batches.

Serve as an **Appetizer** or an **Entrée**--Sprinkle with hot sauce or make my **Special Dip Sauce** for my deep fried chitterlings and steamed crabs *(1/2 teaspoon hot sauce; 1 teaspoon vinegar; 1 teaspoon maple syrup, 1 tablespoon butter*--Multiply these ingredients as your servings increase and to suit desired taste; Add ½ teaspoon Old Bay® Seasoning to this dip for Crabs--steamed and fried).

PIGS' FEET | SERVES 4-6

Ingredients:
6 pigs' feet
6 cups water
1 medium onion
1 tablespoon sugar
1 tablespoon sea salt
1 tablespoon sage
1 tablespoon crushed pepper
2 tablespoon maple syrup
1 large can sauerkraut (optional)
1 cup apple cider vinegar, plus 2 tablespoons

Preparation:
Wash pigs' feet thoroughly.

Instructions:

1. In a crockpot, combine water, crushed pepper, vinegar, onion, sugar, sea salt and sage.
2. Turn crockpot on high and allow feet to cook for 1 to 2 hours.
3. When almost done and tender, add another sprinkle of crushed peppers and 2 tablespoon vinegar and 2 tablespoon of maple syrup; add I large can sauerkraut (optional—that sweet & sour taste) and let simmer to meld the flavors. If available, the butcher at the supermarket can split pigs' feet, and they will cook much faster (Careful not to overcook--as the split pigs' feet will fall completely off the bone).

A Variation:
PIG TAILS: For the pig tail lovers, just substitute 6 pigtails for the pigs' feet, using the same ingredients. The cooking time will be half the time. Put in your sauerkraut when almost done and let simmer and let flavors meld together.

Serve with collard greens, potato salad and my corny cornbread. Enjoy!

FRIED PORK CHOPS | SERVES 4-6

Ingredients:

6 pork chops
1 medium onion, sliced
2 cups flour
½ cup olive oil

1 teaspoon sea salt
1 teaspoon pepper
1 teaspoon garlic powder

Instructions:

1. Wash chops and drain. Add salt, pepper and garlic powder. In a freezer bag, add flour. Place chops in flour and shake well to coat.
2. In a skillet, heat olive oil over medium high and fry pork chops for 4 to 5 minutes. Turn and fry until brown.
3. Once chops are brown on both sides, remove from skillet and lay on paper towels to drain.
4. Pour oil from skillet leaving about 2 tablespoons. Add onions and sauté for 10 minutes or until golden brown.
5. Return chops to skillet. Reduce heat, cover and simmer for 5 minutes.

FRIED PORK CHOPS & GRAVY | SERVES 4-6

Ingredients:

6 pork chops
1 medium onion, sliced
½ cup olive oil
2 cups flour

2 cups water
1 teaspoon sea salt
1 teaspoon ground black pepper
1 teaspoon garlic powder
1/4 cup water

Instructions:

1. Wash pork chops and drain. Add sea salt, ground black pepper and garlic powder. In a freezer bag, add flour. Place chops in flour and shake well to coat.
2. In a large skillet, heat olive oil over medium heat and fry pork chops for 4 to 5 minutes. Turn and fry until brown.
3. Once chops are brown on both sides, remove from skillet and lay on paper towels to drain.

Make The Gravy:

4. Pour oil from skillet leaving about 2 tablespoons. Add onions and sauté for 10 minutes or until golden brown. In a kettle, add 2 cups water and bring to a boil.
5. Add 2 tablespoons olive oil and remaining ½ cup flour to hot oil and stir constantly, until flour is brown.
6. Gradually stir in ¼ cup hot water from the kettle. Stir constantly. Continue to add water, until desired gravy consistency. Return chops to skillet with sautéed onions and cover. Let simmer, uncovered for 10 minutes. **Serve with your favorite Sides.**

STUFFED PORK CHOPS | SERVES 4-6

Ingredients:

6 thick-cut (1½ -inches) pork chops

1 teaspoon sage

1 teaspoon garlic powder

1 teaspoon sea salt

½ butter, melted

½ teaspoon cayenne pepper

1 teaspoon pepper

2 tablespoons olive oil

1 egg, lightly beaten

Prepare and cook Pork Chops:

1. Dip pork chop in egg mixture.
2. In a skillet, over medium-high, cook and allow chops to brown on both sides.
3. Remove chops from heat and cut a pocket in each pork chop. Spoon about ½ cup stuffing into each pocket. Secure with a toothpick.
4. Brush casserole dish with olive oil. Place chops in prepared casserole dish.
5. Add smoked paprika on each chop. Bake for 30 to 40 minutes. Cover with aluminum foil once done. Remove toothpicks before serving.

Make The Stuffing

Stuffing Ingredients:

1 pound of hot sausage (16 oz.)

4 cups garlic and herb bread crumbs

6 slices wheat bread, toasted

½ stick butter, melted

1 medium sweet onion, diced

1 medium onion, diced

4 fresh celery stalks, chopped

1 tablespoon sage

1 teaspoon poultry seasoning

1 teaspoon sea salt

1 teaspoon celery seeds

1 teaspoon garlic powder

1 teaspoon sugar

3 eggs, beaten

1 container low sodium chicken broth

Preparation:

Preheat oven to 350°F.

STUFFED PORK CHOPS (CONT.)

Make The Stuffing (Cont.)

Stuffing Instructions:

1. In a skillet, sauté onions, celery and sausage.
2. In a large bowl, beat eggs and add 1 tablespoon water. Combine bread crumbs, wheat bread, sage, poultry powder, salt, celery seeds, garlic powder, sugar, eggs and chicken broth. Stir in sausage and onion mixture. Set stuffing aside.

RIBS | SERVES 6-8

Ingredients:

1 slab of lean pork or beef ribs

1 medium onion, diced

¼ cup brown sugar

¼ cup maple syrup

2 cups BBQ Sauce

1 cup ketchup

1 tablespoon mustard

2 tablespoons apple cider vinegar

1 teaspoon garlic powder

½ teaspoon sea salt

1 teaspoon lemon juice

1 teaspoon Worcestershire sauce or soy sauce

2 tablespoons cornstarch

¼ cup oil or butter

2 tablespoons tomato puree

Preparation:

1. Preheat oven to 375°F
2. In a pot, boil ribs with a tablespoon of sea salt.
3. Mix cornstarch in a cup.
4. Grease casserole dish with olive oil.

RIBS (CONT.)

Instructions:

1. In a medium-sized saucepan, over medium-high heat, sauté onions in oil and stir in other ingredients.
2. Add 1 tablespoon cornstarch at a time until sauce is at desired thickness.
3. Gently remove ribs from pan and place in casserole dish.
4. Pour BBQ sauce on ribs and cover with foil. Bake between 20 to 30 minutes.
5. Once ribs are done, turn off oven and cover dish. Allow ribs to sit for 10 minutes before serving.

STEAMED CRABS | SERVES 4-6

Ingredients:

20 to 30 live jumbo blue crabs

1 cup vinegar

2 quarts water

1 teaspoon cayenne pepper

4 tablespoons Old Bay® seasoning

Preparation:

1. Rinse crabs with kitchen hose.
2. In a large pot, bring water to a boil.
   Add vinegar, cayenne pepper and Old Bay® seasoning.

Instructions:

1. Use tongs to individually place crabs in pot.
2. Boil until back of crab's shells turn red and crabs stop moving.
3. Serve hot or cold—Good with corn on the cob and hush puppies.

A Variation:

BEER BATTERED FRIED CRABS: Remove hard shell and the "dead man" from the steamed crabs, dip crab in the beer batter (use same batter recipe as Batter Fried Chitterlings with an extra teaspoon of apple cider vinegar and ¼ cup beer).

BAKED FISH | SERVES 6-8

Ingredients:

8 pieces Whiting or Lake trout
2 eggs
½ cup olive oil
1 cup cornmeal

1 teaspoon garlic powder
1 teaspoon Old Bay® seasoning
1 teaspoon smoked paprika
1 tablespoon lemon juice

Preparation:

1. Preheat oven to 375°F.
2. Lightly coat baking dish with olive oil.
3. In a bowl, whisk egg. In a separate bowl, combine cornmeal, garlic powder and Old Bay® seasoning.
4. Rinse fish and drain.

Instructions:

1. Dip fish in egg, then cornmeal mixture. Place fish in prepared casserole dish. Bake for 15 minutes.
2. Turn fish with a spatula and thinly brush lemon juice. Bake for 10 minutes.
3. If necessary, turn on broiler for 4 minutes, allowing fish to brown.
4. Cover dish with aluminum foil.

A Variation:

FRIED FISH: Prepare fish in the same manner; except, after coating fish in cornmeal mixture, place the fish in a skillet of hot grease to fry; fry on each side for 3-5 minutes until brown; drain on paper towel.

SALMON LOAF | SERVES 6-8

Ingredients:

2 medium sweet onions, diced
2 (14.75 oz.) cans of salmon
3 eggs
1 teaspoon salt

½ teaspoon cayenne pepper
½ cup self-rising flour
½ cup garlic and herb bread crumbs
¼ stick of butter, melted

Instructions:

1. Preheat oven to 375°F.
2. Combine all ingredients in a large bowl. Shape into a loaf or place in a loaf dish.
3. Pour butter around sides of dish. Leave a little space at top of dish.
4. Bake for 25 to 30 minutes. Insert knife to see if eggs and onions are properly cooking.
5. If salmon loaf is getting too brown, reduce heat to 350°F and cover with aluminum foil.

SALMON CAKES | SERVES 6-8

Ingredients:
2 (14.75 oz.) cans of salmon
1 cup olive oil
2 medium sweet onions, finely chopped
3 eggs
1 teaspoon salt
½ teaspoon cayenne pepper
½ cup self-rising flour
½ cup garlic and herb bread crumbs

Preparations:
1. Open cans of salmon and drain thoroughly.
2. Place salmon in a mixing bowl and flake evenly with a fork. Stir in sweet onions, eggs, sea salt, cayenne pepper, bread crumbs, and self-rising flour. If mixture is loose, add a little more flour and stir until well blended.

Instructions:
1. Shape mixture into patties about the size of an average burger. They should be about 1/3 of an inch thick. Place salmon cakes on a plate with parchment paper.
2. In a skillet, over medium-high, heat olive oil. Once oil is hot, add salmon cakes starting from the back.
3. Cook cakes for 5-7 minutes, uncovered. Once cakes are brown to your desired likeness, gently turn to brown on the next side, about 5-6 minutes. Drain on paper towels. Serve!

A Variation:
SALMON & ONIONS OVER RICE WITH CABBAGE: In a skillet with hot olive oil, sauté onions until partially brown; pour cans of salmon with juice in the skillet; loosen salmon and stir; blend eggs with salmon and stir until eggs cook and salmon juice thickens. Serve over brown rice; and with stir-fried cabbage, onions and shredded carrots.

BAKED SALMON & VEGETABLES | SERVES 6-8

Ingredients:
6-8 pieces of salmon
1 (32 oz.) container of vegetable broth
1 small onion, sliced
1 (16 oz.) bag baby carrots
1 head cabbage, shredded

1 head cauliflower, cut into florets
1 teaspoon sea salt, divided
1 teaspoon garlic powder, divided
2 tablespoons cornstarch

BAKED SALMON & VEGETABLES (CONT.)

Instructions:

1. Preheat oven to 350°F.
2. In a bowl, combine carrots, cabbage, cauliflower, ½ sea salt, ½ garlic powder, cornstarch, vegetable broth and onion.
3. Coat baking sheet with cooking spray. Place salmon on baking sheet and sprinkle with remaining ½ sea salt and ½ garlic powder. Bake for 15 minutes.
4. When salmon is brown, add vegetables. Cover with foil and bake for 10 minutes.

LOBSTER POT | SERVES 6-8

Ingredients:

3 pounds lobsters
8 small red potatoes
½ stick butter
8 ears of corn
8 carrots, peeled
2 teaspoons sea salt
1 teaspoon Old Bay® seasoning
1 tablespoon cayenne pepper

Instructions:

1. Fill a large pot ¾ full of water. Bring to a boil over high-heat. Place all ingredients into pot and add lobsters. Reduce heat to medium-high.
2. Boil until the shells turn bright red, 12 to 20 minutes, depending on the size of the lobsters.
3. Remove lobsters from the pot with tongs and place on a plate to drain and cool.

A Variation:

SHRIMP OR MUSSEL POT

Same recipe as above. Substitute shrimp or mussels for lobster.

Serve hot with my Hattie's Special Crab Dip Butter Sauce (Pg. 70).

Fish and Chips Hattie's Style | Serves 6-8

Ingredients:
8 pieces Whiting or Lake trout
2 cups rice flour
2 cups cornmeal
2 eggs
¾ cups lard
1 teaspoon sea salt, divided
1 teaspoon ground black pepper, divided
1 teaspoon garlic powder
1 teaspoon Old Bay® seasoning
1 teaspoon smoked paprika
1 tablespoon malt vinegar

Preparation:
1. Preheat oven to 325°F.
2. Wash fish and drain.
3. In a small bowl, whisk eggs. Stir in garlic powder, smoked paprika, and malt vinegar.
4. In a freezer bag, add cornmeal, rice flour, sea salt and ground black pepper, and Old Bay® seasoning.
5. Grease casserole dish with lard.

Instructions:
1. Dip fish in egg solution, next in cornmeal.
2. Place in prepared casserole dish. Cook in oven for 15 minutes. Turn fish and cook for 10 minutes.
3. Turn on broiler and allow fish to get brown, about 2 minutes.
4. Cover with aluminum foil. Allow dish to remain in oven for an additional 5 minutes before serving.

Oven Fried Potatoes (Chips)
1. Cut potatoes in half lengthwise and cut halves into wedges.
2. Put olive oil in bowl and mix in sea salt, garlic, smoked paprika and malt vinegar.
3. Put potatoes in bowl and marinade in mixture.
4. Place potatoes on a cookie sheet and put in broiler; Turn over after 5 minutes.
5. Reduce heat to 200°F once done, and let fish stay in oven for 5 minutes.

A Variation:
BRITISH-STYLE FRIED FISH & CHIPS: Instead of oven baked fish and potato wedges, place them in a deep fryer of hot grease and fry until crispy and brown; drain. Serve both hot with a sprinkle of malt vinegar and hot sauce on one or both.

TUNA CASSEROLE | SERVES 6-8

Ingredients:

2 (5 ounce) cans tuna in water, drained
1 (12 ounce) package egg noodles
1 (10.75 ounce) can cream of celery soup
1 (10.75 ounce) can cream of chicken soup
1 (10.75 ounce) can cream of mushroom soup
1 teaspoon garlic powder
1 teaspoon sea salt
1 teaspoon ground black pepper
1 teaspoon sugar
1 (12 oz.) bag frozen corn
1 (12 oz.) bag frozen peas and carrots
¼ teaspoon seasoning salt
2 large eggs
1 cup bread crumbs
½ cup whole milk

Preparation:

1. Defrost frozen vegetables for 1 hour.
2. Preheat oven to 350°F.

Instructions:

1. Bring a large pot of lightly salted water to a boil. Cook egg noodles for 8 minutes, or until al dente; drain.
2. Beat eggs in a large bowl. Add milk, garlic powder, sea salt, sugar, ground black pepper , and thawed vegetables. Stir.
3. When noodles are half done, pour in a colander, running cold water over them, and drain.
4. In a 2-quart saucepan, add all soups and cook until lumps are dissolved.
5. Pour egg-milk mixture into saucepan; stir thoroughly. Pour noodles into sauce. Stir for about 1 minute. Add tuna and continue stirring.
6. Transfer to baking dish. Sprinkle ½ bread crumbs and toss gently. Sprinkle remaining bread crumbs and seasoning salt. Bake for 45 minutes. Let stand for 10 minutes before serving.

Substitute chicken for tuna to make chicken casserole.

CHEESY CAULIFLOWER & BROCCOLI | SERVES 4-6

Ingredients:
½ stick butter, divided
1 small head of broccoli, cut into florets
1 small head of cauliflower, cut into florets
½ cup onion, diced
½ cup sharp cheese
½ cup extra sharp cheese
½ cup cheddar cheese
1 cup milk
1 egg

Instructions:
1. Preheat oven to 375°F. Grease casserole dish with 1 teaspoon butter.
2. Steam cauliflower florets and broccoli florets until tender, about 10 minutes.
3. Melt remaining butter in a saucepan. Whisk in milk and simmer until slightly thickened.
   Take off heat and stir in extra sharp cheese, sharp cheese, onion, and egg until smooth.
4. Spread cauliflower and broccoli in casserole and pour cheese sauce. Sprinkle cheddar cheese.
5. Bake for 30 minutes, cool slightly and serve.
   Mixed Vegetables Can Be Substituted For The Broccoli.

SWEET POTATOES & CARROT CASSEROLE | SERVES 8-10

Ingredients:
3½ pounds small sweet potatoes
(about 7 sweet potatoes), peeled
½ cup golden raisins, divided
1 large carrot, cut into 1½-inch pieces
1 stick butter, divided
⅓ cup brown sugar
⅓ cup maple syrup
1 teaspoon cinnamon
1 teaspoon nutmeg

1 teaspoon ginger
1 teaspoon allspice
½ cup pineapple juice
½ cup pineapple chunks
½ cup orange juice
1 tablespoon lemon juice
2 tablespoons lemon zest
1 tablespoon cornstarch

SWEET POTATOES & CARROT CASSEROLE (CONT.)

Preparations:

1. Preheat oven to 375°F. Grease casserole dish with 1 teaspoon butter. Place sweet potatoes and carrots in 6-qt stockpot; add water to cover. Bring to a boil.
2. Reduce heat. Cook for 15 minutes. Drain and run cold water over potatoes and carrots.
3. Arrange sweet potatoes and carrot slices in prepared casserole dish. Place aside.

Instructions:

1. In a saucepan, melt remaining butter; stir in in lemon zest, lemon juice and raisins. Add brown sugar and orange juice, maple syrup, cinnamon, nutmeg, ginger and pineapple juice.
2. Stir all ingredients and allow to come to a boil. Add pineapple chunks to sauce. If sauce is too syrupy, add cornstarch.
3. Pour sauce over vegetables. Sprinkle allspice and remaining raisins.
4. Bake, uncovered for 25-30 minutes. Check on brownness every 15 minutes. Let stand for 10 minutes before serving.

SEVEN VEGETABLE CHICKEN MEAL | SERVES 8-10

Ingredients:

chicken: 4 breasts, 8 thighs, 8 drumsticks

1 carton chicken broth

1 carton vegetable broth

1 can Cream of Chicken Soup

½ head of cabbage

1 16 oz. bag shredded kale

2 sticks celery

2 cups baby carrots

2 cups sliced carrots

2 cups fresh cauliflower

2 cups fresh broccoli

1 teaspoon sea salt

1 tablespoon poultry seasoning

1 teaspoon celery seeds

¼ cup brown sugar

¼ cup honey

1 teaspoon red crush pepper (optional)

½ teaspoon black pepper (optional)

1 tablespoon garlic powder

1 medium size onion

1 medium size sweet onion

2 tablespoon cornstarch

Instructions:

1. Remove top rack from oven and lower middle rack. Preheat 375°F Wash chicken. Cut chicken breasts in half. Lay chicken pieces in the bottom of roaster (mix up pieces).
2. Pour chicken broth and vegetable broth over pieces and 2 cups of water. Sprinkle sea salt, garlic powder, red crush pepper (optional), black pepper (optional), poultry seasoning, celery seeds. Place roaster in oven. Cook for 40 minutes.
3. Cut cabbage in half and cut core and place on cutting board and cut. Cut celery at angel. Cut each baby carrot at an angle. Shave skin off long carrots and cut into slices (should equal two cups). Cut onion into 4 to 5 slices.
4. Prepare cornstarch (cornstarch and ¼ cup water in small bowl and mix).

SEVEN VEGETABLE CHICKEN MEAL (CONT.)

Instructions:

5. While chicken is cooking, place in large bowl, shredded cabbage, shredded kale, sliced onion (4 to 5 slices), celery, cauliflower, broccoli, baby carrots, sliced carrots.

6. Check chicken. Add baby carrots, sliced carrots and cabbage first. Cook for about 5-10 minutes.

7. Add onion, kale, broccoli, cauliflower, celery, brown sugar and honey (vegetables should be evenly submerged). Using tongs, pull chicken up to the top. Place back in oven and cook for 10 minutes.

8. Remove cover from roaster and turn on broiler. Cook chicken and vegetables until brown.

9. Prepare Cream of Chicken Soup as directed on can and place to the side.

10. Once chicken and vegetables are brown to your satisfaction, add Cream of Chicken Soup and cornstarch mixture, cover and turn off oven. Keep in oven for 30 minutes.

Variations:

SEVEN VEGETABLE SALMON MEAL & SEVEN VEGETABLE BEEF MEAL

Just substitute your desired meat. Try other vegetables in your oven roast. Or, You can just use ALL VEGETABLES for a delicious vegetarian oven roast.

HATTIE'S SPECIAL CRAB BUTTER SAUCE
(Makes Dipping Sauce for about a Dozen Crabs)

Ingredients:

1/2 cup Apple Cider Vinegar (Raw Ole Fashioned or regular vinegar)
2 Sticks Butter
4 tablespoons Hattie's Butter Sauce (or Maple Syrup)
4 Tablespoons Old Bay Seasoning
1/4 teaspoon cayenne pepper (optional)
1/4 teaspoon sea salt

Instructions:

1. Melt butter in a saucepan over medium-low heat.

2. Add in the saucepan all the other ingredients: Vinegar, Old Bay Seasoning, cayenne pepper, and sea salt.

3. Stir as the ingredients begin to heat up together—taste for the desired spicy, sweet, sour, and buttery flavors. Let the dip mixture get hot, but do not let it boil.

4. Turn off the heat and let stand for about 5 minutes. Serve Hot in individual little dipping containers (This same Sauce can be used to drizzle over your corn on the cob--which is usually served with steamed or fried crabs. ENJOY!

MORE ENTREE RECIPES
IN THE "AND BEYOND" COOKBOOK SECTION

BEEF BRISKET
RECIPE BY BEVERLY THOMAS

SKILLET BARBEQUE CHICKEN THIGHS
RECIPE BY CHARRELL THOMAS

SAUSAGE & GRAVY
RECIPE BY BARBARA A. MUNDEN

CHOPPED PORK BARBECUE
BY BETTIE GOGANIOUS

OXTAILS
BY COURTNEY RENEE LLOYD-WIGGINS

SEAFOOD CASSEROLE
BY JACKIE G. OWENS

SHRIMP FRIED RICE
BY JEAN W. LEE

ZUCCHINI LASAGNA | SERVES 6-8
RECIPE BY CHARRELL THOMAS

CHICKEN & BEEF SHEPHERD'S PIE
A FAVORITE BRITISH DISH WHEN LIVING IN SCOTLAND

FISH & CHIPS
HATTIE'S STYLE & TRADITIONAL BRITISH VERSION

SALADS

Growing up with a vegetable garden was so delightful as we harvested fresh produce as well as fruits from the orchard, bushes and vines. After trying my salad recipes hopefully you'll be inspired to purchase locally grown produce.

Garden Salads
Broccoli Salad
Ambrosia Salad
Hattie's Fruit Bowl
Egg Salad
Macaroni Salad
Spinach, Tomato & Chicken Salad

GARDEN SALAD | SERVES 6-8
WITH BROCCOLI, CAULIFLOWER, CHERRY TOMATOES, CRANBERRIES, RAISINS & WALNUTS

Ingredients:

2 cups baby spinach (fresh, shredded)

2 cups arugula (fresh, shredded)

2 cups kale (fresh, shredded)

¼ red onion, sliced

¼ sweet onion, sliced

1 cup broccoli florets

1 cup cauliflower florets

2 cups cherry tomatoes

⅓ cup dried cranberries

⅓ cup raisins

⅓ cup chopped walnuts (optional)

Instructions:

1. In a large bowl, place all ingredients and toss.
2. Add *Hattie's Special Salad Sauce* (Pg. 182) or your favorite dressing and toss again. ENJOY!

BROCCOLI SALAD | SERVES 6-8
WITH CAULIFLOWER, TOMATOES & CARROTS

Ingredients:

3 cups broccoli, chopped in pieces

1 cup cauliflower, cut into florets

2 cups cherry tomatoes

1 cup carrots, shredded

1 cup cucumbers, sliced

½ red onion, sliced

2 boiled eggs, sliced (optional)

Instructions:

1. In a large bowl, place all the ingredients and toss.
2. Add *Hattie's Special Salad Sauce* or your favorite dressing and toss again.

Garden Salad & Mandarin Oranges | Serves 6-8

Ingredients:

1 small bag baby spinach

2 cups arugula

2 cups kale, chopped

½ cup sweet onion, diced

1 cup cherry tomatoes, diced

1 cup shredded carrots

1 cup cucumbers, sliced

1 (15 oz.) jar of mandarin oranges, drained

⅓ cup almonds, thinly sliced

Instructions:

1. In a large bowl, place all ingredients and toss.
2. Add *Hattie's Special Salad Sauce (Pg. 182)* and toss again or your favorite dressing.

Garden Salad w/ Strawberries & Pecans | Serves 6-8

Ingredients:

1 small bag baby spinach

2 cups arugula

2 cups kale, stemmed and finely chopped

½ cup sweet onion, diced

1 cup cherry tomatoes

1 cup carrots, shredded

2 cup fresh strawberries, diced

⅓ cup pecans, chopped

Instructions:

1. In a large bowl, place all the ingredients and toss.
2. Add *Hattie's Special Salad Sauce* or your favorite dressing and toss again.

GARDEN SALAD WITH APPLES | SERVES 6-8

Ingredients:

1 small bag baby spinach

2 cups arugula

2 cups kale, stemmed and finely chopped

½ cup sweet onion, diced (optional)

1 cup cherry tomatoes

1 cup carrots, shredded

1 cup cucumbers, sliced

1 medium Granny Smith apple, diced

⅓ cup pecans, chopped (optional)

Instructions:

1. In a large bowl, place all the ingredients and toss.
2. Add *Ha ie's Special Salad Sauce (Pg. 182)* or your favorite dressing and toss again.

HATTIE'S FRUIT BOWL | SERVES 20-24

Ingredients:

1 small cantaloupe

1 small honey dew

1 cup each, diced Granny Smith & Honey Crisp apples

1 cup each seedless green & red grapes

1 can pineapple chunks

1 large can fruit cocktail (low sugar)

1 large can sliced peaches , halfed

1 large can mandarin oranges

1 large can crushed pineapple

1 large can frozen pineapple juice

2 cup strawberries (halved), divided

1 cup blueberries, divided for garnish

1 cup blackberries, divided for garnish

Preparation:

1. Dice cantaloupe & honey dew melons in ½ inch chunks.
2. Dice the apples in ½ inch chunks, leave skin on

Instructions:

1. In a large bowl, place all diced fruit and mix.
2. Pour in canned fruits & gently toss.
3. Add pineapple juice & toss throughout.
4. Let marinade for an hour before serving.
5. Garnish with strawberries, blackberries and blueberries.

Ambrosia Salad | Serves 4-6

Ingredients:

1 (8 oz.) container whipped cream

1 (8 oz.) container sour cream

1 (5.3 oz.) container Greek yogurt

1 (11 oz.) can mandarin oranges, drained and halved

1 cup unsweetened shreddded coconut

½ cup diced walnuts and almonds

1 (8 oz.) can crushed pineapple drained

1 (8 oz.) can chunk pineapple, drained

1 (10 oz.) jar Maraschino cherries, drained and halved

Instructions:

1. Take sour cream, whipped cream and 1 cup of yogurt and mix in bowl.
2. Add coconut and drained crushed pineapples.
3. Add drained chunk pineapples (cut chunks in half, if desired) and nuts.
4. Add ¾ of the mandarin oranges in salad (save the rest to garnish).
5. Add ¾ of the cherries in salad (save the rest to garnish).
6. Stir delicately from the bottom so as not to mush the mandarin oranges.
7. Taste to see if salad is sweet enough; if not, add sweetener of choice.
8. Pour in clear bowl for the visual effect.
9. Garnish top by alternating mandarin oranges and cherries and put a cherry in the middle.

Egg Salad | Serves 6-8

Ingredients:

12 eggs

1 teaspoon sea salt

1 tablespoon sweet relish

½ teaspoon cayenne pepper

1 tablespoon vinegar

1 tablespoon maple syrup

1 tablespoon regular mustard

1 tablespoon Dijon mustard

2 tablespoon sour cream

1 cup mayonnaise

Instructions:

1. Place eggs in a pot and add water to cover eggs. Bring to a boil. Turn off stove and let eggs set in the hot water for 15 minutes.
2. Remove from hot water. Peel eggs. Remove yolk in a small bowl.
3. Combine all ingredients in a large bowl.
4. Refrigerate for at least an hour.

Macaroni Salad | Serves 6-8
Protein Options: Diced Chicken | Turkey | Italian Sausage | Shrimp | Crab

Ingredients:

1 medium bag of macaroni

1 medium onion, chopped

1 green bell pepper, chopped

2 stalks of fresh celery

1 teaspoon celery seeds

1 cup of mayonnaise

¼ cup of sour cream

1 tablespoon mustard

2 tablespoon apple cider vinegar

1 tablespoon maple syrup

¼ cup sweet relish

1 teaspoon sea salt

½ teaspoon cayenne pepper

1 red bell pepper, chopped

2 eggs

protein options (see above)

Macaroni Salad (cont.)

Preparation:

1. Boil macaroni until desired tenderness .
2. Run cold water over macaroni.
3. Dice protein of your choice and cook, if necessary.

Instructions:

1. Boil eggs and peel and dice once cool.
2. When macaroni is done, in a colander, rinse under cold water.
3. Once drained completely, put macaroni in a large bowl.
4. Mix remaining ingredients in a separate bowl. Gently fold mixture into macaroni.

Spinach, Tomato & Chicken Salad | Serves 6-8

Ingredients:

1 small bag of baby spinach
1 cup cherry tomatoes
2 boiled eggs, diced
2 cooked chicken breasts, diced

Instructions :

1. In a large bowl, place all ingredients and toss.
2. Add *Hattie's Special Salad Sauce* (Pg. 182)
   or add your favorite dressing and toss again.

VEGETABLES & VEGETARIAN

Growing up in the country, eating vegetables came naturally. Now days, processed food is the norm. Many in the new generation think fast food is a meal. In this section, you will find vegetable recipes that are healthy and easy to prepare.

Oven Roasted Brussels Sprouts
Stir-Fry Cabbage, Carrot & Onions
Collard Greens with Smoked Turkey Necks
Stir-Fry Collards with Onions & Carrots
Stir-Fry Kale
French Style String Beans
Mashed Cauliflower Pattie Cakes
Caramelized Apple Slices
Green Tomatoes
Sweet Potatoes
Stewed Red Tomatoes

OVEN ROASTED BRUSSELS SPROUTS | SERVES 6-8

Ingredients:

1 (12 oz.) bag of Brussels sprouts
½ teaspoon garlic powder
½ teaspoon sea salt
2 tablespoon olive oil

Instructions:

1. Preheat oven to 375°F.
2. Cut sprouts in half.
3. Put sprouts in a bowl and sprinkle with garlic powder, sea salt and olive oil.
4. Toss in a bowl with seasonings.
5. Place on cookie sheet and put in oven.
6. Bake for 40 minutes.

This dish can be Broiled, Grilled or Stir Fried

STIR-FRY SHREDDED
CABBAGE, CARROTS & ONIONS
SERVES 6-8

Ingredients:

1 small head of cabbage

1 cup carrots, shredded

1 medium onion, diced

¼ cup olive oil

or unflavored coconut oil

1 teaspoon sea salt

1 teaspoon crushed red peppers

1 teaspoon organic, raw sugar

1 tablespoon maple syrup

Preparations:

1. Clean and shred cabbage and carrots.
2. Drain in colander.

Instructions:

1. In a large skillet, heat olive oil over medium-high for 3 minutes. Add onions and sauté for about 30 seconds. Add ½ of cabbage and stir. Cook for about 2 minutes.
2. Turn onions and cabbage and add remaining ½ of cabbage and carrots. Cook for 2 minutes and turn. Stir in sea salt, crushed peppers, sugar and maple syrup.
3. Toss ingredients consistently until cabbage is almost done. Reduce heat to low and continue to toss.
4. Cover skillet and turn off heat. Allow to rest for 5 minutes.

COLLARD GREENS WITH SMOKED TURKEY NECKS I SERVES 6-8

Ingredients:

2 to 2 ½ pounds fresh collards
6 (about 4-inches long) smoked turkey necks
1 cup carrots, shredded
1 medium onion, cut into ½-inch pieces
1 cup olive oil or unflavored coconut oil
1 teaspoon sea salt
1 teaspoon crushed red peppers
1 teaspoon organic, raw sugar
1 tablespoon maple syrup
1 tablespoon vinegar
2 cups vegetable broth
1 (6 oz.) almonds, slivered

Preparations:

1. Wash collards and drain.
2. Cut collards 1-inch thick. Remove excess stem and vein.

Instructions:

1. In a pot, boil turkey necks in enough water to only cover the necks. Cook for 45 minutes on low boil.
2. Add collards to turkey necks and water. Cook for 1 hour or more, depending on desired tenderness.
3. In a large skillet, heat olive oil for 3 minutes. Add onions and sauté for about 30 seconds. Add collard greens to onions. Cook, uncovered, for about 2 minutes.
4. Turn onions and collards together and add carrots. Cook for 2 minutes. Turn again. Stir in vinegar, sea salt, crushed peppers, sugar, and maple syrup. Toss ingredients consistently until collards are almost done. Add shredded almonds and stir.
5. Reduce heat to low and continue to toss. Turn off stove and allow dish to rest for 10 minutes before serving.

This recipe can also be prepared with no meat by using vegetable broth in place of turkey necks.

STIR-FRY COLLARDS WITH ONIONS, CARROTS | SERVES 6-8

Ingredients:

8 cups collards, (2 bunches)

1 cup carrots, shredded

1 medium onion

¼ cup olive oil

1 teaspoon sea salt

1 teaspoon crushed red peppers

1 teaspoon organic raw sugar

1 tablespoon maple syrup

1 tablespoon vinegar

1 (6 oz.) almonds, slivered

Preparations:

1. Thoroughly wash collards and drain.
2. Cut collards ¼-inch thick. Remove excess stem and vein.

Instructions:

1. Heat oil In a skillet.
2. Sauté sliced onions for about 30 seconds. Add collards and cook for about 2 minutes
3. Add shredded carrots, and toss ingredients. After 2 minutes, toss again. Add vinegar, salt, crushed peppers, sugar and maple syrup.
4. Continue to toss ingredients until collards are almost done. Add slivered almonds.
5. Reduce heat and continue to toss. Turn off stove and allow to rest for 5 minutes.

STIR FRY KALE | SERVES 6-8

Ingredients:

8 cups kale, (2 bunches)
1 cup carrots, shredded
1 medium onion, sliced
¼ cup olive oil
1 teaspoon sea salt
1 teaspoon crushed red peppers
1 teaspoon organic raw sugar
1 tablespoon maple syrup

Preparations:

1. Thoroughly wash kale and drain.
2. Cut kale 1-inch thick.

Instructions:

1. Heat oil in skillet on medium high until oil is hot.
2. Stir in sliced onions and sauté for about 30 seconds.
3. Add kale to onions.
4. Let everything cook for about 2 minutes.
5. Turn over onions and kale together and add shredded carrots. After 2 minutes, turn over again.
6. Add sea salt, crushed peppers, sugar and maple syrup.
7. Toss ingredients consistently until kale is cooked to your preferred crunch.
8. Turn heat down low and continue to cook, tossing every 2 to 3 minutes.
9. Turn off stove and allow kale to rest for 5 minutes. *Serve with your favorite Entrée.*

FRENCH STYLE STRING BEANS | SERVES 6-8

Ingredients:

1 pound fresh or frozen string beans

6 ozs. slivered almonds

1 teaspoon garlic powder or fresh garlic

1 medium onion, sliced

¼ cup olive oil

¼ cup unflavored coconut oil

1 teaspoon sea salt

1 teaspoon crushed red peppers

1 teaspoon organic raw sugar

Preparations:

1. Snap beans or thaw if frozen.
2. Rinse and drain beans in colander.

Instructions:

1. In a skillet, add oil until hot. Stir in sliced onions and sauté for about 30 seconds on medium high.
2. Add beans and saute together for about 2 minutes.
3. Let cook for another 2 minutes; then, turn again.
4. Add vinegar, salt, crushed peppers, sugar and maple syrup. Toss ingredients until beans are almost done to desired crunchiness.
5. Add almonds. Reduce heat to low and gently toss.
6. Turn off stove and allow them to rest 5 minutes. **Serve with your Favorite Entrée.**

CAULIFLOWER PATTIE CAKES | SERVES 4-6

Ingredients:

1 head cauliflower, blended small pieces

1 tablespoon garlic powder

¼ stick butter

½ cup buttermilk

1 tablespoon whole milk

½ cup oat bran, reserve 1 tablespoon

½ cup almond flour, reserve 1 tablespoon

4 tablespoons olive oil

1 teaspoon salt

1 teaspoon sugar

½ cup sour cream

2 eggs

Instructions:

FRIED CAULIFLOWER PATTIES

1. Pour olive oil in pan and allow to get hot.

2. Mix all ingredients in a bowl; Add the remaining flour and oat bran, as needed.

3. Form cauliflower balls, the size of a hamburger patty, flatten into patties.

4. Place patties in hot pan cook until one side is brown and turn over until both sides are brown.

5. Reduce heat to allow egg inside to get completely done.

OVEN BAKED CAULIFLOWER PATTIES

1. Bake patties for 15 minutes on each side.

2. Turn off oven and leave dish until ready to serve.

SOUPS & SIDES

Every winter, I cook a big pot of soup at least once a week while listening to music or watching a good movie. I'll turn my soups in to a well-rounded dinner by adding either a nice warm side dish or a cool nutritious salad.

Macaroni & Stewed Tomatoes
Potato Corn Chowder
Cheesy Potato Soup
Hattie's Potato Soup
Beef Stew
Beef Vegetable Soup
Chicken Stew
Vegetable/Vegetarian Soup
Baked Beans with Brown Sugar
Baked Beans with Peppers & Onions
Black-Eyed Peas
Great Northern Beans
Small Butter Beans
Large Butter Beans
Herbal Stuffing
Hattie's Three Cheese Mac & Cheese

MACARONI & STEWED TOMATO SOUP I SERVES 6-8

Ingredients:

1 (16 oz.) box elbow macaroni

1 (28 oz.) cans whole tomatoes

1 small sweet onion, diced

1 teaspoon sea salt

1 teaspoon black pepper

2 tablespoons sugar

1 tablespoon brown sugar

¼ stick butter

¼ teaspoon garlic powder

3 quarts water

Preparation:

1. Blend can of whole tomatoes at low speed for about 30 seconds. Do not liquefy—leave some chunks. Set aside.
2. Dice sweet onion. Set aside.

Instructions:

1. In a large saucepan, over medium-high heat, add water and sea salt. Bring to a rapid boil.
2. Stir in elbow macaroni. Cook for 5 minutes, allowing pasta to get al dente done—just starting to get rubbery.
3. Remove from heat. Pour macaroni in colander. Run hot water over the macaroni to rinse off excess starch. Drain and place to the side.
4. Wash large saucepan, place back on medium-high heat, add butter; After butter melts, add onions and sauté for about 5 minutes.
5. Put macaroni back into saucepan and stir in the sautéed onions; Pour in the tomatoes in the blender and stir. Allow mixture to come to a slow boil.
6. Add sugars, black pepper, garlic powder. Reduce heat to low and finish cooking about 8 minutes or until macaroni expands and is tender—Do Not Overcook. Serve Hot--as a meal or Side.

Anecdote: *This was my cousin Bubba's favorite soup when I was a teenager staying with his mother. He would make a pot of this soup every time he came home from the Air Force. I loved watching him slurp this soup as if it were the best tasting food in the world. He taught me how to prepare this soup, and I started having it already prepared when he came home on military leave.*

POTATO CORN CHOWDER | SERVES 4-6

Ingredients:
6 medium Russet potatoes
2 cups vegetable broth
2 cups chicken broth
1 teaspoon garlic powder
1 teaspoon sea salt
1 teaspoon pepper
½ stick butter
1 cup milk
1 cup buttermilk, divided
1 cup sour cream, divided
4 tablespoons cornstarch, divided
2 tablespoons sugar
1 (12 oz.) bag frozen corn
1 (14.75 oz.) can creamed corn
⅓ cup green scallions, chopped

Instructions:

1. Peel and dice potatoes into ¼ inch pieces.
2. Place potatoes and ¼ cup water in a medium pot over high heat. Bring to a boil.
3. Stir in ½ cup buttermilk and ½ cup sour cream, sugar, milk, butter, ground black pepper, sea salt, garlic powder, chopped scallions, broth, frozen corn and creamed corn. Bring to a boil.
4. Reduce heat to low and stir constantly. As soup thickens, stir in remaining ½ buttermilk and ½ sour cream. Add 1 tablespoon cornstarch at a time until desired thickness is reached.
5. Reduce heat to low and simmer, stirring constantly for 3 to 5 minutes. Let stand for 5 minutes. Serve!

CHEESY POTATO SOUP | SERVES 4-6

Ingredients:

6 medium Russet potatoes
2 cups vegetable broth
2 cups chicken broth
1 teaspoon garlic powder
1 teaspoon sea salt
1 teaspoon ground black pepper
½ stick butter
1 cup milk

1 cup buttermilk divided
1 cup sour cream, divided
4 tablespoons cornstarch, divided
2 tablespoons sugar
1 cup sharp cheese, shredded
1 cup mozzarella cheese, shredded
1 cup white cheddar, shredded

CHEESY POTATO SOUP (CONT.)

Instructions:

1. Peel and dice potatoes into ¼ inch pieces.
2. Place potatoes and ¼ cup water in a medium pot over high heat. Bring to a boil.
3. Stir in ½ cup buttermilk and ½ cup sour cream, sugar, milk, butter, ground black pepper, sea salt, garlic powder, chicken broth, vegetable broth and all cheeses. Bring to a boil.
4. Reduce heat to low and stir constantly. As soup thickens, stir in remaining ½ cup buttermilk and ½ cup sour cream. Add 1 tablespoon cornstarch at a time until desired thickness is reached.
5. Reduce heat and simmer, stirring constantly for 3 to 5 minutes.

HATTIE'S POTATO SOUP | SERVES 6-8

Ingredients:

6 medium Russet potatoes
2 cups low sodium vegetable broth
2 cups low sodium chicken broth
1 teaspoon garlic powder
1 teaspoon sea salt
1 teaspoon ground black pepper

½ stick butter
1 cup milk
1 cup buttermilk, divided
1 cup sour cream, divided
4 tablespoons cornstarch
2 tablespoons sugar

Instructions:

1. Peel and dice potatoes into ¼ inch pieces.
2. Put potatoes on the stove with ¼ cup of water.
3. Let potatoes come to a boil and stir as they boil.
4. As potatoes are cooking add ½ buttermilk and ½ sour cream. Add remaining ingredients.
5. Heat starts out on high and you may turn heat down to medium once you see bubbles in the water. Stir constantly.
6. Add 1 tablespoon cornstarch at a time until desired thickness is reached.
7. Reduce heat to low and simmer, stirring constantly for 3 to 5 minutes.
8. Rest for 5 minutes; Serve Hot!

BEEF STEW | SERVES 8-10

Ingredients:

2 pounds lean beef, cubed

1 carton vegetable broth (32 oz.)

1 carton beef broth (32 oz.)

1 teaspoon garlic powder

¼ teaspoon ground black pepper

1 large sweet onion, divided

1 package mixed peas, corn & carrots

1 cup white potatoes, cubed

1 cup cauliflower, cut into florets

1 cup of broccoli, cut into florets

1 cup green beans (optional)

2 cups kale, shredded

1 cup baby carrots

2 cups water

2 tablespoons cornstarch, divided

2 tablespoons brown sugar

1 teaspoon red crushed pepper (optional)

Instructions:

1. Add beef, beef broth and vegetable broth, 2 cups water, garlic powder and black pepper in crockpot. Cover and cook for 45 minutes.

2. Add potatoes first, and then stir. Add ½ sweet onion and ½ onion, kale and baby carrots. Lastly, stir in cauliflower, broccoli, mixed vegetables and green beans. Cover and cook for 30 minutes.

3. Mix cornstarch with a quarter cup water in a separate bowl and stir. Set aside.

4. Stir in brown sugar and remainder ½ diced sweet onion into crockpot. Add crushed pepper. For thicker stew, add 1 tablespoon cornstarch. Check for thickness after 1 minute before adding more.

5. Reduce heat to low. Turn crockpot off and let stew rest for 30 minutes. **Serve While Hot!**

BEEF VEGETABLE SOUP | SERVES 8-10

Ingredients:

2 pounds lean beef

1 carton beef broth (32 oz.)

1 carton vegetable broth (32 oz.)

1 cup baby carrots

1 cup sweet onion, chopped

1 cup onion, chopped

1 cup green peas

1 cup kale, shredded

1 cup kernel corn

1 carrot, peeled and sliced

6 white Russet potatoes, cubed (optional)

1 teaspoon garlic powder

1 teaspoon sea salt

1 teaspoon ground black pepper

2 tablespoons cornstarch, divided

¼ cup brown sugar

¼ cup maple syrup

3 cups water

Instructions:

1. Cut beef into ½-inch cubes. In a crockpot, add beef, beef broth, vegetable broth, water, garlic powder, sea salt, and ground black pepper on HIGH. Cook for 45 minutes to 1 hour.

2. Add onions and kale. Stir in remaining vegetables, brown sugar and maple syrup. Cover and bring to a boil.

3. Stir in 1 tablespoon cornstarch at a time, stirring for about 30 seconds, until desired thickness is reached. Turn off crock pot. Let stand for 15 minutes, allowing vegetables to continue cooking. **Serve Hot!** ~ Can be served as an **Entree** or an **Appetizer**.

CHICKEN STEW | SERVES 8-10

Ingredients:

1 pound chicken (8 thighs, 6 to 8 drumsticks)

1 cup cauliflower, cut into florets

1 (32 oz.) carton chicken broth

1 cup of broccoli, cut into florets

1 (32 oz.) carton vegetable broth

1 cup green beans (optional)

1 teaspoon garlic powder

2 cups kale, shredded

1 teaspoon ground black pepper

1 cup baby carrots

1 large sweet onion, divided

2 cups water

1 large onion, divided

2 tablespoons cornstarch, divided

1 package frozen peas, corn & carrots

2 tablespoons brown sugar

1 cup white potatoes, cubed (optional)

1 teaspoon red crush pepper (optional)

Instructions:

1. Add chicken, chicken broth and vegetable broth, and 2 cups water, garlic powder and black pepper in crockpot. Cover and cook for 45 minutes.

2. Add potatoes, and stir. Add ½ sweet onion and ½ onion, Stir in kale and carrots. Lastly, stir in cauliflower florets, broccoli florets, and peas, corn and carrots. Cover and cook for 30 minutes..

3. Mix cornstarch with a quarter cup of water in a separate bowl and stir. Set aside.

4. Stir in brown sugar and remaining ½ diced sweet onion and onion into crockpot. Add pepper.

5. For thicker stew, add cornstarch. Wait 1 minute before adding more.

6. Turn crockpot off and let chicken stew rest for 30 minutes. Serve Hot.

VEGETABLE SOUP | SERVES 6-8

Ingredients:

1 (32 oz.) carton of beef broth

1 (32 oz.) carton of vegetable broth

1 cup baby carrots

1 cup sweet onion, chopped

1 cup onion, chopped

1 cup green peas

1 cup kale, shredded

1 cup kernel corn

1 carrot, peeled & sliced

6 white Russet potatoes, cubed (optional)

1 teaspoon garlic powder

1 teaspoon sea salt

1 teaspoon black pepper

2 tablespoons cornstarch, divided

¼ cup of brown sugar

¼ cup of maple syrup

3 cups of water

Instructions:

1. In a crockpot, add beef broth, vegetable broth, water, garlic powder, sea salt, and black pepper on high. Cook for 45 minutes.

2. Add onion and kale. Stir in remaining vegetables, brown sugar and maple syrup.

3. Cover and bring to a boil. Stir for about 30 seconds. Add 1 tablespoon cornstarch at a time, stirring for about 30 seconds, until desired thickness is reached.

4. Turn off crockpot. Let stand for 15 minutes, allowing vegetables to continue cooking. Serve Hot!

Can Be Served As An Appetizer, A Side or A Meal.

Baked Beans with Brown Sugar | Serves 6-8

Ingredients:

1 (28 oz.) can baked beans

2 tablespoons maple syrup

2 cups brown sugar

1 tablespoon mustard

1 tablespoon Dijon mustard

2 tablespoons butter

Instructions:

1. In a skillet, melt butter over medium heat. Stir in brown sugar and cook until dissolves.
2. Stir in baked beans and remaining ingredients. Cook for 2 minutes. Reduce heat to low, cover, and simmer for 10 minutes.
3. Let rest for 5 minutes. Serve Hot!

Baked Beans with Brown Sugar & Onions

Same instructions as above but sauté onions before adding brown sugar.

Baked Beans with Bacon, Brown Sugar & Onions

Same instructions as above but sauté onions before adding brown sugar. After Step 2, cook 6 slices of bacon and chop into fine pieces and add to beans.

BAKED BEANS WITH PEPPERS & ONIONS | SERVES 6-8

Ingredients:
1 (28 oz.) can baked beans
2 tablespoons maple syrup
½ cup brown sugar
1 tablespoon mustard
1 tablespoon Dijon mustard

2 tablespoons butter
1 medium onion, diced
1 green bell pepper, diced
1 red bell pepper, diced

Preparations:
1. Dice onion
2. Dice green & red pepper

Instructions:
3. In a large skillet, melt butter over medium heat.
4. Sauté onion, green pepper and red pepper with butter.
5. Add brown sugar and stir until sugar dissolves.
6. Pour in baked beans and remaining ingredients. Stir well; Cook for 2 minutes.
7. Reduce heat to low; Cover and simmer for 10 minutes, Turn off Heat; Let stand for 5 minutes.

GREAT NORTHERN BEANS | SERVES 6-8

Ingredients:
2 medium-sized ham hocks or smoked turkey necks
2 pounds Great Northern Beans, sorted and soaked
1 teaspoon sea salt
¼ teaspoon ground black pepper
2 tablespoons maple syrup

¼ cup brown sugar
3 cups water
1 (32 oz.) carton vegetable broth
1 teaspoon garlic powder
1 medium sweet onion, diced

Instructions:
1. Add vegetable broth and 7 cups of water to crock pot. Add ham hocks or smoked turkey. Stir in sea salt, ground black pepper and garlic powder. Cook on High.
2. When water comes to a slow boil, add soaked beans. Cook, covered, for 5 hour.
3. Stir in sweet onion, sugar, and maple syrup. Cover and cook for an additional 45 minutes.
4. Reduce to Low and cook for 5 hour until beans are tender. Allow beans to rest for 30 minutes before serving.

Can Be Served As An Appetizer, A Side or A Meal.

BLACK-EYED PEAS | SERVES 6-8

Ingredients:

2 medium-sized ham hocks or smoke turkey necks (optional)
2 pound bag hard black-eyed peas, sorted & soaked
2 tablespoons maple syrup
1 (32 oz.) carton vegetable broth
1 teaspoon garlic powder

1 teaspoon sea salt
¼ inch black pepper
¼ cup brown sugar
3 cups water
1 medium sweet onion, diced

Instructions:

1. In a crockpot, pour in water and vegetable broth. Add smoked turkey necks or ham hocks.
2. Sprinkle in sea salt, black pepper and garlic powder. Cook on High.
3. When water comes to a slow boil, add soaked peas; Cover & cook for 1 hour.
4. Stir in diced sweet onion, sugar, and maple syrup. Cover and cook for another 45 minutes to an hour, still on high.
5. After 45 minutes, reduce temperature to Low and cook for 1 additional hour or until peas are tender—Taste for desired tenderness, sweetness or need for more salt or garlic.
6. Turn off and let crockpot set for at least 30 minutes before serving—giving the peas a chance to absorb all of the flavors from your juice.

Serve your Black-Eyed Peas as a "Side Dish", a "Soup", over rice (called "Hoppin' John") or with stewed tomatoes mixed in the center of your peas—giving that sweet and salty taste.

SMALL BUTTER BEANS | SERVES 6-8

Ingredients:

2 medium-sized ham hocks or smoked turkey necks

2 pound bag small butter beans, sorted and soaked

1 teaspoon sea salt

¼ teaspoon ground black pepper

2 tablespoons maple syrup

¼ cup brown sugar

3 cups water

1 (32 oz.) carton vegetable broth

1 teaspoon garlic powder

1 medium sweet onion, diced

Instructions:

1. Add vegetable broth and water to crockpot. Add ham hocks or smoked turkey.
2. Stir in sea salt, ground black pepper and garlic powder. Cook on High.
3. When water comes to a slow boil, add soaked beans. Cook, covered for 1 hour.
4. Stir in sweet onion, sugar and maple syrup. Cover and cook for an additional 45 minutes.
5. Reduce heat to Low and cook for 1 hour until beans are tender. Turn off heat and let beans stand for 30 minutes.

LARGE BUTTER BEANS | SERVES 6-8

Ingredients:

2 medium-sized ham hocks or smoked turkey necks

2 pound bag small butter beans, sorted and soaked

1 teaspoon sea salt

¼ teaspoon ground black pepper

2 tablespoons maple syrup

¼ cup brown sugar

3 cups water

1 (32 oz.) carton vegetable broth

1 teaspoon garlic powder

1 medium sweet onion, diced

LARGE BUTTER BEANS (CONT.)

Instructions:

1. Add vegetable broth and water to crockpot. Add ham hocks or smoked turkey.
2. Stir in sea salt, ground black pepper and garlic powder. Cook on High.
3. When water comes to a slow boil, add soaked beans. Cook, covered, for 1 hour.
4. Stir in sweet onion, sugar, and maple syrup. Cover and cook for an additional 45 minutes.
5. Reduce heat to Low and cook for 1 hour until the beans are tender. Turn off crockpot and allow beans to rest for 30 minutes.

HERBAL STUFFING | SERVES 6-8

Ingredients:
1 (15 oz.) box garlic and herb bread crumbs
6 toasted slices of wheat bread
½ stick of butter
1 sweet onion, diced
1 onion, diced
2 stalks of celery, cut in 1-inch pieces
1 tablespoon sage
1 teaspoon poultry powder
1 teaspoon salt
1 teaspoon celery seeds
1 teaspoon garlic powder
1 teaspoon sugar
3 eggs
3 cups broth from turkey
1 (16 oz.) container chicken broth

Preparation: MAKING THE STUFFING
1. Dice onions and celery. Toast bread and break into pieces and put in a bowl.
2. Melt butter and beat eggs.
3. Preheat oven to 400°F.
4. Put onions, celery and bread in a bowl and mix. Pour 1 cup chicken broth over bread pieces. Add seasonings and eggs into bowl and stir well.
5. Sprinkle 1 cup of breadcrumbs, mix and add the other 1 cup.

Instruction: COOKING THE TURKEY
1. Sprinkle sea salt and pepper inside turkey. Turn turkey over and scoop stuffing inside. Sprinkle a dash of salt and paprika on turkey. Lay stalks of celery and peeled onions around turkey.
2. Add 1 cup water and 1 cup chicken broth on sides of turkey.
3. Lay turkey giblets in liquid. Place heavy duty foil around roaster and put the top on the roaster (do not allow the foil to touch the turkey).
4. Allow turkey to bake for 4 hours before checking. Once turkey is brown, place foil over breasts and legs and put in the broiler.
5. Once turkey is done and fully brown, remove foil from legs and breast and allow to rest for 20 minutes before serving.

Serve Stuffing with your turkey, gravy, and your favorite Sides. **ENJOY!**

HATTIE'S THREE-CHEESE MAC & CHEESE | SERVES 6-8

Ingredients:
1 (16 oz.) box elbow macaroni
1 cup extra sharp cheddar cheese, cubed
1 cup sharp cheddar cheese, cubed
1 cup mild cheddar cheese, cubed
1 teaspoon ground black pepper
½ teaspoon garlic powder
1 teaspoon sea salt
1 teaspoon sugar
1 cup buttermilk
½ stick butter
2 cups milk
8 eggs
1 teaspoon smoked paprika (for garnish)

Preparations:
1. Preheat oven to 375°F; Cooking time: 45 min--1 hr.
2. In a large saucepan, fill with water; add 1 tsp of salt.
3. Beat 8 eggs in a medium-sized bowl.
4. Pre-dice the 3 cheeses into ½-inch cubes and put in three separate bowls; Set aside.

Instructions:
1. Add macaroni to boiling water. Stir to prevent macaroni from sticking. Remove macaroni before it cooks completely and pour in a colander. Run hot water over macaroni to remove excess starch.
2. Place colander on a plate to drain macaroni. Rinse pot to remove residual starch. Pour macaroni back into pot. Turn on heat to low and melt half of the butter into macaroni. Stir in half the shredded cheddar cheese to macaroni and allow to melt. Add half extra sharp cheese and stir so that cheese can partially melt. Add half of sharp cheese and the other half extra sharp cheese and gently fold in all cheeses throughout the macaroni. Turn off heat; Remove from stove and wait 5 minutes.
3. Pour eggs in pot and stir thoroughly. Add buttermilk, milk, salt; other half melted butter and mix in thoroughly. Add pepper, sugar and garlic into mixture and stir thoroughly.
4. Pour macaroni mixture in large casserole dish; leave ⅛ of an inch from the top of the dish. Stir in half of remaining shredded cheese within the mac & cheese just before placing it in the oven; push cheese down into liquid. Place dish on center rack in oven.
5. After Mac & Cheese is almost done (after about 45 minutes), open oven and sprinkle remaining extra sharp shredded cheese on mac & cheese. Then, sprinkle the smoked paprika on top of the shredded cheese. Once done inside and brown outside to desire color, turn oven off and allow the dish to set for 10 to 15 minutes (Sometimes, I turn on the broiler and brown the cheese more, if more cheese brownness is desired).

CARAMELIZED APPLE SLICES | SERVES 4-6

Ingredients:

1 cup dark brown sugar
½ cup light brown sugar
¼ cup maple syrup
¼ stick butter, divided
1 tablespoon nutmeg
1 tablespoon cinnamon

1 teaspoon ginger
1 teaspoon allspice
1 teaspoon sea salt
4 Granny Smith apples
1 cup raisins

Instructions:
1. In a large pot with water, add apples. Bring to a boil for 1 minute.
2. In a large skillet, melt remaining 3 tablespoons butter. Stir in brown sugar, syrup and spices, except nutmeg. Cook until it is bubbling. Reduce heat.
3. Pour apples into a colander. Drain and add to skillet. Stir constantly. Stir in 1 tablespoon cornstarch if it's not thick enough.
4. Stir in raisins. Place mixture in prepared casserole dish. Sprinkle nutmeg and brown sugar on top.
5. Bake for 20 minutes. Once apples are done, turn on broiler for 5 to 10 minutes for desired brownness.

VARIATION: *Add 3 pears (sliced) to make a "Caramelized Apples & Pears" scrumptious dish.*

CRUSTED BAKED GREEN TOMATOES | SERVES 6-8

Ingredients:

5 4 firm medium green tomatoes

½ teaspoon of sugar

2 cups garlic and herb bread crumbs, finely ground

¼ teaspoon of cayenne pepper

2 eggs

2 tablespoons olive oil

Preparations:

1. Preheat oven to 375°F.
2. Slice tomatoes, about ¼" thick.
3. Finely grind bread crumbs; Mix in salt, sugar, garlic powder & cayenne pepper (optional) & stir.
4. Beat eggs.
5. Grease baking sheet with olive oil.

Instructions:

1. Dip tomatoes in egg mixture and allow excess to drip off.
2. Using tongs, place each tomato slice individually into bread crumb mixture and coat thoroughly.
3. Lay coated slices on a greased baking sheet (no more than 12 slices at a time).
4. Place slices in oven for 15 minutes on one side.
5. Flip slices over and let them bake another 7 to 10 minutes until done and brown.

FRIED GREEN TOMATOES | SERVES 6-8

Ingredients:
4   Firm medium green tomatoes
1   cup of wheat flour
1   cup of rice flour
1   cup olive oil, divided

Batter:
1   cup garlic and herb bread crumbs
2   cup wheat flour
1   cup rice flour
4   eggs
1   teaspoon of baking powder
1   teaspoon of sugar
½   teaspoon of sea salt
1   cup of vegetable broth
½   teaspoon of apple cider vinegar
½   teaspoon of cayenne pepper

Preparations:
1. Beat eggs.
2. Pour in remaining ingredients for batter and mix until smooth.
3. Slice tomatoes, about ¼-inch thick.

Instructions:
1. Heat oil in large skillet over medium heat until hot. Dip tomatoes in egg mixture and allow excess to drip off. Using tongs, place each tomato slice individually into batter.
2. Let excess batter dip off and place in hot grease (Place up to 6 in a skillet at a time). Fry slices on one side for 5 to 7 minutes; Flip slices over and let them cook for another 5 to 7 minutes until they are done and brown.
3. Drain on paper towel; Place on baking sheet and place in warm oven to stay warm until the next batch is done. Add remaining olive oil in skillet and repeat the procedure for the next 6 slices.

Serve as a Side or an Appetizer.

OLD-FASHIONED STEWED TOMATOES | SERVES 6-8

Ingredients:

2 cans whole tomatoes
2 slices whole wheat bread, diced in ½-inch pieces
2 tablespoons of cornstarch
½ cup brown sugar
¼ cup sugar
1 teaspoon vanilla extract
¼ teaspoon nutmeg
¼ teaspoon cinnamon
¼ teaspoon ginger
2 tablespoons of butter
¼ cup water

Preparations:

1. Add 2 cans of whole tomatoes in blender. Blend at medium speed for about 1 minute (not liquefied). Make sure some of the tomato pieces are still in the blender. Place to the side.
2. Mix cornstarch with ¼ cup of water and place to the side.
3. Dice whole wheat bread (*Options: Use other bread choices or none--just use more cornstarch*).

Instructions:

1. In a large skillet over medium-high heat, add brown sugar, sugar and stir until sugar is moist.
2. Slowly, pour tomatoes, vanilla extract, nutmeg, cinnamon, and ginger in the 2-quart saucepan and stir for about 1 minute or until mixture bubbles.
3. Add bread pieces and stir. Bring to a bubble again. Cover and heat on low for about 10 minutes.
4. After 10 minutes, remove top. If stew is thick, add a little more water and/or butter. Allow to come to a near boil (Taste for desired sweetness).
5. Add cornstarch and pour into the tomato stew and stir around thoroughly in the pot. Let Set 5 minutes before serving.

You can eat this old-fashioned favorite dish as
a sweet "Side Dish", a "Dessert", pour over
steamed rice or mix it in black-eyed peas
(for a sweet and salty taste).

SWEET & TANGY STEWED TOMATOES | SERVES 6-8

Ingredients:

2   cans whole tomatoes
½   cup green bell pepper, diced small
¼   cup yellow bell pepper (optional), diced small
1   (12 oz.) package frozen whole corn, thawed
2   slices whole wheat bread, diced in ½-inch pieces
2   tablespoons of cornstarch
½   cup brown sugar
¼   cup sugar
1   teaspoon vanilla extract
¼   teaspoon nutmeg
¼   teaspoon cinnamon
¼   teaspoon ginger
2   tablespoons of butter
¼   cup water

Preparations:

1. Remove corn from freezer 30 minutes before preparing dish.
2. Mix cornstarch with ¼ cup of water and place to the side.

Instructions:

1. Place tomatoes in a blender. Blend at medium speed for 1 minute (do not liquefy) Place aside.
2. Dice whole wheat bread. Place aside.
3. In a large skillet over medium-high heat, add peppers, and corn. Sauté for 1 minute. Add brown sugar, sugar and stir until sugar is moist.
4. Melt butter in a 2-quart saucepan over medium-high heat; Slowly, pour tomatoes, vanilla extract, nutmeg, cinnamon, and ginger into saucepan and stir until mixture bubbles.
5. Add bread and stir. Bring to a near bubble. Cover and heat on low for about 10 minutes. Aft er 10 minutes, remove top. If tomato stew is too thin, add 1/3 of the cornstarch mixture; cook slowly for another 2 minutes; If too thick, add a little more water and/or butter.
6. Bring to a near boil. Taste for desired sweetness. When desired thickness is reached, turn off heat and let stand for 2 minutes.

Enjoy the Old-Fashioned Traditional dish--You can pour this tomato stew over rice; mix it with black-eyed peas; or eat as a sweet side dish.

BREADS

What's a southern comfort meal without bread to feed the soul? My stepmother baked mouth watering breads: rolls, biscuits, and cornbread from scratch, to accompany whatever entree or side dish she was creating.

Mama's Southern Buttermilk Biscuits
Southern Butter Yeast Rolls
Mama's Hot Garlic Buttered Rolls
Buttermilk Corny Cornbread
Hush Puppies
Waffles

MAMA'S BUTTERMILK BISCUITS | YIELDS 12 BISCUITS

Ingredients:
4 cups all-purpose flour, plus ¼ cup
½ teaspoon baking soda
2 tablespoon baking powder
2 ½ teaspoon sea salt
¾ cup lard (cold & solid), divided
2 cups buttermilk, very cold
4 tablespoons butter, melted

Instructions:

1. Preheat oven to 375ºF. Grease bread pan with 1 tablespoon lard.
2. In a large bowl, mix flour and all remaining dry ingredients (baking powder, baking soda, salt) together.
3. Cut the cold lard into the flour mixture using a cold fork. Knead the lard and flour mixture in bowl for about 5 minutes, until it looks like coarse meal.
4. Make a hole in center of dough mixture and pour in cold buttermilk. Stir briefly until it's combined.
5. Add flour loosely on waxed paper. Coat your hands with flour and knead the dough, turning in each four directions.
6. Add more loose flour and place dough on the lightly floured surface and roll the dough to ½ inch thick.
7. Use a biscuit cutter to form the dough to the desired size. Dip biscuit cutter in the loose flour and repeat.
8. Place the biscuits in greased bread pan. Bake for 15-20 minutes.
   Turn oven off, brush the top with melted butter, and let biscuits stand in oven for 5 minutes.
9. Serve the hot biscuits with homemade preserves, apple butter or **Hattie's Honey Butter Sauce.**

HATTIE'S HONEY BUTTER SAUCE

4 tablespoon of honey
½ stick butter, melted
1 tablespoon buttermilk

Mix together; Stir until smooth. Drizzle on top of Hot Biscuits, Pancakes, Waffles, etc.

MAMA'S HOT GARLIC BUTTERED ROLLS | YIELDS 12-14

Ingredients:

4 cups wheat flour, plus ¼ cup for kneading 1 teaspoon sea salt
2 tablespoon sugar, divided
½ cup lard, divided
1½ cups buttermilk, warm
½ cup butter (melted), divided
2 tablespoons butter for greased pan
1 (0.25 oz.) package active dry yeast
2 tablespoons garlic powder, divided
1 large eggs
½ teaspoon basil
½ parsley

Instructions:

1. Preheat oven to 375°F. Grease bread pan with 1 tablespoon lard.
2. In a large mixing bowl, mix the yeast with the warm milk. Set aside--Let it stand until bubbles form.
3. Combine the flour and all remaining dry ingredients (baking powder, baking soda, salt, sugar, parsley, basil, and 2 cloves or 1 tablespoon garlic powder) together.
4. Cut the cold lard into the flour mixture using a fork. Knead the lard and flour mixture in bowl for about 5 minutes, until it looks like coarse meal. Add ¼ cup butter and the egg and continue to mix.
5. Add the flour mixture to the bowl with the yeast and milk; adding a little flour mixture at a time.
6. Knead the dough until well mixed. Put the kneaded dough in another bowl with 2 tablespoons of melted butter. Dip each side of the dough in the butter to cover it. Cover dough with a clean dish towel and place in a warm place to rise for about 1 hour, until they double in size.
7. After dough rises, add loose flour on wax paper. Coat your hand with flour and knead bread again for about 5 minutes. Pinch off dough balls (about 1 ½ inch around or the size of a golf ball).
8. Place dough balls on a greased pan (three across and four down—leaving some space between dough balls). Cover pan with a dish towel for about 30 minutes and let rise until dough balls double in size. Halfway through rising, brush garlic butter mixture on top of the rolls. Then let them finish rising.
9. Place in preheated oven and bake for 20 to 25 minutes. After 15 minutes, brush top of rolls with more garlic butter sauce. SERVE Hot (*with more garlic butter inside--optional*) with your favorite Entrée.

The secret to a good cook is to coordinate whatever you're cooking so that all of the dishes are finished cooking, ready and hot about the same time. Your hot biscuits or rolls should be timed just right so that they are the last dish to be placed on the table while still piping hot with your melted sweet cream or honey butter.

BUTTERMILK CORNY CORNBREAD | SERVES 10-12

Ingredients:

2 cups coarse cornmeal

2 cups regular cornmeal

1 cup self-rising flour

4 eggs

2 cups buttermilk, divided

4 tablespoons sour cream

4 tablespoons butter (melted), divided

1 (14.75 oz.) can of cream corn

¼ cup sugar or maple syrup

1 teaspoon sea salt

1 package of fried pork skins
  cut into small pieces, optional

Instructions:

1. Preheat oven to 350°F.
2. Using a medium bowl, mix together both corn meals and flour. Whisk eggs in a separate large bowl with 1½ cups buttermilk, sour cream, sugar, pork skins, 2 tablespoons butter, and sea salt.
3. Stir in can of creamed corn into liquid egg mixture. Add flour mixture into liquid and stir well (use a mixer, if desire, but not necessary). If flour is too thick, pour in remaining ½ cup buttermilk.
4. Pour the remaining 2 tablespoons melted butter in bread pan or casserole dish. With a butter knife, make super 8's to spread the melted butter throughout the cornbread batter.
5. Place batter in center of the oven. Bake for 45 minutes to an hour. **Knife test:** If the knife comes out clean, your cornbread is done. Turn off oven and leave in oven for 5 minutes. SERVE!

Serve hot with my Honey Butter Sauce and your favorite Entrée—
Fried Fish or Pigs Feet, Potato Salad or Beans.

HUSH PUPPIES | YIELDS 15

Ingredients:

1 cup buttermilk, divided

2 cups self-rising flour

4 tablespoons lard, divided

½ cup milk, divided

½ cup water, divided

2 cups Washington Self-rising Corn Meal®

½ cup sugar

½ teaspoon sea salt

½ teaspoon garlic powder

1 (14.75 oz.) can of cream corn

1 (8.5 oz.) box of Jiffy® Corn Muffin Mix

1 cup onion, diced and sautéed

2 eggs, beaten

1 egg, lightly beaten

Preparation:

1. Preheat oven to 375° F.
2. Mix 1 egg and water together, set aside.
3. Grease bread pan with 1 tablespoon butter.
4. Sauté onions in 2 tablespoons hot lard until edges brown.

Instructions:

1. In a large bowl, stir together ½ cup buttermilk, onions, sugar, sea salt, garlic powder, and 1 egg.
2. Stir in Jiffy® Mix, Washington Corn Meal®, and flour.
3. Mix until smooth and thick. Add remaining buttermilk and make dough to the consistency for forming corn dough balls (about size of a golf ball).
4. Roll and elongate dough ball. Bake or fry hush puppy balls.

Hush Puppies can be Baked or Fried:

Baked: Place each elongated ball on a greased baking sheet. Brush each side with egg mixture. Bake for about 10 minute, Turn over and bake another 5 to 7 minutes.

Fried: Don't brush with egg mixture when frying. Fry dough in lard on each side for about 7 to 10 minutes, until brown. Drain on paper towel, Serve warm.

WAFFLES | SERVES 4-6

Ingredients:

3 eggs
1 cup buttermilk
1 cup wheat flour
1 cup almond flour
¼ stick butter, melted
fruit of choice (optional)
1 tablespoon baking soda
1 tablespoon baking powder
¼ cup maple syrup or honey
¼ cup sour cream or Greek yogurt
1 tablespoon olive oil or cooking spray

Preparations:
1. Beat 3 eggs; Add buttermilk, butter & stir.
2. Mix dry ingredients together and combine with the egg & buttermilk mixture to make the waffle batter (Reserve some buttermilk if needed for a consistency that's too thick).

Instructions:
1. Set electric waffle griddle to 350° F.
2. Spray waffle griddle and pour in ½ cup batter.
3. Add fruits or nuts into batter on the griddle.
4. Should be done after about 5 minutes.
5. Serve with my *Hattie's Special Syrup*

Hattie's Special Syrup
1 cup of Maple syrup
½ cup of honey
½ cup of brown sugar
3 tablespoon of butter
¼ teaspoon of hot sauce
¼ teaspoon of wine vinegar
¼ cup confectionary sugar
¼ teaspoon of cornstarch

Instructions

Put butter and confectionery and brown sugar in a sauce pan and heat on medium high until hot (do not boil); Stir until smooth; Add in all of the other ingredients; Stir until all are combined; Turn heat on low (Add a few drops of cornstarch mixed with water, if you wish a thicker syrup). Stir well. **Serve!**

DESSERTS

These old-fashioned desserts will have you feeling like a kid again and are guaranteed to satisfy you and your family's sweet tooth. When I eat my desserts, memories of watching my stepmom preparing them come to mind.

Cakes
Breads
Brownies
Puddings
Cobblers
Pies

Sweet Potato Pie*
Ballistic Brownies*
Blueberry Delight*
Rice Pudding*
Coconut Custard Pie*
Corn Pudding*
Red Velvet Cake*
Old Fashioned Pound Cake*
Banana Pudding*
HELP-LESS Pie*
Lemon Chess Pie*

*Family dessert recipes in the "And Beyond" section.

PINEAPPLE UPSIDE DOWN CAKE

SERVES 12

Ingredients:
1 (14 oz.) can sliced pineapples
1 (8 oz.) can crushed pineapples
½ cup brown sugar
½ cup raw honey
4 eggs
2½ cup regular sugar
½ cup of almond or cashew milk
1 stick of butter, melted, divided
10 oz. jar maraschino cherries
2 tablespoons baking powder
2 teaspoons pineapple extract
4 cups all-purpose flour or cake flour
2 teaspoons vanilla extract, divided
4 tablespoons lemon Juice

Preparation:
1. Preheat oven to 375° F
2. Get cake mixer/blender ready.
3. Drain pineapple slices. Save the pineapple juice.
4. Drain cherries
5. Sift flour to remove all of the lumps and pour into a large bowl and set aside.
6. Beat eggs. Melt butter. Mix your cornstarch with water and stir until smooth. Put these aside.
7. Get cake pan ready (Use a deep round flat-bottom cake pan or a rectangular cake pan):
   Coat the bottom & sides of pan with melted butter and plain flour or baking spray. Set aside.

PINEAPPLE UPSIDE DOWN CAKE (CONT.)

A. The Pineapple Sauce:

1. In a saucepan on medium high, melt ¼ stick butter. Add the pineapple juice from the slices and the whole can of crushed pineapples, 2 tablespoon (half) of the lemon juice, 1 teaspoon vanilla extract, brown sugar and 1½ cup regular sugar (or organic sugar) and honey.

2. Heat on stove until the juice and crush pineapple get hot and the sugars dissolve and come to a slow boil and start getting thicker. Add the raw honey and stir.

3. Add the mixed cornstarch (a teaspoon at a time) to your hot pineapple mixture. Stir thoroughly for at least 2 minutes until the mixture becomes thicker.

4. Add another teaspoon of cornstarch, if needed, and stir constantly until to the desired thickness. If not, repeat the teaspoon of cornstarch until using up the remainder mixed cornstarch. Turn stove on low and stir about every 2 minutes until thick.

B. The Cake Batter:

1. Pour beaten eggs, ½ cup buttermilk, and ½ cup almond milk in your large mixing bowl. Mix with a mixer (medium speed) for 2 minutes.

2. Add other ¾ stick melted butter; other 1 teaspoon vanilla extract, and 2 tablespoon lemon juice. Mix all liquids together with a Mixer (medium speed) for 2 minutes.

3. Then, pour 1/3 of the flour or cake flour in the liquid in the mixing bowl; Mix together thoroughly on **medium** speed. Add another 1/3 flour and blend thoroughly; Then, mix the remainder of flour until it is all blended smoothly in the liquid. Tip: Allow flour to get fully moist before adding another 1/3 amount; Move the mixer in a circle and continue until all cake flour has been added to the liquid and batter is smooth (The consistency of the batter should be a little thicker than pancake batter).

4. Put the mixer on high speed and mix the cake batter for 5 minutes—moving the mixer in circles (clockwise and counterclockwise). If batter becomes too thick, add in the remainder of the milk and mix for another 5 minutes on high speed; Set aside.

5. Check on your Pineapple Sauce mixture on the stove and STIR (Your Pineapple Sauce mixture on the stove should now be to your desired thickness; if not, you can add the remainder 1 teaspoon of cornstarch and stir consistently until desired thickness. Turn the stove off).

6. Lay drained Pineapple Slices on the bottom of the round or rectangular baking pan—Place slices around on the bottom of the round cake pan (or for a rectangular pan, place 3 slices across the top of baking pan and 5 slices down the side--3 x 5).

7. Put a drained cherry in the middle of each hole of the pineapple slices placed in the bottom of the baking pan.

PINEAPPLE UPSIDE DOWN CAKE (CONT.)

8. Gently pour warm thick pineapple sauce mixture over the cherries and pineapple slices at the bottom of the baking pans (you can use a large dipper to spread the pineapple sauce mixture over the pineapple slices and cherries, careful not to disturb the placement of the slices and the cherries). Make sure pineapple mixture in evenly distributed over all of the slices at the bottom of pan.

9. Using a spatula, scrap the sides of the saucepan to remove all of the thick pineapple sauce and spread it evenly on top of the pineapple slices and centered cherries. Your pineapple mixture should be enough to cover the top of the pineapple slices.

Back to the Cake Batter:

10. Mix the cake batter another 1 minute on high speed. Pour cake batter over the pineapple sauce, slices and cherries until all are fully covered (Use a large dipper and spread batter from left to right on top of the pineapple slices and cherries and the thick pineapple sauce mixture).

11. Turn baking pan around (90 degrees) and repeat the process pouring cake batter in the other direction across from left to right. Repeat process in all four directions until all pineapple slices and sauce are fully covered and all cake batter is used.

12. Use spatula to remove remaining batter from the sides of the bowl and to spread the batter evenly in the cake pan on top of the sauce and pineapples.

13. Place cake in the center of the middle shelf of a pre-heated oven. Bake from 45 minutes to 1 hour. View cake after 30 minutes to see if cake is browning. Turn in opposite direction (180°) and bake for another 20 minutes. Test for doneness by sticking a toothpick in the center of the cake. If the toothpick comes out with cake residue on it, the cake is not done enough yet; but, if it comes out mostly clean, the cake is done enough. Turn off oven and let cake set in oven for another 10 minutes to set (*A Very Important Process: Mama would describe this process as letting the cake now "soak", meaning allowing all of the sauce, flavors, eggs and butter to soak into the batter making the cake as moist as it can be while ensuring its final doneness. This important process makes the difference between a done and moist cake or a done and dry cake*).

14. Remove cake from oven, cover the top with a clean dish cloth and let it set for another 10 minutes. Using a knife or spatula, cut around all of the sides of the cake down to the bottom of the pan to loosen the cake. Using oven gloves, place a large flat-bottom plate (or platter) tightly on the top of the cake pan and flip over quickly (*The flat-bottom of the plate should cover the entire top of the cake pan with room left around sides to catch any excess sauce that may still be in the bottom of the cake pan*).

15. Place plate on the counter and wait a minute to let cake fall down in the plate on its own. Lift pan slowly to ensure the whole cake is on the plate and no cake is still stuck to the bottom or sides of the pan. Sprinkle a thin coat of powdered sugar on top (optional). Can Serve Warm or Chilled.

OLD FASHIONED GINGERBREAD | SERVES 6-8

Ingredients:

2 ½ cups all-purpose flour
1 stick butter, melted, divided
1 cup buttermilk
1 cup milk
2 large eggs
1 teaspoon vanilla extract
1 teaspoon almond extract
4 tablespoons ground ginger
1 tablespoon mace
1 teaspoon cinnamon
1 teaspoon nutmeg
½ cup dark brown sugar
1 teaspoon confectioners sugar
2 cups molasses
1 cup raw honey, divided
1 teaspoon baking powder
½ cup cocoa
½ teaspoon sea salt

Preparation:
1. Preheat oven to 350° F.
2. Grease large 9 x 13-inch rectangular baking pan.
3. In a small bowl, beat eggs. Set aside.
4. **Prepare Raw Honey Mixture:** In a separate bowl, combine ¼ stick melted butter with ¼ cup raw honey. Mix well. Set aside.

Instructions:
1. Mix all dry ingredients (sea salt, cocoa, baking powder, spices) in a large bowl, except brown sugar and confectioners sugar.
2. In a medium bowl, combine brown sugar, beaten eggs and remaining ¼ stick melted butter. Stir in molasses, remaining ¾ cup honey, buttermilk, milk, vanilla extract and almond extract.
3. In a small bowl, beat eggs. Set aside.
4. Pour liquid mixture in large bowl with dry ingredients. Mix thoroughly.
5. Pour batter mixture in prepared pan. Bake for 25 to 30 minutes.
6. Turn pan around (180 degrees) and bake for an additional 15 minutes, until a toothpick inserted in the center comes out clean.
7. Brush top with melted butter and raw honey mixture. Finish by sprinkling confectioners sugar on top.

Mama's Old-Fashioned Fruitcake | yields 1 large cake

Ingredients:

1½ cups candied yellow pineapple, chopped
1 bag of ready-mixed candied fruit
1 cup candied currants
1 cup brown seedless raisins
1 cup white seedless raisins
2 cups chopped pecans or walnuts
1½ cups butter, room temperature
2 cups firmly-packed light brown sugar
1 cup firmly-packed dark brown sugar
6 eggs, room temperature
1 tablespoon baking soda
1½ teaspoons ground cinnamon
1½ teaspoons ground mace
1½ teaspoons nutmeg
1 teaspoon sea salt
1 teaspoon almond extract
1 teaspoon lemon extract
2 teaspoons vanilla extract
1 cup rum or brandy (for the spiked cake only)
1 cup of Grandma's Molasses (Reserve ½ cup for soaking)
4 cups all-purpose flour, Plus ¼ cup for coating the moist fruits
1 cup apple juice (reserve ½ cup for soaking the dried/candied fruits)
1½ cups candied red maraschino cherries (1 cup halved & ½ cup chopped)
1½ cups candied green maraschino cherries (1 cup halved & ½ cup chopped)

Preparations:

1. Grease a 10-inch tube regular flat-bottom cake pan. Line with parchment paper.
2. In a large bowl, combine candied pineapple, ½ cup each of red and green maraschino cherries, candied cherries, raisins, currants, and pecans or walnuts. Add ½ cup apple or grape juice and molasses. Stir until well blended. Let stand 1 hour or overnight.
3. Drain the soaked and moist fruits (keep the juice) and coat fruit evenly with the ¼ cup flour. Set aside.
4. Preheat oven to 275°F.

MAMA'S OLD-FASHIONED FRUITCAKE (CONT.)

Instructions:

1. In a large bowl, cream butter. Gradually add both brown sugars, stirring until light and fluffy; Add eggs, one at a time, beating well after each addition.
2. In another large bowl, combine flour, baking soda, cinnamon, nutmeg and mace; Gradually add this dry mixture to butter mixture (⅓ at a time and mix well): Add the juice left from the soaked fruits, and the almond and vanilla extract, Mix well,
3. Fold in the soaked flour-coated fruit mixture until well blended; Spoon into prepared cake pan.
4. Bake 3 hours and 20 minutes.
5. Remove from oven and cool on a wire rack for 30 minutes. Loosen the cake from the sides of the cake pan and flip over on to a wide plate; Peel paper liner from the sides of cake, and let cool completely.
6. Wrap one cake in a brandy-soaked cheesecloth; store in an airtight container for one week. After one week, store in the refrigerator.

Fruitcake Variations:

FRUITCAKE LOAF: Grease and flour a loaf pan; Use the same Fruitcake recipe batter and pour in the loaf pan; Bake at 275°F degrees for 25 minutes; Rotate 180° in the oven; Bake for another 15 minutes; Test for doneness; Make a great breakfast coffee bread or can be a dessert.

FRUITCAKE MUFFINS: Grease and flour a muffin pan (or use the muffin parchment paper holders); Use the same fruitcake recipe batter and pour in each of the muffin holders; Bake at 275°F for 15 minutes; Rotate 180° in the oven; Bake for another 10 minutes; Test for doneness; Makes a great breakfast muffin or can be a dessert.

MAMA'S FRUITCAKE SECRETS &TIPS:

A. Baked in a Cooler Oven: 275°F is the right temperature; test the doneness as all ovens are different.
B. Put A Pan of Hot Water on Lower Oven Shelf: Pre-boiled water kept the Fruitcake moist as it baked
C. Line the Cake Pan: Mama would cut a brown paper bag to fit the bottom and other pieces to fit the sides. She sketched the shape of the pan on the brown paper bag for an accurate fit.
D. Soaked Dried Fruits Overnight: When making two cakes, Mama would soak half of the dried fruits overnight in warm water and the other half in molasses (or, in Rum, Brandy and molasses).
E. Coat Softened Fruit with Flour: Mama coated fruits to keep them from sinking to bottom while baking.
F. Fruitcakes Months in Advance: Mama would make her two Christmas Fruitcakes every September and would wrapped them in cheese cloth. The liquor soaked cake was also wrapped with foil.
G. Storage of the Fruitcake Until Christmas: The cakes were then placed in an air tight container and stored in the china cabinet in the dining room.

Mama's Sweet Cream Butter Pound Cake | Serves 10-12

Ingredients:

2 sticks unsalted sweet cream butter, softened
1 ½ stick salted butter
2 ¼ cups all-purpose flour
1 ½ cup sugar
½ cup honey
½ cup coconut milk
3 large egg whites
3 large eggs
1 ½ tablespoon baking powder
2 tablespoons vanilla extract
½ teaspoon almond extract
½ teaspoon lemon extract
½ teaspoon sea salt

Preparations:

1. Preheat oven to 350'F.
2. Grease 12-inch Bundt pan or a Loaf Pan with 2 tablespoons butter and dust with ¼ cup flour.
3. In a small bowl, whisk egg whites until fluffy. Set aside.
4. In a separate bowl, combine remaining 2 cups flour, sea salt and baking powder. Set aside.

Instructions:

1. Using a mixer, in a large bowl, mix sugar, remaining 3 sticks and 2 tablespoons butter and honey on low speed for 1 minute. Add each egg one at a time and mix completely after each egg.
2. Add flour, sea salt and baking powder mixture. Mix thoroughly at low speed for 1 minute. Add extracts and coconut milk. Mix at medium speed for 5 minutes.
3. Fold fluffy egg whites into batter with a spatula. Mix at low speed for 7 minutes.
4. Pour the batter into prepared Bundt pan and gently shake pan to even out the batter.
5. Bake for 35-40 minutes. Turn the cake pan (180 degrees) and cook for an additional 20 to 30 minutes, until a toothpick inserted into center comes out clean.
6. Turn off oven and allow cake to sit in the oven for 5 minutes before removing to finish cooling for 10 to 20 minutes. Loosen the edges of the cake with a table knife; then turn the pan upside down on a large plate. Serve warm with Tea or vanilla ice cream.

HATTIE'S BUTTERMILK BROWNIES | SERVES 6-8

Ingredients:

1 (1 lb. 6.25 oz.) box brownie mix

2 egg whites

½ cup molasses

½ stick butter, melted

2 teaspoon butter, melted

¾ cups sour cream

1 cup buttermilk

1 teaspoon vanilla extract

1 cups chopped walnuts (optional)

Preparation:

1. Preheat oven to 350° F.
2. Grease and flour a 13 x 9-inch baking pan.
3. In a small bowl, mix egg whites until fluffy. Fold in egg whites into brownie batter. Set aside.

Instructions:

1. Prepare brownie batter as instructed on box, except add butter and buttermilk, instead of water.
2. In the bowl with the brownie batter, add the other ingredients: fluffy egg whites, vanilla extract & sour cream.
3. Using a mixer, mix batter thoroughly at medium speed for 5 minutes.
4. Pour batter in prepared baking pan. Bake for 20 minutes. Turn pan (180 degrees) and bake for an additional 10 minutes, or until toothpick inserted in center of brownie comes out clean.
5. When done, brush melted butter on the top of brownie. Sprinkling confectioners sugar on top. Cool for 10 minutes before serving.

Feel Free to Use Pecans or Almonds in Place of Walnuts, or Use No Nuts.

BROWNIES WITH CREAM CHEESE | SERVES 6-8

Ingredients:

1 (1 lb. 6.25 oz.) box brownie mix

1 (4 oz.) cream cheese, softened

2 egg whites

1 cup granulated sugar

½ cup molasses

¼ stick butter, melted

2 teaspoons butter, melted

1 teaspoon vanilla extract

2 teaspoons milk

½ cup confectioners sugar

2 tablespoons flour (for coating baking pan)

Preparation:

1. Preheat the oven to 350° F.
2. Prepare brownie batter as directed on box, add the 1/4 stick butter.
3. In a small bowl, mix egg whites until fluffy. Fold in egg whites into brownie batter. Set aside.
4. Coat a 9 x 13-inch baking pan *(can use butter and flour or baking spray)*.

Instructions:

1. Cream Cheese Mixture: In a medium bowl, beat thoroughly cream cheese, granulated sugar, vanilla extract, and milk.
2. Brownie Mix: Prepare brownie mix according to instructions on box, add the butter.
3. Pour brownie batter evenly into coated baking pan, first. Pour cream cheese mixture & molasses on top of batter.
4. With a knife, swirl super 8's through mixtures, creating a marble design.
5. Bake for 20 minutes; Turn pan (180 degrees) and bake for an additional 15 minutes or until toothpick inserted in center of brownie comes out clean.
6. Brush remaining melted butter on top and sprinkle with confectioners sugar. Cool for 30 minutes before serving.

NOTE: Feel free to use organic, gluten-free brownie mix instead of the regular brownie mix.

BREAD PUDDING WITH BROWN & WHITE RAISINS | SERVES 8-12

Ingredients:

8 cups bread
1 stick butter, melted, divided
4 cups whole milk
3 cups almond milk
2 cans evaporated milk
2 tablespoons lemon juice
2 cups of regular sugar
2 cups raw brown sugar

2 tablespoons nutmeg, divided
2 tablespoons cinnamon, divided
2 tablespoons allspice, divided
2 tablespoons vanilla extract
2 tablespoons ginger, divided
6 to 8 eggs
1 cup each white & brown raisins

Preparation:

1. Preheat oven to 375° F.
2. Dice bread in ½ inch pieces
3. Place bread cubes/pieces in a big mixing bowl, Set aside.
4. Beat the eggs and put them in a large bowl.
5. Grease a large rectangular clear baking dish or baking pan with melted butter.

Instructions:

1. Add all 3 milks to your big bowl with beaten eggs; Stir.
2. Add vanilla and lemon extracts, the sugars, and ½ teaspoon each of the three spices. Stir liquid until sugars dissolved and all ingredients are mixed well.
3. Pour ¾ stick melted butter into the liquid. Stir. Pour liquid over ½ of the bread pieces. Push bread down in the solution and let bread soak for about 10 minutes. Then, stir all the ingredients together.
4. Add the other half of the bread to the solution. Push bread down in the solution (*I like to have two dimensions of soaked bread: The first half dimension of bread will be more dissolved and will make a more custardy consistency; and the second half dimension is not as dissolved and will give the pudding body*).
5. Taste for desired sweetness and spicy taste (Add more milk or spices and/or sugar here, if needed). Fold in coated raisins or other fruits: peaches, apples, pears, fruit cocktail or crushed pineapples (optional). Gently stir again.
6. Pour bread pudding batter in a large greased baking dish. Sprinkle ½ tablespoon nutmeg and the other spices over the top. Put in the middle of the preheated oven--on middle rack.

Bread Pudding with brown & white raisins (cont.)

7. Cook 1 hour to 1 hour & 20 minutes *(During the cooking process, the last bread pieces may come up out of the juice, take spoon to push back down into juice and continue to bake).* Stick a knife into the center to see if it's done after 45 minutes. If the knife comes out with residue, the pudding is not done yet; but, if it comes out clean, the pudding is done.
8. When done, turn oven off and let the Bread Pudding set in the oven for another 10 to 15 minutes to finish setting.

Tip: Add foil on top if bread pudding gets brown before it gets all the way done inside—Oven temperature variations may affect this--whether oven is gas or electric.

Variations: Instead of Raisins (or in addition to), add a cup of chocolate chips or nuts. Other Options: Add a can of Peaches, Apples or Crushed Pineapples (feel free to include part of the canned fruit/s juice; but, do reduce the milk so as not to have the batter too loose).

Serve Warm with Hattie's Rum Butter Honey Glaze

Hattie's Rum Butter Honey Glaze | serves 4-6

Ingredients:
½ cup honey
½ stick melted butter
1 cup confectioners sugar
2 tablespoons rum extract or 1 tablespoon rum liquor
1 teaspoon lemon extract or lemon juice
2 tablespoons milk
1/8 teaspoon sea salt

Instructions:
1. Melt butter in saucepan over medium heat.
2. Mix confectioners sugar with the milk in a bowl. Stir & Mix well.
3. Pour sugar and milk mixture into the saucepan with the melted butter.
4. Bring to near boil. Stir continuously. Turn heat down to low.
5. Add in the honey and stir. Add lemon extract or juice and rum extract or rum liquor. Stir until smooth.
6. Add more milk, if too thick; or more confectioners sugar, if too loose. Simmer on low for about 5 to 7 minutes. Drizzle Glaze/Rum Sauce on top of warm Bread Pudding. **YUM!** ENJOY!

CORN PUDDING | SERVES 4-6

Ingredients:

12 ears fresh corn, husked or 1 (10-16 oz.) bag frozen corn, thawed

2 (14.07 oz.) cans creamed corn

4 eggs

2 tablespoon nutmeg, divided

1 tablespoon cinnamon

1 teaspoon allspice

1 tablespoon vanilla extract

1 cup heavy cream

2 tablespoons cornstarch

2 tablespoons self-rising flour

2 tablespoons

5 tablespoons butter, divided

¾ cup sugar

½ cup light brown sugar

1 (3 oz.) box tapioca pudding mix (optional)

1 teaspoon sea salt

Preparations:

1. Preheat the oven to 350°F.
2. Grease casserole dish with remaining 1 tablespoon butter.

Instructions:

1. In a small bowl, combine cornstarch and flour with 3 tablespoons water to create a paste.
2. In a large bowl, beat eggs. Stir in bowl with eggs, corn, creamed corn, spices, sea salt, vanilla extract, heavy cream, flour, 4 tablespoons butter, sugar, light brown sugar and tapioca pudding mix (optional).
3. Pour corn pudding in a casserole dish. Sprinkle additional nutmeg on top. Bake 40 to 50 minutes or until firm.
4. Halfway through cooking, turn dish 180 degrees. If pudding is too brown, reduce heat and cover with foil.

Serve warm as a dessert or as a side dish.

Raspberry and Blueberry Cobbler | Serves 4-6

Ingredients:
1 package fresh or frozen raspberries and blueberries
1 pie crust, top and bottom
2 tablespoons cornstarch
1 tablespoon lemon extract
1 tablespoon cinnamon
2 tablespoons vanilla extract
1 tablespoon allspice
1 tablespoon ginger
¾ cup brown sugar, divided
1 stick butter, divided
½ cup granulated sugar
½ cup water or pineapple juice

Preparations:
1. Preheat oven to 375° F.
2. Grease with a butter a 6 x 9-inch baking dish. Line the baking dish with pie crust.
3. Take your finger and tuck the bottom crust evenly around the sides.

Instructions:
1. In a saucepan, over medium-high heat, combine ½ stick butter, ½ cup brown sugar, raspberries, blueberries, granulated sugar, 1½ teaspoon nutmeg, cinnamon, allspice, ginger and lemon extract. Bring to a light boil (if liquid is too thick, add more water or pineapple juice. If liquid is not thick enough, add 1 teaspoon of cornstarch at a time and stir). Stir gently.
2. Stir in raspberries and blueberries. Simmer for 5 minutes over medium heat.
3. Pour filling in the bottom of the crust and spread evenly. Before adding top crust, add 4 slices of butter evenly around on top of the fruit mixture .
4. Sprinkle remaining 1 ½ teaspoon nutmeg and 1 tablespoon brown sugar on top.
5. Place top crust evenly over dish. Take a fork to press down the crust sides to keep it together and scrape off the excess crust around the dish.
6. Cut 6 slits in top crust, making sure the raspberries and blueberries are visible through slits for breathing and bubbling while cooking. Brush melted butter across the top and the edges of the crust. Place dish on a sheet of foil and bake for 30 to 40 minutes until golden brown.
7. Let rest for about 10 minutes so crust and fruit mix will set.

DESSERTS

Strawberry Cobbler | Serves 4-6

Ingredients:

4 cups fresh strawberries, halved

1 pie crust, top and bottom

2 tablespoons cornstarch

1 tablespoon lemon extract

1 tablespoon cinnamon

2 tablespoons vanilla extract

1 tablespoon allspice

1 tablespoon ginger

¾ cup brown sugar, divided

1 stick butter, divided

½ cup granulated sugar

½ cup water or pineapple juice

Preparations:

1. Preheat oven to 375°F.
2. Grease with a butter a 6 x 9-inch baking dish. Line the baking dish with pie crust.
3. Take your finger and tuck the bottom crust evenly around the sides.

Instructions:

1. In a saucepan, over medium-high heat, combine ½ stick butter, ½ cup brown sugar, strawberries, granulated sugar, 1 ½ teaspoon nutmeg, cinnamon, allspice, ginger and lemon extract. Bring to a light boil (if liquid is too thick, add more water or pineapple juice. If liquid is not thick enough, add 1 teaspoon of cornstarch at a time and stir). Stir gently.
2. Stir in the strawberries. Simmer for 5 minutes over medium heat.
3. Pour filling in the bottom of the crust and spread evenly. Before adding top crust, add 4 slices of butter evenly around on top of the fruit mixture . Sprinkle remaining 1 ½ teaspoon nutmeg and 1 tablespoon brown sugar on top.
4. Place top crust evenly over dish. Take a fork to press down the crust sides to keep it together and scrape off the excess crust around the dish.
5. Cut 6 slits in top crust, making sure the strawberries are visible through slits for breathing and bubbling while cooking. Brush melted butter across the top and the edges of the crust. Place dish on a sheet of foil and bake for 30 to 40 minutes until golden brown.
6. Let rest for about 10 minutes so crust and fruit mix will set.

CHERRY COBBLER | SERVES 4-6

Ingredients:
3 cups fresh cherries, pitted
1 pie crust, top and bottom
1 tablespoon nutmeg, divided
1 teaspoon lemon extract
1 tablespoon cinnamon
2 tablespoons vanilla extract
1 tablespoon allspice
1 tablespoon ginger
¾ cup brown sugar, divided
1 stick butter, divided
½ cup granulated sugar
2 tablespoons cornstarch
½ cup water or pineapple juice

Preparations:
1. Preheat oven to 375°F.
2. Grease with a butter a 6 x 9-inch baking dish. Line the baking dish with pie crust.
3. Take your finger and tuck the bottom crust evenly around the sides.

Instructions:
1. In a saucepan, over medium-high heat, combine ½ stick butter, ½ cup brown sugar, cherries, granulated sugar, 1½ teaspoon nutmeg, cinnamon, allspice, ginger and lemon extract. Bring to a light boil (if liquid is too thick, add more water or pineapple juice. If liquid is not thick enough, add 1 teaspoon of cornstarch at a time and stir). Stir gently.
2. Stir in cherries. Simmer for 5 minutes over medium heat.
3. Pour filling in the bottom of the crust and spread evenly. Before adding top crust, add 4 slices of butter evenly around on top of the fruit mixture. Sprinkle remaining 1 ½ teaspoon nutmeg and 1 tablespoon brown sugar on top.
4. Place top crust evenly over dish. Take a fork to press down the crust sides to keep it together and scrape off the excess crust around the dish.
5. Cut 6 slits in top crust, making sure the cherries are visible through slits for breathing and bubbling while cooking. Brush melted butter across the top and the edges of the crust. Place dish on a sheet of foil and bake for 30 to 40 minutes until golden brown.
6. Let rest for about 10 minutes so crust and fruit mix will set.

PEACH COBBLER | SERVES 4-6

Ingredients:

6 fresh peaches, peeled and sliced
1 pie crust, top and bottom
1 tablespoon nutmeg, divided
1 teaspoon lemon extract
1 tablespoon cinnamon
2 tablespoons vanilla extract
1 tablespoon allspice
1 tablespoon ginger
¾ cup brown sugar, divided
1 stick butter, divided
½ cup granulated sugar
½ cup water or pineapple juice

Preparations:

1. Preheat oven to 375°F.
2. Grease with a butter a 6 x 9-inch baking dish. Line the baking dish with pie crust.
3. Take your finger and tuck the bottom crust evenly around the sides.

Instructions:

1. In a saucepan, over medium-high heat, combine ½ stick butter, ½ cup brown sugar, peaches, granulated sugar, 1½ teaspoon nutmeg, cinnamon, allspice, ginger and lemon extract. Bring to a light boil (if liquid is too thick, add ½ cup water. If liquid is not thick enough, add 1 teaspoon of cornstarch at a time and stir). Stir gently.
2. Stir in peach slices. Simmer for 5 minutes over medium heat.
3. Pour filling in the bottom of the crust and spread evenly. Before adding top crust, add 4 slices of butter evenly around on top of the fruit mixture. Sprinkle remaining 1 ½ teaspoon nutmeg and 1 tablespoon brown sugar on top.
4. Place top crust evenly over dish. Take a fork to press down the crust sides to keep it together and scrape off the excess crust around the dish.
5. Cut 6 slits in top crust, making sure the peaches are visible through slits for breathing and bubbling while cooking. Brush melted butter across the top and the edges of the crust. Place dish on a sheet of foil and bake for 30 to 40 minutes until golden brown.
6. Let rest for about 10 minutes so crust and fruit mix will set.

APPLE COBBLER | SERVES 4-6

Ingredients:
4 granny smith apples, peeled and sliced
1 pie crust, top and bottom
1 tablespoon nutmeg, divided
1 teaspoon lemon extract
1 tablespoon cinnamon
2 tablespoons vanilla extract
1 tablespoon allspice
1 tablespoon ginger
¾ cup brown sugar, divided
1 stick butter, divided
½ cup granulated sugar
2 tablespoons cornstarch
½ cup water or apple juice

Preparations:
1. Preheat oven to 375°F.
2. Grease with a butter a 6 x 9-inch baking dish. Line the baking dish with pie crust.
3. Take your finger and tuck the bottom crust evenly around the sides.

Instructions:
1. In a saucepan, over medium-high heat, combine ½ stick butter, ½ cup brown sugar, sliced apples, granulated sugar, 1 ½ teaspoon nutmeg, cinnamon, allspice, ginger and lemon extract. Bring to a light boil (if liquid is too thick, add more water or apple juice. If liquid is not thick enough, add 1 teaspoon of cornstarch at a time and stir). Stir gently.
2. Stir in sliced apples. Simmer for 5 minutes over medium heat.
3. Pour filling in the bottom of the crust and spread evenly. Before adding top crust, add 4 slices of butter evenly around on top of the fruit mixture. Sprinkle remaining 1 ½ teaspoon nutmeg and 1 tablespoon brown sugar on top.

4. Place top crust evenly over dish. Take a fork to press down the crust sides to keep it together and scrape off the excess crust around the dish.
5. Cut 6 slits in top crust, making sure the apples are visible through slits for breathing and bubbling while cooking. Brush melted butter across the top and the edges of the crust. Place dish on a sheet of foil and bake for 30 to 40 minutes until golden brown.
6. Let rest for about 10 minutes so crust and fruit mix will set.

Apple & Pear Cobbler | Serves 4-6

Ingredients:

4 granny smith apples, peeled and sliced

2 pears, peeled and sliced

1 pie crust, top and bottom

2 tablespoons cornstarch

1 tablespoon nutmeg, divided

1 teaspoon lemon extract

1 tablespoon cinnamon

2 tablespoons vanilla extract

1 tablespoon allspice

1 tablespoon ginger

¾ cup brown sugar, divided

1 stick butter

½ cup granulated sugar

½ cup water or apple juice

Preparations:

1. Preheat oven to 375°F.
2. Grease with a butter a 6 x 9-inch baking dish. Line the baking dish with pie crust.
3. Take your finger and tuck the bottom crust evenly around the sides.

Instructions:

1. In a saucepan, over medium-high heat, combine ½ stick butter, ½ cup brown sugar, sliced apples, sliced pears, granulated sugar, 1 ½ teaspoon nutmeg, cinnamon, allspice, ginger and lemon extract. Bring to a light boil (if liquid is too thick, add more water or apple juice. If liquid is not thick enough, add 1 teaspoon of cornstarch at a time and stir). Stir gently.
2. Stir in apples and pears. Simmer for 5 minutes over medium heat.
3. Pour filling in the bottom of the crust and spread evenly. Before adding top crust, add 4 slices of butter evenly around on top of the fruit mixture. Sprinkle remaining 1 ½ teaspoon nutmeg and 1 tablespoon brown sugar on top.
4. Place top crust evenly over dish. Take a fork to press down the crust sides to keep it together and scrape off the excess crust around the dish.
5. Cut 6 slits in top crust, making sure the apples and pears are visible through slits for breathing and bubbling while cooking. Brush melted butter across the top and the edges of the crust. Place dish on a sheet of foil and bake for 30 to 40 minutes until golden brown.
6. Let rest for about 10 minutes so crust and fruit will set.

BLACKBERRY COBBLER | SERVES 4-6

Ingredients:

3 cups of fresh blackberries

1 pie crust, top and bottom

2 tablespoons cornstarch

1 tablespoon nutmeg

1 teaspoon lemon extract

¼ cup water or pineapple juice

1 tablespoon cinnamon

1 tablespoon ginger

¾ cup brown sugar, divided

1 stick butter, divided

½ cup granulated sugar

Preparations:

1. Preheat oven to 375°F.
2. Grease with a butter a 6 x 9-inch baking dish. Line the baking dish with pie crust.
3. Take your finger and tuck the bottom crust evenly around the sides.

Instructions:

1. In a saucepan, over medium-high heat, combine ½ stick butter, ½ cup brown sugar, blackberries (add 2 tablespoons milk if berries are too tart), granulated sugar, 1 ½ teaspoon nutmeg, cinnamon, allspice, ginger and lemon extract. Bring to a light boil (if liquid is too thick, add water or pineapple juice. If liquid is not thick enough, add 1 teaspoon of cornstarch at a time and stir). Stir gently.
2. Stir in the blackberries. Simmer for 5 minutes over medium heat.
3. Pour filling in the bottom of the crust and spread evenly. Before adding top crust, add 4 slices of butter evenly around on top of the fruit mixture. Sprinkle remaining 1 ½ teaspoon nutmeg and 1 tablespoon brown sugar on top.
4. Place top crust evenly over dish. Take a fork to press down the crust sides to keep it together and scrape off the excess crust around the dish.
5. Cut 6 slits in top crust, making sure the blackberries are visible through slits for breathing and bubbling while cooking. Brush melted butter across the top and the edges of the crust. Place dish on a sheet of foil and bake for 30 to 40 minutes until golden brown.
6. Let rest for about 10 minutes so crust and fruit mix will set.

MIXED FRUIT COBBLER | SERVES 4-6

Ingredients:

Frozen or fresh blackberries, raspberries, cherries

1 pie crust, top and bottom

1 tablespoon nutmeg, divided

1 teaspoon lemon extract

1 tablespoon allspice

1 tablespoon cinnamon

1 tablespoon ginger

¾ cup brown sugar, divided

1 stick butter, divided

½ cup granulated sugar

2 tablespoons cornstarch

½ cup water or pineapple juice

Preparations:

1. Preheat the oven to 375°F.
2. Grease with butter a 6 x 9-inch baking dish. Line the baking dish with pie crust.
3. Take your finger and tuck the bottom crust evenly around the sides.

Instructions:

1. In a saucepan, over medium-high heat, combine ½ stick butter, ½ cup brown sugar, blackberries, raspberries & cherries, granulated sugar, 1 ½ teaspoon nutmeg, cinnamon, allspice, ginger and lemon extract. Bring to a light boil (if liquid is too thick, add more water or pineapple juice. If liquid is not thick enough, add 1 teaspoon of cornstarch at a time and stir). Stir gently.
2. Stir in the fruit. Simmer for 5 minutes over medium heat.
3. Pour filling in the bottom of the crust and spread evenly. Before adding top crust, add 4 slices of butter evenly around on top of the fruit mixture. Sprinkle remaining 1 ½ teaspoon nutmeg and 1 tablespoon brown sugar on top.
4. Place top crust evenly over dish. Take a fork to press down the crust sides to keep it together and scrape off the excess crust around the dish.
5. Cut 6 slits in top crust, making sure the fruits are visible through slits for breathing and bubbling while cooking. Brush melted butter across the top and the edges of the crust. Place dish on a sheet of foil and bake for 30 to 40 minutes until golden brown.
6. Let rest for about 10 minutes so crust and fruit mix will set.

APPLE PIE | SERVES 8

Ingredients:

6 Granny Smith apples
1 cup granulated white sugar
½ cup brown sugar
4 tablespoons lemon juice
2 tablespoons vanilla extract
2 tablespoons nutmeg
2 tablespoons cinnamon
2 tablespoons allspice
1 tablespoon ginger

9 tablespoons butter, divided
1 large egg white
3 tablespoons cornstarch
2 tablespoons flour
½ cup apple juice or cider
¼ cup orange juice
½ cup raisins (optional)
½ cup water or pineapple juice

Preparations:

1. Preheat oven to 375°F.
2. Peel and slice apples into 2" thick slices.
3. Line a 9-inch plate with bottom crust. Trim pastry's edges even with a knife.
4. Melt remaining 1 tablespoon butter in microwave and brush pie crust pastry with butter. Bake for 10 minutes (halfway done). Set aside.
5. Beat egg white until foamy to brush over pastry.

Instructions:

1. In a saucepan, over medium-high heat, combine 8 tablespoons butter, ½ cup brown sugar, granulated sugar, 1 ½ teaspoon nutmeg, cinnamon, allspice, ginger and lemon extract. Bring to a light boil (if liquid is too thick, add more water or pineapple juice. If liquid is not thick enough, add 1 teaspoon of cornstarch at a time and stir). Stir gently.
2. Stir in apples. Simmer for 5 minutes over medium heat.
3. Pour filling in the bottom of the pie crust and spread evenly. Before adding top crust, add 4 slices of butter evenly around on top of the fruit mixture. Sprinkle remaining 1½ teaspoon nutmeg and 1 tablespoon brown sugar on top.
4. Place top crust evenly over dish. Take a fork to press down the crust sides to keep it together and scrape off the excess crust around the dish.
5. Cut 6 slits in top crust, making sure the apples are visible through slits for breathing and bubbling while cooking. Brush melted butter across the top and the edges of the crust. Brush foamy egg white over pastry. Sprinkle with additional brown sugar (optional).
6. Place dish on a sheet of foil and bake for 40 to 50 minutes until golden brown and the filling is bubbly. Let rest for about 10 minutes before serving.

BLACKBERRY PIE | SERVES 8

Ingredients:

4 cups fresh or frozen blackberries (thawed)
1 cup granulated white sugar
½ cup brown sugar
4 tablespoons lemon juice
2 tablespoons vanilla extract
2 tablespoons nutmeg
2 tablespoons cinnamon
2 tablespoons allspice
2 Tablespoons brown sugar

1 tablespoon ginger
9 tablespoons butter, divided
1 large egg
3 tablespoons cornstarch
2 tablespoons flour
½ cup apple juice or cider
¼ cup orange juice
½ cup water or pineapple juice

Preparations:

1. Preheat oven to 375°F.
2. Line a 9-inch plate with bottom crust. Trim pastry's edges even with a knife.
3. Melt remaining 1 tablespoon butter in microwave and brush pie crust pastry with butter. Bake for 10 minutes (halfway done). Set aside.
4. Beat egg white until foamy to brush over pastry.

Instructions:

1. In a saucepan, over medium-high heat, combine 8 tablespoons butter, ½ cup brown sugar, granulated sugar, 1 ½ teaspoon nutmeg, cinnamon, allspice, ginger and lemon extract. Bring to a light boil (if liquid is too thick, add more water or pineapple juice. If liquid is not thick enough, add 1 teaspoon of cornstarch at a time and stir). Stir gently.
2. Stir in blackberries. Simmer for 5 minutes over medium heat.
3. Pour filling in the bottom of the pie crust and spread evenly. Before adding top crust, add 4 slices of butter evenly around on top of the fruit mixture. Sprinkle remaining 1½ teaspoon nutmeg and 1 tablespoon brown sugar on top.
4. Place top crust evenly over pie crust pan. Take a fork to press down the crust sides to keep it together and scrape off the excess crust around the dish.
5. Cut 6 slits in top crust, making sure the blackberries are visible through slits for breathing and bubbling while cooking. Brush melted butter across the top and the edges of the crust. Brush foamy egg white over pastry. Sprinkle with additional brown sugar (optional).
6. Place dish on a sheet of foil and bake for 40 to 50 minutes until golden brown and the filling is bubbly. Let rest for about 10 minutes before serving.

PEACH PIE | SERVES 4-6

Ingredients:

6 cups fresh peaches, sliced and peeled
1 can peaches (keep syrup)
1 cup granulated white sugar
½ cup brown sugar
4 tablespoons lemon juice
2 tablespoons vanilla extract
2 tablespoons nutmeg
2 tablespoons cinnamon
2 tablespoons allspice

1 tablespoon ginger
9 tablespoons butter, divided
1 large egg white
3 tablespoons cornstarch
2 tablespoons flour
½ cup apple juice or cider
¼ cup orange juice
½ cup water or pineapple juice

Preparations:

1. Preheat oven to 375°F.
2. Line a 9-inch plate with bottom crust. Trim pastry's edges even with a knife.
3. Melt remaining 1 tablespoon butter in microwave and brush pie crust pastry with butter. Bake for 10 minutes (halfway done). Set aside.
4. Beat egg white until foamy to brush over pastry.

Instructions:

1. In a saucepan, over medium-high heat, combine 8 tablespoons butter, ½ cup brown sugar, granulated sugar, 1½ teaspoon nutmeg, cinnamon, allspice, ginger and lemon extract. Bring to a light boil (if liquid is too thick, add more water or pineapple juice. If liquid is not thick enough, add 1 teaspoon of cornstarch at a time and stir). Stir gently.
2. Stir in peach. Simmer for 5 minutes over medium heat.
3. Pour filling in the bottom of the pie crust and spread evenly. Before adding top crust, add 4 slices of butter evenly around on top of the fruit mixture. Sprinkle remaining 1½ teaspoon nutmeg and 1 tablespoon brown sugar on top.
4. Place top crust evenly over pie crust pan. Take a fork to press down the crust sides to keep it together and scrape off the excess crust around the dish.
5. Cut 6 slits in top crust, making sure the peaches are visible through slits for breathing and bubbling while cooking. Brush melted butter across the top and the edges of the crust. Brush foamy egg white over pastry. Sprinkle with additional brown sugar (optional).
6. Place dish on a sheet of foil and bake for 40 to 50 minutes until golden brown and the filling is bubbly. Let rest for about 10 minutes before serving.

HATTIE'S SWEET POTATO PUDDING PIE | SERVES 8-10

Ingredients:

4 sweet potatoes, peeled and mashed

1 teaspoon sea salt

2 tablespoons fresh lemon juice

1 teaspoon vanilla extract

¼ cup butter, soften

1 tablespoon butter

½ teaspoon ground nutmeg

½ teaspoon ground cinnamon

¾ cup evaporated milk

1 egg white, beat until fluffy

2 eggs, beaten

¼ cup brown sugar

½ cup walnuts, crushed

½ cup shredded coconut

½ cup light brown sugar (plus 2 tablespoons)

1 package of pudding mix

Instructions:

1. Preheat the oven to 350°F.

2. Lay out crust into 9-inch casserole dish.

3. In a large mixing bowl, combine sweet potatoes, sea salt, lemon juice, vanilla extract, soften butter, nutmeg, cinnamon, milk, eggs, pudding mix, sugar, coconut and walnuts (Optional). Mix well. Fold in the fluffy egg white.

4. Pour into pie crust. Sprinkle light brown sugar on top. Bake for 25 to 30 minutes. Turn dish 180 degrees and continue cooking for 10 to 15 minutes, or until pie test is done with a knife.

This sweet potato pudding pie can be served as a side dish or a dessert.
If you would like to make it a side dish, skip using the pie crust. Enjoy!

RECIPE FOR HATTIE'S HOMEMADE PIE CRUST
(FOR PIES, PUFFS, COBBLERS, CASSEROLES, & OTHER CRUST DISHES--VARY THE AMOUNT OF INGREDIENTS ACCORDING TO VARIOUS RECIPES OR PERSONAL PREFERENCES)

Ingredients:

(Enough ingredients for a Crust for a cobbler size (3 in. high x 6 in x 9 in baking dish) or for two medium-size deep-dish pies--with a bottom & top crust)

4 cups Self-Rising Flour, plus another ½ cup for rolling pin & rolling out;

1 cup cold Lard* (1 ½ "hands full" of Lard—Sorry, I could not resist. My stepmom measured lard by the hands full for her delicious flaky pie and other crusts, melt-in-your-mouth biscuits, fluffy rolls, etc.);

½ cup cold butter; plus 2 tablespoons melted butter; and

1½ cup ice water.

Instructions:

These Crust Ingredients and Instructions are the same for ALL fruit pies, puffs, cobblers, casseroles, quiches, and any other dish that calls for a crust of any kind, either on the bottom and/or on top.

1. Mix lard, butter, and 4 cups flour together in a large bowl--until mixture is crumbly (just enough so there are no lard, butter, or flour lumps—do not over handle);

2. Form an indenture (a little hole) in the center of your flour mixture in the bowl and add about a tablespoon of the cold water at a time;

3. Mixing with a fork (or your hand, as my stepmom did) in a circle—blending in a little more of the flour mixture at a time from the outer edges of the bowl; Add more cold water, and Mix until consistency is like dough; Knead the dough just enough so all ingredients are mixed in;

4. Divide dough in half; roll in a ball on a flat surface; put in separate freezer bags and refrigerate for about two hours—will keep the clumps of lard and butter intact to make for a flakier crust;

5. Then, when ready, spread some of remaining flour on your rolling pin all around— to keep the dough from sticking to the rolling pin as you roll the dough on a flat surface (I roll my dough on wax paper sprinkled with flour to prevent dough from sticking as I roll it out);

Instructions (Cont.):

6. Roll dough, start in the middle, and roll in both directions until desired thickness is even all the way around. You may need to sprinkle a little more of remaining flour on top of the dough on the flat surface as you finish rolling it out;

7. Follow respective recipes that call for a Crust **(Make your crust dough thicker for your cobblers & thinner for your pies, puffs, casseroles, quiche, and other dishes that call for a crust—thickness is a personal preference).**

Optional: Brush melted butter across the top and the edges of the crust after baking for about 10 minutes.   Be Creative With Your Crust Uses! Enjoy!

*Lard is a southern staple that's used in all crusts, biscuits, rolls, frying chicken, and various other recipes (See Resource Directory in the back of cookbook for articles on **"The Benefits of Lard— A Good Fat"**).

SMOOTHIES & BEVERAGES

Smoothies are not only delicious, but when made with the right ingredients smoothies can serve as a healthy meal replacement. I've also included power-energy smoothies that are excellent to start the day or after intensive workouts.

Boostie Energy Smoothies
Fruit & Veggie Green Smoothie
Citrus Sorbet Smoothie
Nutty Buddy Smoothie
Savory Vegetable Smoothie
Watermelon Smoothie
Charrell's Pre-Workout Smoothie*
Cheryl's Tropical Green Smoothie*
Sean's Power He-Man Smoothie*
Cameron's Power Smoothie*
*Family smoothie recipes in the "And Beyond" section.

ENERGY BOOSTIE SMOOTHIE | SERVES 1-2

Ingredients:
1 cup baby spinach leaves
1 cup kale, shredded
½ Granny Smith apple, cut in chunks
2 tablespoons fresh lemon juice
½ ripe banana
½ cup strawberries
1 cup coconut water
1 cup almond milk
½ cup ice cubes (optional)

Instructions:
1. Put all ingredients into blender.
2. Blend at medium high speed, until desired smoothness.
3. Add ice cubes for desired thickness.

FRUIT & VEGGIE GREEN SMOOTHIE | SERVES 1-2

Ingredients:

Ingredients:
1 cup spinach leaves
1 cup pineapple chunks
1 cup kale
2 apples cut into chunks
¼ cup shredded carrots
½ container plain yogurt
½ ripe banana
½ container fruit yogurt
2 strawberries
½ cup crushed ice

Instructions:
1. Put all ingredients into blender.
2. Blend at medium-high speed, until desired smoothness.
3. Add ice cubes for desired thickness.

CITRUS SORBET SMOOTHIE | SERVES 1-2

Ingredients:

1 orange, peeled
1 tangerine, peeled
2 teaspoons lemon
2 teaspoons lime
4 pineapple chunks
4 apple, cut into chunks
½ ripe banana
5 oz. coconut pineapple water
4 oz. sparkling water
1 teaspoon honey
1 teaspoon coconut oil
1 (4 oz.) container lemon yogurt

Instructions:

1. Put all ingredients into blender.
2. Blend at medium high speed until desired smoothness.
3. Add ice cubes for desired thickness. Enjoy!

NUTTY BUDDY SMOOTHIE | SERVES 1-2

Ingredients:

4 oz. almond milk
2 oz. coconut water
2 oz. cashew milk
1 teaspoon maple syrup
1 tablespoon almond butter

1 teaspoon coconut oil
½ ripe banana
2 strawberries
4 blackberries
sprinkle of cinnamon

Instructions:

1. Put all ingredients into blender.
2. Blend at medium speed, until desired smoothness.
3. Add ice cubes for desired thickness.

SAVORY VEGETABLE SMOOTHIE | SERVES 1-2

Ingredients:
1 cup spinach leaves
1 cup kale
½ celery stalk,
¼ bell pepper
½ small tomato
¼ cup shredded carrots
4 pineapple chunks
4 Granny Smith apple chunks
dash of salt
pinch of cayenne pepper
½ teaspoon apple cider vinegar
1 tablespoon maple syrup
¼ cup ice cubes

Instructions:
1. Put all ingredients into blender.
2. Blend at medium-high speed until desired smoothness.
3. Add ice cubes for desired thickness. Enjoy!

WATERMELON SMOOTHIE | SERVES 1-2

Ingredients:
1 cup diced watermelon
6 oz. coconut water
6 oz. pineapple water, optional
2 oz. almond or coconut milk
2 tablespoons lemon juice
2 tablespoons strawberry and vanilla protein powder
½ cup crushed ice cubes (optional)

Instructions:
1. Put all ingredients into blender.
2. Blend at medium high speed until desired smoothness.
3. Add ice cubes for desired thickness. Enjoy!

WATERMELON REFRESHING DRINK

Put ice cubes in the watermelon juice and 2 tablespoon of lemon juice. Serve in a tall glass with a slice of lemon on the rim of glass and two fresh strawberry halves in the glass for color.

WATERMELON COCKTAIL

Add rum, vodka or Amaretto to the watermelon juice to make a nice refreshing summer cocktail. You can serve over crushed ice or blend the crushed ice and ingredients in the blender for a more slushy watermelon cocktail.

WATERMELON ICEE

Add coconut water (no milk nor protein powder) and lemon juice in the blender with plenty of ice.

WATERMELON SORBET

The watermelon Icee (above) can be more of a sorbet if 2 tablespoons almond milk and 2 tablespoons cashew milk are added to the blender.

AND BEYOND

This section shares selected recipes from my family and friends. Recipes ranging from desserts to main dishes. This chapter also includes favorite dishes and customs from when my family lived in Greece and Scotland.

Family

Skillet Barbecue Chicken Thighs
Zucchini Lasagna
Iron Girl Smoothie
Sweet & Spicy Green Beans
Vegan Spicy Black Beans
Power He-Man Smoothie
Power Smoothie
Ballistic Brownies
Yogurt Delight
Potato Salad
Rice Pudding with Raisins
Sweet Potato Pie
Hot Sausage & Brown Gravy
Salmon Cakes
Coconut Custard Pie
Corn Pudding
Oven Chopped Barbecue
Potato Salad
Seafood Casserole
Beef Brisket
Rum Ball
Sweet Potato
Red Velvet Cake
Zucchini Bread
Butternut Squash Soup
Split Pea Soup
Old Fashion Coconut Pie
Poor Boy Cake/Pie
Old Fashion Pound Cake
Grandma's Sweet Potato Pie
Southern Banana Pudding
Chocolate Pie
Shrimp Fried Rice

Friends

Broccoli & Cheese Muffins
Oxtails
7-Up Pound Cake
Monkey Bread
Lemon Chess Pie
Old-Fashioned Spoon Bread

Dishes From Abroad

Greek Watermelon Salad
Beef Shepherd's Pie
Chicken Shepherd's Pie

SKILLET BARBECUE CHICKEN THIGHS | SERVES 6 - 8
BY CHARRELL W. THOMAS, M.D., MY OLDER DAUGHTER

Ingredients:

8 boneless and skinless** chicken thighs

½ large red onion or shallots

1 tablespoon coconut oil

½ cup barbecue sauce

½ teaspoon sea salt

½ teaspoon chili powder

½ teaspoon garlic powder

½ teaspoon black pepper -optional-

1- 2 tablespoons chopped cilantro (optional)

Preparations:

1. Preheat the oven to 375°F.
2. Preheat large cast iron skillet on medium high.
3. Wash thighs and pat dry.
4. Season thighs with garlic powder, chili powder, sea salt and pepper. Set aside.
5. Peel & thinly slice a red onions or shallots.

Instructions:

1. In a large cast iron skillet, heat coconut oil over medium-high. Add seasoned thighs in the skillet (on flat side down). Cook until the bottom side is golden brown, about 2 to 3 minutes.
2. Flip the thighs over and let the other side brown, for 2 to 3 minutes.
3. While cooking, add the red onions or shallots in the skillet between the thighs and saute for about 1 to 3 minutes.
4. Pour in the barbecue sauce over the top of the chicken thighs.
5. Place the cast iron skillet in the preheated oven. Cook 20 to 30 minutes until done, depending on the size of the chicken thighs.
6. Remove the skillet of cooked chicken from the oven, sprinkle with cilantro. Serve immediately.

Serve with vegetable of your choice for a delicious low carb meal (350 to 400 calories per serving).

**Note: See Article in the Resource Directory in the back of Cookbook on "Good Fats"

Zucchini Lasagna | Serves 6 - 8
by Charrell W. Thomas, M.D. (my older daughter)

Ingredients:

1 jar of Spaghetti Sauce

2 eggs

4 cup shredded mozzarella cheese, divided

1/2 cup grated parmesan cheese

1/2 cup green pepper, diced

1 teaspoon dried oregano (or 1 teaspoon Italian seasoning)

1 tablespoon Stevia Blend®

6 medium zucchini, sliced

1 tablespoon olive oil

1 cup onions, diced

1 pound ground turkey

1 teaspoon black pepper

2 cups ricotta cheese

Cooking spray

Preparations:

1. Preheat the oven to 425°F.
2. Slice the zucchini with mandolin or sharp knife length-wise ¼ inch thick.
3. Dice onions and peppers, in small pieces.
4. Spray bottom of casserole dish with cooking spray.

Making the Ricotta Cheese Mixture:

1. Combine 2 cups ricotta cheese, 2 eggs, and black pepper in bowl.
2. Stir in 3 cups of shredded mozzarella cheese and grated parmesan cheese.
3. Mix well. Set aside.

ZUCCHINI LASAGNA (CONT.)

Instructions:

A: **Preparing the Zucchini Slices--To Use in Place of Pasta Noodles**
1. Lay zucchini slices on a cookie sheet. Spray slices evenly with cooking spray.
2. Sprinkle with dried oregano or Italian seasoning.
3. Place slices in preheated oven and roast for about 10 minutes.
4. Remove slices from oven and set aside to cool.
5. Reduce oven to 300°F to bake the lasagna later.

B: Preparing the Meat Sauce
1. In a skillet, heat olive oil over medium high. Sauté ground turkey, onion, and bell pepper together until meat is cooked; Stir in jar of spaghetti sauce and Stevia Blend®. Mix well.
2. Add salt and pepper for taste.

C. Layering the Lasagna Dish
1. In a casserole dish, spread 2 tablespoons of spaghetti sauce in the bottom. Then, arrange the cooled zucchini slices on top of the sauce.
2. Next, spread 1/3 of the ricotta cheese mixture evenly on top of the zucchini slices; cover the cheese mixture with spaghetti sauce.
3. Repeat the layering process, build last layer with a heavier amount of ricotta cheese mixture on the top layer; Sprinkle the remaining mozzarella cheese on the top of the ricotta cheese mixture.
4. Place in a preheated oven (300°F) and cook for 45 minutes; Once done, let stand for 15 minutes.

CHARRELL'S PRE-WORKOUT SMOOTHIE

Ingredients:
2 scoops whey protein
1 scoop collagen protein
½ banana
½ cup strawberries (frozen or fresh)
1 tablespoon coconut oil
2 cups unsweetened almond milk
a sprinkle of pure Stevia® to sweeten

Instructions:
1. Pour all ingredients into blender. Add ice cubes (optional).
2. Blend at medium high, until desired smoothness.

"IRON GIRL" TROPICAL GREEN SMOOTHIE
BY CHERYL WASHINGTON, ESQ., (MY YOUNGER DAUGHTER)

Ingredients:
1 ½ cups spinach
1 ripe banana
1 cup pineapple
1 tablespoon flax or chia seeds
1 cup water or coconut water
½ to 1 cup unsweetened vanilla almond milk
Ice (optional)
2 tablespoons protein powder (optional)
Stevia/Xylitol® Blend (to taste)
1 teaspoon vanilla extract
⅛ teaspoon cinnamon
⅛ teaspoon sea salt
ice (optional)

Instructions:

1. Combine spinach and water in blender.

2. Blend until smooth.

3. Add remaining ingredients and blend on high speed until smooth.

4. Add ice cubes for thickness (optional).

SWEET AND SPICY GREEN BEANS | SERVES 6 - 8
BY CHERYL WASHINGTON

Ingredients:

2 pounds organic green beans (pre-washed)
1 organic red pepper cut into thin strips
1 organic sweet onion cut into thin strips
1 tablespoon coconut oil
2 to 3 tablespoons balsamic vinegar
2 to 3 tablespoons organic maple syrup

½ teaspoon garlic powder
½ teaspoon onion powder
½ teaspoon sea salt
⅛ teaspoon pepper
⅛ teaspoon cayenne pepper

Instructions:

1. Boil 3 cups water in a medium sauce pan.
2. Add green beans to boiling water and cook for 5 minutes.
3. Meanwhile, heat coconut oil in frying pan.
4. Add red bell peppers and onions and sauté until partially caramelized.
5. Drain water from green beans.
6. Add green beans to frying pan with the partially sautéed onions and peppers.
7. Continue sautéing.
8. Add balsamic vinegar, maple syrup, sea salt, pepper and spices.
9. Continue cooking until green beans are tender to your taste. **Enjoy!**

"CAN'T BELIEVE THEY'RE VEGAN SPICY BLACK BEANS"
SERVES | 4 - 6
BY CHERYL WASHINGTON

Ingredients:

1 large can organic black beans
2 tablespoons coconut oil
1 jar organic hot salsa
2 tablespoons bouillon paste ("not chicken")
1 large organic sweet onion, diced
1 organic green pepper, diced
1 organic red pepper, diced
½ teaspoon sea salt

½ teaspoon pepper
1 tablespoon chili powder
1 tablespoon cumin
1 teaspoon garlic powder
1 teaspoon onion powder
½ teaspoon balsamic vinegar
½ teaspoon Stevia Blend ® or Xylitol Blend
2 cups water (for desired consistency)

Instructions:

1. In a large stock pot, Sauté onion and all bell peppers in coconut oil until tender.
2. Drain beans and add to pot with onions and bell peppers.
3. Add salsa
4. Add water and bouillon paste, stir.
5. Add all spices and stir.
6. Add balsamic vinegar and Stevia® blend; stir.
7. Simmer for 30 to 40 minutes, stirring frequently.
8. Garnish with avocado and cilantro. Enjoy!!

"POWER HE-MAN" SMOOTHIE
By Sean Thomas, My son-in-law

Ingredients:

12 oz. purified water
1 scoop vegetable-based protein meal smoothie mix
1 scoop protein and greens smoothie mix
½ cup frozen fruit of your choice
½ cup vanilla yogurt
1 granola bar
1 handful of ice cubes (6 or 7)

Instructions:

1. Put all ingredients into blender.
2. Blend at medium high speed, until smooth.
3. Add ice cubes for desired thickness.

CAMERON'S "POWER" SMOOTHIE
By Cameron Thomas (My Older Granddaughter)

Ingredients:

2 cups unsweetened Vanilla Almond milk
1 to 2 scoops protein/greens powder
½ scoop whey protein
1 scoop collagen protein powder
2 tablespoons Chia seeds
4 strawberries
½ banana
½ cup blueberries

Instructions:

1. Pour all ingredients into blender. (Add ice cubes optional)
2. Blend at medium high speed, until desired smoothness
3. Add ice cubes for desired thickness (Optional). Enjoy

My granddaughter, Cam, has this smoothie for breakfast many mornings which helps her keep her energy level up for school and for her many active extra-curricular activities.

REAGAN'S BALLISTIC BROWNIES
BY REAGAN THOMAS (MY YOUNGER GRANDDAUGHTER)

Ingredients:

1 package Oreo® sandwich cookies
1 package vanilla sandwich cookies
1 box Brownie mix
2 cups chocolate chip cookie dough
Cooking spray

Preparations:

1. Preheat oven to 350°F
2. Mix brownie batter according to instructions, Set aside.
3. Spray an 8 x 8 baking pan with cooking spray.

Instructions:

1. Press cookie dough into bottom of the pan.
2. Arrange cookies in a rows on top of the cookie dough (alternate the vanilla & chocolate cookies).
3. Pour the brownie batter evenly on top of cookie layer to create a brownie layer (approximately ⅓ inch).
4. Place baking pan in preheated oven and bake for 30-45 minutes.
5. Make sure each layer of the brownies is sufficiently cooked.
6. Test brownies with toothpick until done and desired brownness.
7. If the toothpick comes out clean, turn the oven off and allow brownies to sit for another 20 minutes.
   Let cool prior to serving.

RAY'S BLUEBERRY YOGURT DELIGHT   I SERVES 1 - 2
BY REAGAN THOMAS

Ingredients:

¼ cup fresh blueberries

1 (4 oz.) container Greek vanilla yogurt

½ banana, sliced

2 squirts whipped cream (low fat)

Instructions:

1. Slice ½ of a banana.
2. Put ½ of the container (2 oz.) of Greek Vanilla Yogurt in a   tall dessert glass (or any desired dish).
3. Place the banana slices on top of the Greek Vanilla yogurt in dish.
4. Put the remaining Greek vanilla yogurt on top of the banana slices and spread out evenly.
5. Sprinkle the fresh blueberries on top of the Greek Yogurt.
6. Squirt a dab of whipped cream on top of the blueberries.
7. Chill in the refrigerator for a few minutes.

Ray will double or triple the ingredients--a great and tasty way to reinforce math skills--when she is given permission to have friends over. This Dish may be eaten as a Dessert, for Breakfast or as an anytime Snack.

POTATO SALAD   Serves 8 - 10
BY AUDREY MEREDITH (MY STEP-SISTER)

*Anecdote: My step sister, Audrey ("Tootie Boo"), taught me how to cook many southern dishes; how to iron a starched woman's blouse and a man's shirt with an iron you heat on the wood-burning stove; how to starch a crinoline slip with Argo® starch for her wide petticoat skirts (the style at the time); how to dance certain dances to American Bandstand music and other songs on the radio; how to fold a fitted sheet later in life after the remaining family moved away from Meherrin, Va. to Baltimore, MD; and other useful lessons and information. As a social worker supervisor for social services, she was instrumental in assisting us in opening a foster boys home, called **Aunt Hattie's Place (AHP).** After her retirement, "Aunt" Audrey became a member of the Board of Directors of AHP; later the Chair of the Board until its closure in December 2016, after being opened for over 20 years.*

Ingredients:

6 medium white potatoes
4 eggs
¾ cup celery, diced
¾ cup mayonnaise (Hellman's®)
½ teaspoon salt
¾ cup sweet relish

½ teaspoon pepper
2 eggs (for garnish only)
1 tablespoon sugar
1 teaspoon yellow mustard (as desired-optional)
¾ cup onion, diced

Preparations:
1. Cook the whole potatoes until done. Do not overcook.
2. Cool potatoes in cold water. Drain and peel with a knife.
3. Dice potatoes in cubes. Put potatoes in large bowl.
4. Boil eggs, peel and dice 4 of the boiled eggs (Reserve 2 for slicing for garnish).
5. Dice onions and celery, small pieces.

Instructions:
1. Mix all ingredients into the diced potatoes: Mayonnaise, onions, relish, celery, salt, pepper, mustard, and sugar. Fold in the 4 diced boiled eggs (optional).
2. Keep in this bowl or transfer to a decorative bowl.
3. Arrange the two eggs slices on top of the potato salad and sprinkle parsley on top of the eggs and the top of potato salad for garnish.
4 Cover with clear wrap or foil and place in the refrigerator.
5. ˙ Let stay in refrigerator for 30 minutes to chill.

RICE PUDDING | SERVES 6 - 8
BY AUDREY MEREDITH

Ingredients:

2 cups rice, cooked
1 cup whole milk
2 sticks butter
6 tablespoons vanilla extract
½ cup all-purpose flour (for coating raisins)

3 tablespoons nutmeg (1 tablespoon as garnish)
1 cup brown raisins
2 cups sugar (1 tablespoon as garnish)
6 eggs

Preparations:

1. Cook rice (according to package directions).
2. Preheat oven to 350°F.
3. Beat eggs.
4. Soak raisins in ½ cup water for 30 minutes.
5. Coat Raisins with flour

Instructions:

1. In the same cooked rice pan, stir in the butter, sugar, nutmeg and vanilla extract.
2. Add beaten eggs and stir well.
3. Coat the raisins with all-purpose flour.
4. Fold the coated raisins into your rice pudding mixture.
5. Pour in loaf pan. Sprinkle the sugar and nutmeg on top of the rice pudding.
6. Place in preheated oven. Cook for about 30 to 40 minutes, until brown and thick.
7. Take out of oven. Let it cool for about 15 minutes. Serve and Enjoy!

NOTE: *Mama taught me that coating the raisins (or other dried fruits) with flour will keep all of them from dropping to the bottom of the rice pudding or any other dish that she cooked; such as bread pudding, fruitcakes, etc.*

SWEET POTATO PIE
Serves 8 - 10
BY AUDREY MEREDITH

Ingredients:

6 medium sweet potatoes

2 cups whole milk

1 stick butter

6 eggs

4 tablespoons vanilla extract

2 cups sugar

2 tablespoons sugar, garnish

2 tablespoons nutmeg

2 tablespoons nutmeg, garnish

Preparations:
1. Preheat Oven to 350°F.
2. Beat the eggs.
3. Cook potato whole until completely done.
4. Cool and peel the potatoes.
5. Make your pie crust out of any of your pie crust ingredients, or purchase two 9-inch pie crusts.

Instructions:
1. Mash cooked sweet potatoes with potato masher or by hand.
2. Add butter and sugar to mashed potatoes. Mix well with a mixer on medium-high.
3. Add in nutmeg, vanilla extract and eggs. Mix all the ingredients together well.
4. Add milk and beat until nice and smooth. Pour the potato mixture into two 9-inch pie pan with crust.
5. Sprinkle 1 tablespoon nutmeg and 1 tablespoon of sugar on top. Bake the pies until they start browning (about 30 to 40 minutes).
6. Check for doneness by sticking a toothpick in the center. If it comes out clean, its done.
7. Take pies out of the oven and set them aside until they cool (about 30 minutes).

Serve by itself or with ice cream or whipped cream. ENJOY!

COUNTRY SAUSAGE & GRAVY
BY BARBARA MUNDEN, FIRST COUSIN

Ingredients:

1 package red smoked link sausage (mild or hot)
1 small onion, diced
3 teaspoons all-purpose flour
¼ cup cooking oil
1 teaspoon seasoning salt
½ teaspoon garlic salt

Instructions:

1. Cut sausage in half (length-wise).
2. Fry in the hot oil on both sides. Remove sausage.
3. Put flour in the grease and stir until flour turns light brown.
4. Stir in the onion and stir until both turns brown.
5. Add ¾ cup warm water to the browned flour and onions.
6. Stir well until there are no lumps (If too thick, add more water).
7. After gravy is smooth and right consistency, place the browned sausages in the gravy.
8. Cover the skillet. Turn heat to low and let simmer 5 to 7 minutes.
9. Turn off heat and let skillet set for about 3 minutes. It's Ready to Serve.

Serve for breakfast or any time of the day. If you serve it for breakfast, put sausage and gravy over grits and serve with scrambled eggs. If you serve it for lunch or dinner, put it over rice and serve with another vegetable side dish.

SALMON CAKE   --   Serves 4 - 6

BY BARBARA MUNDEN

Ingredients:

1 can pink salmon

1 small onion

1 egg

1 clove of garlic, crushed

½ cup cooking oil (canola oil or olive oil)

1 teaspoon seasoning salt *(I Use Lawyr's® Season Salt)*

½ teaspoon black pepper

I stalk celery, chopped fine (optional)

1 tablespoon self-rising flour

Instructions:

1. Mix all ingredients with can of salmon.
2. Heat oil.
3. Make small salmon cakes.
4. Put cakes in hot grease.
5. Brown salmon cakes on both sides until crispy.
6. Remove from pan and lay on paper towel to drain.
7. Serve with any side of your choice.

Suggestions: Can be serve with grits for Breakfast; with rice and garden peas for Dinner; or as a Salmon Cake sandwich with hot sauce for Lunch.

COCONUT CUSTARD PIE | MAKES TWO 9-INCH PIES
BY BETTIE GOGANIOUS (MY FAVORITE COUSIN'S WIFE)

Ingredients:

3 teaspoons vanilla or coconut extract (optional)

2 cups of white sugar (sweeten to taste)

3 cups sweet coconut, flaked or shredded

2 frozen deep 9" pie crusts, thawed

4 tablespoons all-purpose flour

1 cup butter, melted

3 cups whole milk

4 eggs

Instructions:

1. Preheat oven at 325° F.
2. In a large bowl, mix milk, sugar, eggs, coconut, and extract (optional).

3. Gradually add flour and melted butter while stirring until all mixture is well combined.

4. If using frozen crusts, thaw until crusts are warm and soft. If Homemade, gently knead crusts making sure there are no splits.

5. Pour 2/3 of the custard mixture in the crust almost to the top; Save the remaining mixture to add later after the custard settles when baking. Bake pie for 20 minutes.

6. Once the pies start bubbling, gently stir in the remaining custard mixture (The previous mixture amount would have settled down--this technique makes for a more fluffy and custardy dimension). Careful not to break crust. Bake for another 15 to 20 minutes.

7. Insert clean toothpick near center to test for doneness. If toothpick comes out clean, it's done. If not, bake for an additional 5 minute. Let cool for a few minutes. ENJOY!

MAMA'S CORN PUDDING | SERVES 10 - 12
BY BETTIE GOGANIOUS

Ingredients:

2 (15 oz.) cans whole yellow kernel corn

4 cans yellow cream corn

6 large beaten eggs

½ cup melted butter

1 pint whole milk

1 cup sugar (sweeten to taste)

1 teaspoon sea salt

½ teaspoon ground black pepper

5 tablespoons all-purpose flour or cornstarch

Instructions:

1. Preheat oven to 375°F.
2. Drain whole kernel corn. If kernels are hard, mash with fork.
3. In a large bowl, mix all corn together. Add milk and stir well.
3. In a separate bowl, beat eggs and add them to mixture; Stir.
4. Add butter and sugar (taste for sweetness) to mixture. Add more, if desired.
6. Add salt and black pepper to taste.
7. Add flour (or cornstarch) into mixture. Stir well.
8. Pour pudding mixture in a butter-greased baking pan or casserole dish. Place in preheated oven.
9. Bake for 45 minutes. Mid-way done, stir mixture, especially around edges, and continue to bake for another 15 to 20 minutes. Turn off oven and let set in oven for a few minutes. Serve Warm

This dish can be used as a Dessert or a Side Dish.

CHOPPED PORK BARBECUE | SERVES 12 - 15
BY BETTIE GOGANIOUS

Ingredients:

8 to 10 pounds fresh pork shoulder or Boston butt with or without bone

1 tablespoon crushed red pepper,

1 tablespoon sea salt

1 tablespoon ground black pepper

2 cups apple cider vinegar (brand of choice)

2 to 3 tablespoons seasoning salt

1 tablespoon hot sauce (adjust to taste)

1 tablespoon liquid smoke (optional)

1/3 cup brown sugar

Instructions:

1. Preheat oven to 275°F.
2. Wash meat with cold water and pat dry.
3. Remove excess fat and visible veins. Don't remove fat skin layer.
4. Spread small amount of liquid smoke over meat (optional).
5. Sprinkle salt all over the meat. Wrap meat with heavy duty aluminum foil (Refrigerate overnight, if possible, or 5 to 6 hours for best flavor).
6. In deep roasting pan, slow bake wrapped meat for 4-6 hours (depending on the oven) or until meat falls from the bone. Check to make sure meat isn't drying out.
7. Add 2 cups of vinegar, hot sauce, crushed red pepper and brown sugar into a pot.
8. Slowly bring to a boil, stirring constantly until sugar dissolves. Let's sauce simmer for 10 minutes.
9. When meat is done, remove excess fat and any remaining veins, leaving the fat skin. Chop the meat in small 1-in pieces. Add half of the sauce. Mix in meat thoroughly.
10. Add more sauce, salt, pepper, vinegar, red pepper, hot sauce to suit your taste.
11. Mix sauce thoroughly into meat. Bake chopped barbecue for about 30 minutes for browning, stirring meat two or three times. Do not overbake (meat should be moist, not hard or dry).

This dish can be used in many ways; especially, good for a family reunions and other family gatherings.
"My brother, William, Jr., always did the family barbecue before his death on August 15, 2015.
This is what I remember seeing him do", said Bettie.

POTATO SALAD | SERVES 8 - 10
BY BETTIE GOGANIOUS

Ingredients:

5 pounds red potatoes

1 large celery stalk, diced fine

1/2 cup onions, diced

1/2 cup sweet salad cubes or sweet relish

6 hard boil eggs, peeled & dice 4 eggs (keep 2 for garnish)

1 or 1 1/2 tablespoons yellow mustard (adjust to taste)

1 cup Miracle Whip® Mayonnaise

1 cup Kraft Sandwich Spread®

½ teaspoon sea salt

½ teaspoon black pepper

½ teaspoon paprika (to desired taste).

Instructions:

1. Bring potatoes to a boil in a large pot of lightly salted cold water.
2. Reduce heat to medium and cook until tender (Do Not Overcook).
3. Drain potatoes thoroughly and let cool another 10 minutes.
4. Peeled and diced potatoes in ½-inch cubes.
5. In a large bowl, combine diced potatoes, sweet salad cubes, celery, mustard, Miracle Whip® Mayonnaise and sandwich spread. Mix well by folding in the ingredients.
6. Fold in the diced eggs. Add salt and black pepper (to desired taste).
7. Slice the remaining two eggs and place on top of the potato salad. Sprinkle lightly with paprika to garnish.
8. Refrigerator for two hours prior to serving.

*Bettie's Note: Salad spread gives it more of a sweet pickle taste.
Enjoy as a Side Dish with your favorite meat and vegetables.

SEAFOOD CASSEROLE | SERVES 8 - 10
BY JACKIE GOGANIOUS OWENS

Ingredients:

1 pound crab meat

1 pound medium-to-large raw shrimp, shelled and deveined

1 pint of mayonnaise or 7 to 8 tablespoons

1 medium-size green bell pepper, seeded and chopped

¼ teaspoon cayenne pepper (add more to taste}

1 tablespoon sugar

1 tablespoon of ground mustard.

1 tablespoon of regular mustard.

Preparations:

1. Preheat oven to 350°F.
2. Mix all wet ingredients together &
   mix all the dry ingredients together.
3. Cut shrimp in half.

Instructions:

1. In a medium bowl, mix all wet ingredients: Crab meat, shrimp, mayonnaise and mustard.
2. In a separate small bowl, mix together all dry ingredients: Sugar, cayenne pepper, dry mustard
   and 1 green bell pepper (or ½ green bell pepper and ½ red bell pepper, optional).
3. Fold the dry ingredients mixture into the wet ingredients mixture. Stir Thoroughly.
4. Pour the seafood mixture into a 9 x 13 baking dish and place baking dish in preheated oven.
5. Bake for 30 minutes or until brown on top.
6. Remove from oven and let casserole to set for 5 minutes before serving.
   Serve while hot as an Appetizer (on Bruschetta bread or with chips) or as a Side Dish.

If you would like to have a more colorful holiday dish, you can use ½ green bell pepper and
½ red bell pepper--A red pepper has a sweeter taste than a green pepper

BEEF BRISKET | SERVES 6 - 8

by Beverly "Bev's" Thomas, Charrell's Mother-In-Law
Bev's Late Mom, Floraetta Tedder's Recipe

Ingredients:

3 to 4 pounds beef brisket
1 tablespoon dry mustard
1 pack Lipton Onion Soup & Dip Mix® (Recipe Secret)
¾ cup water
1 to 2 cups Oven Pit Barbecue Sauce®
3 or 4 dashes Worcestershire Sauce®

Preparations:

1. Preheat oven to 325 degrees.
2. Rinse and pat meat dry.
3. Rub dry mustard over meat.

Instructions:

1. In a bowl, mix Lipton Onion Soup Mix, water, Barbecue Sauce, and Worcestershire Sauce. Pour mixture slowly over meat.
2. Pour 2 small glasses of water around the meat.
3. Seal tightly with foil and bake for 3 1/2 hours for 4 pounds and 3 hours for 3 pounds.

HOLIDAY RUM BALLS | SERVES 6 - 8
BY BEVERLY THOMAS (MY SON-IN-LAW'S MOTHER)

Ingredients:
1 (12-ounce) package vanilla wafers
1 (16-ounce) package pecan pieces
½ cup honey
⅓ cup bourbon
⅓ cup dark rum
½ cup Sugar or brown sugar

Instructions:
1. Add vanilla wafers to a food blender and crush until crumbs are fine. Transfer to a large bowl.
2. Place pecans in processor and finely chop.
3. Stir into vanilla wafer crumbs. Stir in honey, bourbon, and rum.
4. Shape into 1-inch balls and roll in sugar or additional vanilla wafer crumbs.
5. Place in an airtight container. Store in refrigerator up to one month.

SWEET POTATO PIE | MAKES TWO 9" PIES
BY REVEREND STEVE THOMAS' MOTHER, MARTHA ELIZABETH THOMAS' RECIPE

Ingredients:
2 9" pie crusts
3 large sweet potatoes
3 eggs
½ can Pet Evaporated Milk®
2 sticks of butter
1 ½ cups sugar
½ teaspoon salt
4 teaspoons freshly ground nutmeg
2 teaspoons vanilla extract

Instructions:
1. Peel sweet potatoes and cut into 4 or 5 parts. Boil until fork tender.
2. Pour off water and mix potatoes well. Add all ingredients and mix well.
3. Pour mixture into pie pans with crust.
4. Bake approximately one hour at 350°F until brown on top and crust is brown .

RED VELVET CAKE | Serves 8 - 10
BY ESTELLE MCCORMICK (COUSIN)

Ingredients:

1 cup Wesson Oil®
1½ cups sugar
1 oz. red food coloring
2 eggs
2 cups Pillsbury® flour
1 cup buttermilk
1 teaspoon cocoa powder
½ teaspoon salt
1 teaspoon baking soda

Instructions:

1. Combine and cream together flour, oil, sugar, cocoa, salt, and soda.
2. Add eggs (mix one at a time).
3. Add food coloring, mixing well until all coloring is dissolved into batter.
4. Add buttermilk. Mix until batter is smooth.
5. Pour batter into the greased and floured cake pans.
6. Bake for 1 hour at 375°F in pre-heated oven until done.
7. Remove from pans and cool cakes for frosting*.

RED VELVET FROSTING
BY ESTELLE MCCORMICK

Ingredients:

2 regular size (8 ounces) packages cream cheese
1 box confectioner sugar
1 teaspoon vanilla extract
1 cup chopped nuts (your preference) (optional)

Instructions:

1. Combine all ingredients for frosting, mix well until frosting consistency creates peaks.
2. Spread frosting on bottom cake layer; Place middle layer on top of the iced bottom layer. Then, frost the third (top) layer and the sides of cakes.
3. Sprinkle one cup of your favorite chopped nuts over cake (optional).

ZUCCHINI BREAD | Serves 6 - 8
BY ESTELLE McCORMICK

Ingredients:

1 cup vegetable oil

1 ¾ cups sugar

2 cups grated zucchini

1 teaspoon baking soda

1 teaspoon salt

2 teaspoons cinnamon

3 teaspoons vanilla extract

2 cups chopped nuts

Instructions:

1. Preheat oven at 350° F.
2. Beat eggs, add sugar and oil.
3. Add flour, and vanilla extract.
4. Mix in the zucchini and other ingredients.
5. Fold in nuts. Pour in greased loaf pan.
6. Bake in oven for 1 hour.
7. Turn off oven. Stay in oven for 1 hour after baked.

Great with cream cheese. Enjoy!

BUTTERNUT SQUASH SOUP | SERVES **6-8**
BY JOYCE MADISON, COUSIN

Ingredients:

2 Butternut squash,
4 cups chicken stock, plus more, if necessary
¼ teaspoon black pepper
1 teaspoon ground allspice
1 teaspoon ground cinnamon
1 stick butter
⅛ teaspoon sugar

Instructions:

1. Baked in oven, peel, seed & cut into 1-inch chunks
2. In a large pot, mash the butternut squash until it is smooth.
3. Add the chicken stock and stir until the consistency is smooth (not too thick).
3. Add all spices: pepper, allspice, cinnamon, nutmeg, stirring occasionally for about 10 minutes.
4. Add butter and sugar. Bring to a boil over high heat.
5. Reduce the heat to low and simmer partially covered for about 30 minutes.

SPLIT PEA SOUP WITH ROSEMARY | SERVES **6 - 8**
BY JOYCE MADISON

Ingredients:

5 slices bacon
1 small onion, chopped
1 leek, thinly sliced
1 large carrot, chopped
2 cloves garlic, minced

4 (10.5 oz.) cans chicken broth
1 ½ cups green split peas
2 bay leaves
1 teaspoon fresh rosemary, chopped

Instructions:

1. Place bacon in a large sauce pan and cook over medium heat until crisp.
2. Stir in onion, leek, carrot and garlic. Cook until the vegetables are soft, about 8 minutes.
3. Pour in chicken broth. Stir in split peas, bay leaves, and rosemary.
4. Bring to a boil. Reduce heat to low. Cover and simmer about 1 hour, stirring occasionally until peas are fully cooked.

GRANDMA'S SWEET POTATO PIE | Makes Two 9" Pies
BY REBECCA "BECK" LEE RANDOLPH

Ingredients:
3 large sweet potatoes (cooked well done)
½ cup brown sugar
1 cup sugar for each pie (2 cups)
1 teaspoon vanilla extract
1 stick butter for each pie (2, melted)
1 teaspoon nutmeg
1 teaspoon cinnamon
6 small eggs
1 teaspoon lemon extract (optional)
1 (12 ounce) can evaporated milk

Instructions:
1. Preheat oven to at 350°F.
2. Mix all ingredients together in a mixing bowl until smooth.
3. Pour ingredients equally into the two pie crusts (9").
4. Bake pies until done and browned (approximately 1 hour).

POOR BOY CAKE/PIE | SERVES 6 - 8
BY REBECCA LEE RANDOLPH

Ingredients:
1 stick butter (melted)   1 can fresh fruit
1 cup milk   1 cup flour
1 teaspoon cinnamon   1 cup sugar

Instructions:
Step 1
1. Preheat oven to 350°F.
2. In a round Pyrex Dish, melt 1 stick butter.
3. Sprinkle in cinnamon. Mix well.

Step 2
1. In a separate bowl, mix 1 cup flour (self-rising).
2. Add 1 cup sugar and 1 cup milk.
3. Mix well.

MIX together Step 1 and 2 into Baking Dish
1. Pour 1 can fresh fruit (peaches, cherries, apples or your favorite fruit) into center of mixtures above.
2. Bake until brown and crust covers the bowl (for approximately 1 hour).

Serve while hot. Add a scoop of your favorite ice cream. Enjoy!

"AND BEYOND"

OLD FASHIONED COCONUT PIE | Makes Two 9" Pies
BY REBECCA LEE RANDOLPH

Ingredients:
1 ½ bag coconut flakes (14 ounces size bag)
1 cup sugar
6 eggs (pre-cracked and beaten in a separate bowl).
1 tablespoon cornstarch
1 can evaporated milk
1 teaspoon vanilla extract
1 stick butter for each pie, melted
½ teaspoon lemon extract

Instructions:
1. Preheat the oven to 350˚F.
2. Mix all the ingredients in the bowl with the beaten eggs.
3. Pour mixture into pie crusts (9"), and place in oven.
4. Bake until pies are done and browned (DO NOT over bake).
5. When pies begin to puff up, turn off oven.
6. Cool for about 30 minutes and serve.

OLD FASHIONED POUND CAKE | SERVES 8-10
BY REBECCA LEE RANDOLPH

Ingredients:
2 cups Domino® Sugar
5 eggs - room temperature-
½ teaspoon baking powder
1 cup milk (can)
1 teaspoon lemon extract

2 sticks butter - room temperature
½ cups Crisco® - room temperature
3 cups cake flour
1 teaspoon almond extract
1 teaspoon vanilla extract

Instructions:
1. Preheat the oven to 325°F
2. Mix butter, Crisco® and sugar.
3. Add 5 eggs, 3 cups flour.
4. Add ½ teaspoon of baking powder to flour, 1cup milk, 1 teaspoon each of vanilla, lemon and almond extract.
5. Alternate adding flour and milk, ending with flour.
6. Mix thoroughly until smooth. Pour into greased cake pan.
7. Bake in oven for 1 hour and 15 minutes.
8. Test for doneness. Cool & Serve.

PAT'S SOUTHERN BANANA PUDDING | SERVES 12 - 14

BY PATRICIA "TRISH" LEE ADAMS, CHILDHOOD FRIEND AND CLASSMATE AT LEVI ELEMENTARY SCHOOL (BECK'S SISTER; KIN TO MY STEPMOM)

Ingredients:

3 cups cold milk

2 packages (4-serving size each) JELL-O® Vanilla Flavor Instant Pudding and pie filling

30 NILLA Wafers

3 medium bananas, sliced

1 tub (8 oz.) COOL WHIP Whipped topping, thawed

Instructions:

1. Pour milk into large bowl. Add dry pudding mixes.
2. Beat with wire whisk 2 minutes or until well blended. Let stand 5 minutes.
3. Arrange half of the wafers on bottom and up the sides of a 2-quart serving bowl.
4. Top with layers of half each of the banana slices and then pudding. Repeat all layers and cover with whipped topping.
5. Refrigerate for 3 hours or until ready to serve. Store leftover dessert in refrigerator.

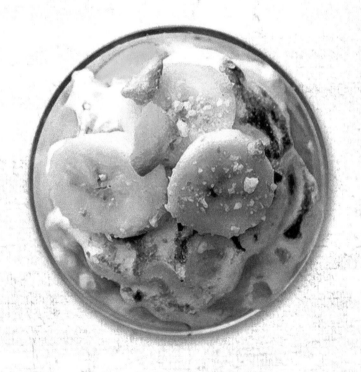

"HELP-LESS" CHOCOLATE PIE | SERVES 6 - 8
BY SHAUNDA A. EPPES, DAUGHTER OF CHILDHOOD FRIEND, TRISH ADAMS

Ingredients:

3 tablespoons unsweetened cocoa powder

4 tablespoons unsalted butter, melted

1 teaspoon pure vanilla extract

1 packaged pie dough crust

¾ cup evaporated milk

1½ cups sugar

¼ teaspoon sea salt

2 large eggs, beaten

Whipped cream

Instructions:

1. Preheat oven to 350°F.
2. Set pie crust into a 9-inch pie plate and crimp the edges, then prick the crust lightly with a fork.
3. Line the crust with foil or parchment paper and fill with pie weights or dried beans.
4. Bake for 15 minutes or until set.
5. Remove the foil and weights and BAKE for about 5 minutes longer, just until the crust is dry but not browned.
6. While the crust is baking Whisk the sugar with the cocoa powder, butter, eggs, evaporated milk, vanilla extract and salt in a bowl until smooth.
7. Pour the filling into the pie shell and Bake for about 45 minutes, until the filling is set around the edges but a little jiggly in the center.
8. Cover the crust with strips of foil halfway through baking.
9. Transfer the pie to a rack and let cool completely before cutting. Serve with whipped cream.

SHRIMP FRIED RICE | SERVES 4 - 6
BY JEAN W. LEE, JEAN'S HUSBAND WAS KIN TO MY STEP MOM

Ingredients:

2 cups rice

1 bunch small green onions

½ pound bacon

1 package Lipton Onion Soup®

4 eggs

1 medium onion, diced

1½ pounds shrimp (frozen, medium)

Instructions:

1. Thaw shrimp in tepid water.
2. Fully cook rice.
3. Fry bacon in a large skillet.
4. Put aside slices and bacon grease.
5. In the skillet with some grease, add onion.
6. Saute until soft.
7. Add rice -if needed, add more grease-.
8. Thoroughly mix onions and rice.
9. Stir in onion soup until thoroughly mixed.
10. Put fried rice in a large casserole dish.
11. Add thawed and peeled shrimp.
12. Scramble eggs and let them cool.
13. Break bacon in small pieces.
14. Cut green onions about ½ inches.
15 . Mix eggs, bacon, and onions into fried rice.
16 . You can substitute chicken or pork. Enjoy!

BROCCOLI & CHEESE MUFFINS | SERVES 6 - 8

*BY LOTTIE L. MILLER, DAUGHTER OF MY ELEMENTARY SCHOOL BUS DRIVER,
MR. MILLER, WHO WOULD WAIT IF WE WERE RUNNING LATE FOR SCHOOL.*

Ingredients:

1 box Jiffy® Mix

1 head broccoli, chopped into small pieces

3 eggs

2 sticks of butter

8 ounces cottage cheese

1 stick butter

½ cup sugar

1 or 2 onions, finely diced

Instructions:

1. Preheat oven to 400°F.
2. Mix all ingredients in a large mixing bowl until thoroughly mixed.
3. Spray muffin pan with a baking spray.
4. Pour batter into muffin pan (or in a 9 x 13 baking dish).
5. Place in a preheated oven.
6. Bake for 10 to 20 minutes, until well done.
7. Test for doneness using a toothpick. If toothpick comes out clean, your muffin is done.
8. Remove from the oven. Serve hot with butter and with another breakfast food.

OXTAILS--FALLING OFF THE BONE   Serves 6 - 8
BY COURTNEY WIGGINS-LLOYD, FRIEND & COLLEAGUE AT AUNT HATTIE'S PLACE

Ingredients:
Marinade Ingredients: Stir until mixed

2 teaspoons garlic powder
2 tablespoons onion power
1 tablespoon salt
1 teaspoon cayenne pepper
1 teaspoon black pepper

½ cup of dark brown sugar
2 teaspoons Adobo
2 bay leaves
12 ounces Worcestershire Sauce
48 ounces beef broth

Preparations:
1. Put 3-4 pounds of oxtails in an air-tight container.
2. Marinate for 3 hours, then refrigerate.

Stew Pot Preparations:
1 large onion sliced
1 medium green pepper sliced
1 stick butter
Sauté sliced onion and green peppers in butter directly in bottom of pot.

Dredge Mixture Ingredients:
½ teaspoon salt
½ teaspoon pepper
1 cup all-purpose flour
1 teaspoon garlic powder
1 teaspoon onion powder
½ teaspoon Adodo®

Instructions:
1. Frying: ¼-inch Canola in frying pan on medium high.
2. Heat Canola oil in frying pan to medium high heat
3. Place marinated oxtails flat side into flor dredge on both sides and fry for 3-5 on each side.
4. Place each oxtail into stew pot on top of caramelized onions and greens peppers.
5. Pour marinade mixture into pot over oxtails.
6. Bring to a boil then turn on medium low heat.
7. Cook on medium low heat for 3-4 hours until tender.

Gravy (Optional)
1. Put 1 cup of broth from cooked oxtail in separate pan.
2. Add slowly ¼ cup of all-purpose flour.
3. Stir until smoothness and thickness as desired.
4. Pour gravy into pot of cooked oxtails. Stir gently.

7-UPCAKE   Serves 10 - 12

by Leona Davis, friend met at Martha's Vineyard

Ingredients:

3 cups Swans Down® cake flour

¾ cup 7-Up®

3 cup sugar

3 sticks butter

2 lemon for juice, and zest

5 eggs

Baker's Joy® Spray

Preparations:

1. Preheat the oven to 350°F.
2. Squeeze 2 lemons for the juice
3. Break 5 eggs, leave them whole
4. Measure cake flour
5. Spray Baker's Joy® to grease Bundt cake pan
6. Scrap the zest from the 2 lemons
   Let butter get room temperature (A spray of butter & flour-- to prevent cakes from sticking).

Instructions:

1. Cream the butter with sugar and eggs (one at a time). Mix on high speed.
2. Pour the flour into the mixture and combine. Add in the 7-Up and mix well.
3. Add the lemon juice and the lemon zest into the mixture and mix thoroughly.
4. Pour batter into the greased Bundt cake pan. Bake cake for an hour; Test for doneness.
5. When done, turn cake upside down on a plate. While still warm, sprinkle confectioners sugar on top of cake or you can put icing on top of the cake.

A Variation: Sometimes, I put toothpick holes in the top of the cake and pour a mixture of lemon juice and confectioners sugar over the top of the cake and let it seep down in the holes.

A delicious, light, moist and tart cake for any occasion!

MONKEY BREAD
BY LEONA DAVIS

Ingredients:
4 cup bread flour (Gold Medal Flour®)
1/3 cup sugar
1 cup scalded* milk, cooled to warm
1 teaspoon salt

1pack of Fleischmann's® RapidRise Yeast
2 eggs, slight beaten
Baker's Joy ® Spray
1/3 cup soft butter

Preparations:
1. Preheat the oven to 350°F.
2. Melt butter in bowl to dip the dough balls
3. Slightly beat 2 eggs
4. Grease bowl with olive oil
5. Heat milk until scalded (very hot with bubbles—not to boiling); and let it cool to warm
6. Spray Baker's Joy® to grease bundt cake pan
7. "The Sugar Tip": Get the mixture ready (See Instructions in 2a and 2b below):

Instructions:
1. Mix in hot scaled milk the butter, salt, sugar and stir thoroughly;
2. "The Sugar Tip": Mix ¼ cup of warm water from faucet in a bowl; stir in 1 packet of yeast & 1 teaspoon of "The Sugar" Secret Tip:
   a. First, make sure the yeast and the sugar are fully dissolved in the water by moving the bowl around (do not stir–make sure all of the yeast is covered by water);
   b. **"The Sugar Tip":** The sugar is the secret; because it makes the yeast come to "a head" which will be noticeable by a scab-looking film that will form on top of the yeast, water and sugar mixture (This sugar secret tip was shared with me by Sister Beverly from my church. (Leona shared, *"My Monkey Bread has been perfect ever since."*);
3. Pour all the liquids--the yeast, water & sugar mixture and the scalded milk mixture (still hot or warm) into a mixing bowl together; and Stir well;
4. Mix in 2 cups flour and 2 slightly beaten eggs; Beat together on medium high speed until all ingredients are mixed together; Mix in the rest of the flour; and then put mixer on high speed and beat until the dough clings to the side of the bowl;
5. Take out the dough and knead it on a cutting board or a counter until it is smooth (Put flour on a cutting board or on the counter to knead the dough); Put the kneaded smooth dough in a greased bowl; Drizzle olive oil on the top of the dough; Cover with saran wrap (or a clear wrap) and a clean dish towel.

MONKEY BREAD (CONT.)
BY LEONA DAVIS

Instructions:

6. Let it rise for about an hour (or until it doubles in size); Remove the risen dough and roll it out into a square until it is evenly flat all over; Cut in squares (horizontally and vertically); Roll up the squares into little dough balls—about the size of a walnut;

7. Roll dough balls in melted butter; Stack them up on top of each other around in the greased Bundt cake pan (the pan will be about half full when finished); Cover again with saran wrap or clear wrap and a dish towel; and let it rise again for about 45 minutes to an hour;

8. Put in preheated oven and cook for 35 to 40 minutes at 350°F; When done, take a butter knife and go around the edges to loosen the bread from the pan; Put a plate on top of the hot Bundt pan; Use a dish towel, and Turn the hot cake pan over into the plate for the monkey ball-cake shaped bread to fall into the plate;

9. Brush with melted butter (or rub with a stick of soft butter) again; Pull the balls apart from the cake-shaped balls.

Serve Hot or Cold. Next day, warm the cold balls in the oven or the microwave.

BETTY BALDWIN & SHELDON'S RESTAURANT | KEYSVILLE, VA

In addition to her stepmother, Aunt Hattie's two aunts in Norfolk were also great cooks. Great cooks extend beyond the family to friends who've shared their specialty recipes with Dr. Washington for the

View from Sheldon's

cookbook. Sheldon's, a family favorite restaurant In her hometown, is a gathering place for those seeking the farm fresh flavors that she enjoyed growing up. **Sheldon's** has served the community for over 75 years and is still thriving as a favorite spot for near and far faithful customers. Aunt Hattie and her family dine at Sheldon's every time she returns home. The mouthwatering **Lemon Chess Pie** and their succulent **Spoon Bread** are two of her favorites shared by **Betty Baldwin of Sheldon's.**

SHELDON'S FAMOUS LEMON CHESS PIE | SERVES 8 - 10

Ingredients:
5 eggs
Juice of 2 lemons
1½ cups sugar
½ stick butter, melted
⅛ sea salt

Instructions:
1. Using the whip on your electric stand mixer, beat the eggs until very creamy and lemony yellow
2. Add sugar, salt, & butter and beat at least 2 minutes.
3. Add lemon juice and beat more. Pour into unbaked pie crust.
4. Bake at 350°F until center does not shake and it is golden brown. Cool before slicing.

OLD-FASHIONED SOUTHERN SPOON BREAD | SERVES 8 - 10
BETTY BALDWIN & SHELDON'S RESTAURANT

Ingredients:

2 cup milk, scalded

1 cup white cornmeal

4 eggs, separated

2 sticks butter

1 tablespoon sugar

½ teaspoon sea salt

Preparation:

1. Preheat oven to 375ºF
2. Grease a 2-qt casserole dish
3. Separate Yolk and whites from eggs
4. Beat egg yolk until thick & lemon colored.
5. Using clean beater, beat the egg whites until stiff, but not dry.
6. Scald milk (Heat milk until it ALMOST comes to a boil; set for 5 minutes; Take off milk scab)

Instruction:

1. In a heavy saucepan over medium heat, gradually, add the cornmeal to scalded milk.
2. Cook and stir until mixture thickens and is smooth.
3. Blend cornmeal mixture into egg yolks with the butter, sugar and salt. Mix thoroughly.
4. Spread egg yolk mixture over egg whites and gently fold together with spatula.
5. Pour batter into casserole dish. Bake in preheated oven for 35-40 minutes or until a toothpick comes out clean when inserted into center. Serve immediately.

MORE "AND BEYOND" RECIPES
FROM TEACHING & STUDYING IN GREECE AND SCOTLAND

A. Greece (1973 to 1976)-- Family-Favorite Foods & Experiences:

1. Watermelon: In Greece they would serve watermelon at every meal; every way possible, from chunks, slices, in salads, pickled, dessert and as a side dish.

2. Greek Watermelon Summer Salad (*w/Feta Cheese, Olives and Walnuts*).

3. Greek Olive Oil Dipping—*Mixture of Olive Oil, Garlic, and Feta Cheese (Goat cheese) for dipping with Greek hard bread.*

Anecdote: *A Few Other Popular Greek Dishes—That we enjoyed while in Greece, but, I won't even attempt to cook them for fear I won't do justice to these delicious traditional dishes are: Souvalki-- The popular Greek snack food, called the "Greek's hot dog", served with strips of lamb, roasted onions, peppers, garlic & olive oil on a flat bread rolled up; Squid: cut in small 1-inch pieces, battered and deep fried; Babounya Fish (red skin sweet fish—similar to our Whitings or Lake Trout, without the bone); Moussaka; Spanakopita; Baklava; Dolma; and Galaktoboureko.*

There are numerous others, but I will stop here.
I'm getting hungry and missing my favorite Greek foods and friends.

The Traditional Greek Beverages are: Ouzo--A dry anise-flavored liquor made from white grapes—Turns a milky-white color when water is added; Retsina--A white resonated wine with a unique flavor of resin of the pine tree—It was definitely a taste to be acquired which the Greeks and numerous Americans did just that. Since I was practically a teetotaler, just a taste of retsina and/or ouzo was quite sufficient for me at our invited outings with Greek friends.

Expresso strong sweet black coffee served in small cups—Served often.

B. Scotland (1980 to 1983)--Living and Studying in Scotland, U.K.

Anecdote: *My family and I lived in Scotland for two and a half years and had a unique experience difference from most all of the other military families.*

I Studied In Scotland at the University of Glasgow and Spoke at Spoke at Numerous Rotary Clubs: I studied Multiculturalism and Special Education of the Handicapped at the University of Glasgow on a Rotary International Fellowship. I was sponsored by both the Dunoon and the Glasgow Rotary Clubs and was invited to speak at numerous Rotary Clubs breakfasts and suppers all over Scotland. It was an awesome and eye-opening cultural experience. A local Scottish newspaper article stated, **"She [Washington] is a lady with a capital name from a capital city who has captivated all of our hearts here in Scotland."**

High Tea: Daily about 4:00 pm: Everyone stopped for High Tea, including my professors at Glasgow University as well as construction workers. What was the epitome of high culture was to see construction workers drinking tea from a real cup and saucer on the side of the highway, rather than from a mug or a paper cup.

My Family's Favorite Scottish Dishes: Shepherd Pie, Fish and Chips, Scones, Truffle Pudding, Caramel Custard Pudding, Shortbread Cookies, British Teas, and **Haggis** and Mash Potatoes (A Traditional Scottish Dish served on special occasions, such on Burns Night held annually on January 25th, the birthday of the Scottish beloved poet, Robert Burns. This long popular dish in England, was celebrated in **Robert Burns'** lines, **"to a Haggis"** in his poem in 1786).

GREEK WATERMELON SALAD | SERVES 1-2

Ingredients:
½ cup baby spinach
½ cup fresh herb salad mix
1 cup diced watermelon (1 x ½ inch pieces)
3 tablespoons crumble feta cheese, divided
3 tablespoons Coconut Greek yogurt, divided
6 to 8 pitted Greek olives.
2 tablespoons diced walnuts (optional)

Preparations:
1. Place spinach and salad mix in the bottom of a salad dish.
2. Place watermelon pieces on top of your salad greens.
3. Put Greek Yogurt on top of the watermelon pieces.
4. Sprinkle crumble feta cheese on top of your watermelon pieces.
5. Place olives on the top.
6. Garnish with chopped walnuts (or nuts of your choice).
7. Place your Greek Watermelon Summer Salad in the fridge to serve later. It keeps well.
8. Serve with Hattie's Watermelon Summer Salad Dressing*

*Hattie's Special Salad Dressing/Sauce
1 tablespoon apple cider vinegar
1 tablespoon olive oil
1 tablespoon of fresh lemon juice
¼ teaspoon garlic powder
¼ sea salt
1 tablespoon maple syrup or honey
3 tablespoons of the coconut yogurt, divided (1 tablespoon for salad dressing)
Shake up all of the ingredients until the yogurt dissolves; taste for desired sweetness.

Note: *For the **Dressing** for this **Greek Watermelon Salad** above, Use the **Hattie's Special Salad Dressing** ingredients above; Plus, *1/2 cup watermelon juice with 1 cup watermelon chunks, and 2 tablespoons feta cheese crumbs (divided, sprinkle some on top).* **For best results and appearence, make each watermelon salad individually in a salad dish; Cover with clear wrap; Put the one salad dish (or several salads) in the fridge until ready to serve.**

This Watermelon Salad is a refreshing and healthy sweet-and-sour Greek salad.

BEEF SHEPHERD'S PIE | SERVES 6 - 8
A FAMILY FAVORITE WHILE LIVING ABROAD IN SCOTLAND

Ingredients:

Potatoe Mixture	Meat Mixture	
6 medium potatoes	1 pound ground beef	½ cup of beef broth
½ cup sour cream	1 tablespoon garlic, minced	2 tablespoons apple cider vinegar
¼ cup Greek yogurt	1 small onion, chopped	1 tablespoon parsley, divided
1 egg white	½ cup celery, chopped	2 teaspoons maple syrup
1 teaspoon sea salt, divided	½ cup carrots, shredded	2 tablespoons brown sugar
1 teaspoon pepper, divided	½ green bell pepper, chopped	1 tablespoon sage
½ stick butter, melted, divided	¼ cup tomato paste	1 teaspoon nutmeg
1 tablespoon garlic powder	12 oz. frozen mixed vegetables	½ teaspoon paprika, divided
		2 tablespoons cornstarch, divided

Preparations: Make The Mashed Potato Mixture

1. Wash potatoes thoroughly and peel, cut in 1-inch squares. Wash again and Drain.
2. In a large saucepan of 4 cups of water, over medium-high heat, bring potatoes to a boil;
3. Add salt to water, turn down to medium heat. Cover, and cook between 10 to 20 minutes.
4. Check for doneness. The potatoes are done when they are tender all the way through.
5. Drain potatoes, leave in saucepan; Add ¼ cup butter, garlic powder, ¼ teaspoon parsley, and
   ½ teaspoon sea salt, ½ teaspoon pepper; Mash the potatoes until smooth.
6. Add to the mashed potatoes the other ingredients (sour cream & yogurt), and stir until smooth.
   Place to the side. Beat egg white until fluffy (with white peaks).
7. Coat a casserole dish with 1 tablespoons melted butter. Set to the side.
8. Preheat the oven to 375°F
9. Mix cornstarch with ½ cup water

Instructions: Make The Meat Filling

1. In a 12-inch hot skillet, saute the ground beef for 3 to 4 minutes. Add the onion, celery, green bell
   pepper, fresh minced garlic and carrots; sauté for 3 to 4 additional minutes.
2. Stir in tomato paste, beef broth, vinegar, maple syrup, sugar, sage, ¾ teaspoon parsley, nutmeg,
   and bag of mixed vegetables. Bring to a boil, reduce the heat to low, and simmer slowly for 10 to
   12 minutes or until meat mixture is thicker. If mixture is loose, add 2 tablespoons cornstarch
   mixture water and stir thoroughly.

Beef Shepherd's Pie (cont.)

3. Pour meat mixture in prepared casserole dish and spread evenly. Sprinkle a dash of smoked paprika over meat mixture.
4. Using a spatula, fold the egg whites gently into the mashed potatoes. Then, Spread the mashed potatoes evenly on top of the meat mixture in the casserole dish, starting around the edges to create a seal to prevent meat mixture from bubbling out during cooking.
5. Brush melted butter on top of potatoes and then sprinkle garlic powder, ½ teaspoon sea salt and smoked paprika on top.
6. Place in preheated oven and cook for 20 to 25 minutes. Turn dish around 180 degrees and cook another 10 to 15 minutes. Turn on Broiler and cook for 5 minutes to brown top of Shepherd Pie, if not brown enough. Turn off oven, and let set for 5 minutes. **Serve Hot or warm. YUM!**

CHICKEN SHEPHERD'S PIE | SERVES 6 - 8
A FAMILY FAVORITE WHILE LIVING ABROAD IN SCOTLAND

Ingredients:

6 raw chicken breasts (cut into small cubes)
1 (10.5 oz.) can cream of chicken soup
2 tablespoons cornstarch
½ cup chicken broth
1 teaspoon sea salt
¼ stick butter
1 tablespoon fresh garlic, minced, divided
1 teaspoon of smoked paprika
1 tablespoon parsley, divided
½ teaspoon sugar
½ cup sour cream

½ cup Greek yogurt
1 egg white
2 tablespoons powdered sugar
1 tablespoon sage
1 teaspoon nutmeg
6 medium potatoes
1 (12 oz.) bag frozen mixed vegetables
½ teaspoon poultry seasoning
1 tablespoon celery seeds
½ cup water

Preparations: Make The Mashed Potato Mixture

1. Cut chicken breast crosswise into straight, even strips, about 1 ½ inches wide. Turn strips so that the length runs horizontally and cut strips into shorter pieces (½-inch in diameter).
2. Wash potatoes thoroughly and peel, cut in 1-inch squares. Wash again and drain.
3. In a large saucepan, add potatoes to 4 cups water and bring to a boil. Cook between 10 to 20 minutes, covered. Add salt to water while boiling.
4. Check for doneness. Potatoes are done when they are tender all the way through. Drain potatoes and leave in saucepan. Add ¼ butter, ½ fresh garlic, ½ teaspoon parsley, ½ teaspoon sea salt, and powdered sugar. Mash potatoes until smooth. Set aside.
5. Coat casserole dish with butter. In a small bowl, mix 1 tablespoon cornstarch with ½ cup water.
6. Preheat oven to 375°F.

Instructions: Make The Meat Filling

1. In a 12-inch skillet, place chopped chicken, onion, celery, poultry seasoning and bell pepper. Sauté for 3 to 4 minutes.
2. Stir in bag of frozen mixed vegetables, remaining ½ fresh garlic, sage, remaining ½ teaspoon parsley, nutmeg, sour cream, Greek yogurt, chicken broth and cream of chicken soup. Bring to a boil. Reduce heat to low and simmer slowly for 10 to 12 minutes or until meat mixture is thicker. If mixture is loose, add 2 tablespoons premixed cornstarch and water, and stir thoroughly. Turn off stove.

CHICKEN SHEPHERD'S PIE (CONT.)

3. Pour meat mixture in prepared casserole dish and spread evenly. Sprinkle a dash of smoked paprika. Fold egg whites gently into mashed potatoes. Spread mashed potatoes evenly on top of meat mixture in casserole dish, starting around the edges to create a seal to prevent meat mixture from bubbling out.
4. Brush melted butter on potatoes and sprinkle garlic powder, ½ teaspoon sea salt and paprika on top.
5. Place in oven and bake for 20 to 25 minutes. Turn dish around 180 degrees and cook an additional 10 to 15 minutes. Turn on Broiler and cook for 5 minutes to brown top of Shepherd Pie, if not brown enough. Turn off oven, and let set for 5 minutes. Serve Hot or warm. ENJOY!

RESOURCES

MEASUREMENTS | CONVERSIONS | EQUIVALENTS
KITCHEN STABLES | SUBSTITUTIONS | INDEXES
CALORIC & NUTRIENT VALUES FOR VARIOUS FOODS
WEBSITES | OTHER PERTINENT INFORMATION

Measurement

CUP	OUNCES	MILLILITERS	TABLESPOONS
8 cup	64 oz	1895 ml	128
6 cup	48 oz	1420 ml	96
5 cup	40 oz	1180 ml	80
4 cup	32 oz	960 ml	64
2 cup	16 oz	480 ml	32
1 cup	8 oz	240 ml	16
3/4 cup	6 oz	177 ml	12
2/3 cup	5 oz	158 ml	11
1/2 cup	4 oz	118 ml	8
3/8 cup	3 oz	90 ml	6
1/3 cup	2.5 oz	79 ml	5.5
1/4 cup	2 oz	59 ml	4
1/8 cup	1 oz	30 ml	3
1/16 cup	1/2 oz	15 ml	1

Temperature

FAHRENHEIT	CELSIUS
100 °F	37 °C
150 °F	65 °C
200 °F	93 °C
250 °F	121 °C
300 °F	150 °C
325 °F	160 °C
350 °F	180 °C
375 °F	190 °C
400 °F	200 °C
425 °F	220 °C
450 °F	230 °C
500 °F	230 °C
525 °F	274 °C
550 °F	288 °C

Weight

IMPERIAL	METRIC
1/2 oz	15 g
1 oz	29 g
2 oz	57 g
3 oz	85 g
4 oz	113 g
5 oz	141 g
6 oz	170 g
8 oz	227 g
10 oz	283 g
12 oz	340 g
13 oz	369 g
14 oz	347 g
15 oz	425 g
1 oz	453 g

ANECDOTE: I watched my stepmother cook for years and never saw her measure anything. In fact, I don't ever remember seeing a measuring cup or measuring spoons any place in sight. When she cooked, she would simply use a pinch of this, a dash of that or a handful of this and that? This simply means that I had to recreate all of her delicious recipes from memory.

Then, I would start measuring my ingredients over the years as I have cooked her dishes and now have them a part of my repertoire of frequently requested dishes by family, friends and colleagues alike.

This Chart list various substitutions for various other ingredients just in case you are cooking a dish and find yourself out of an ingredient or two for which a recipe calls, you can consider these substitutions to complete your recipe.

The chart will also give you specific measurements as you select the specific substitution for your recipe; for example, how many tablespoons are in a cup? Or, how many cups are in a pint or in a quart? This helpful chart has the answers.

Substitutions of Recipe Ingredients When Cooking

Ingredient/s		Substitution/s
1 teaspoon allspice	=	½ teaspoon cinnamon; plus ⅛ teaspoon cloves plus ¼ teaspoon nutmeg
1 teaspoon baking powder	=	¼ teaspoon soda; plus ½ teaspoon cream of tartar
1 cup butter	=	1 cup sweet milk; plus 1 tablespoon lemon juice or vinegar
1 square chocolate (unsweetened)	=	3 tablespoon cocoa; plus 1 tablespoon butter
1 6-oz package chocolate (semi-sweet)	=	2 squares unsweetened chocolate; plus 2 tablespoon butter; plus ½ cup sugar
3 tablespoon cocoa	=	1 square unsweetened chocolate (omitting 1 tablespoon butter)
1 tablespoon cornstarch	=	2 tablespoons all-purpose flour (for thickening) or 4 teaspoons tapioca
1 cup heavy cream	=	3/4 cup skim milk; plus 1/3 cup butter
1 cup sour cream	=	7/8 cup sour milk; plus 3 tablespoons butter
1 cup dry bread crumbs	=	3/4 cup cracker crumbs
2 large eggs	=	3 small eggs

Substitutions of Recipe Ingredients When Cooking

Ingredient/s		Substitution/s
1 egg	=	2 egg yolks; plus 1 tablespoon water (for cookies)
1 cup all-purpose flour	=	3/4 cup AP Flour; plus 2 tablespoons cake flour
1 cup cake flour	=	1 cup all-purpose flour; minus (--) 2 tablespoons all-purpose flour; plus 2 tablespoons cornstarch or arrowroot powder
1 cup self-rising flour	=	1 cup all-purpose flour; plus 1 1/2 teaspoons baking powder, and 1/2 teaspoon sea salt
1 medium clove garlic	=	1/2 teaspoon of garlic powder; plus 1/8 teaspoon instant flakes or minced garlic; plus ½ teaspoon of sea salt
1 tablespoon fresh herbs	=	1 teaspoon dried herbs or 1/4 teaspoon powdered herbs
1 cup honey	=	1 1/4 cups sugar; plus 1/4 cup liquid or 1 cup corn syrup or molasses
1 cup ketchup	=	1 cup tomato sauce; plus 1/2 cup sugar and 2 tablespoons vinegar
1 cup milk	=	1/2 cup evaporated milk; plus 1/2 cup water OR 4 tablespoons of powdered milk dissolved in 1 cup of water
1 cup of molasses	=	1 cup of honey

Substitutions of Recipe Ingredients When Cooking

Ingredient/s		Substitution/s
1 medium lemon	=	2 to 3 tablespoons of juice or 1/2 teaspoon of lemon extract
1 teaspoon lemon juice	=	1 teaspoon vinegar
1 pound fresh mushrooms	=	6 ounces canned mushrooms
1 tablespoon prepared mustard	=	1 teaspoon dry mustard
1 medium onion	=	1 tablespoon dried minced onion or 1 teaspoon onion powder
1/4 cup chopped fresh parsley	=	1 tablespoon dried parsley flakes
1 teaspoon poultry seasoning	=	$\frac{1}{4}$ teaspoon thyme; plus $\frac{3}{4}$ teaspoon sage
1 teaspoon pumpkin pie spice	=	$\frac{1}{2}$ teaspoon cinnamon; plus $\frac{1}{2}$ teaspoon ginger;
1 cup packed brown sugar	=	1 cup granulated sugar or 2 cups powdered sugar; plus 1 tablespoon molasses
1 cup granulated sugar	=	1 cup light brown sugar, well packed
1 tablespoon tapioca	=	1 1/2 tablespoons all-purpose flour

Substitutions of Recipe Ingredients When Cooking

Substitutions of ingredients in various recipes can be utilized when the indicated recipe ingredients/s are not available in your pantry; such as making homemade biscuits.

Ingredient/s		Substitution/s
1 cup canned tomatoes	=	About 1 1/3 cups chopped tomato, simmered for 10 minutes
1 cup tomato juice	=	1/2 cup tomato sauce; plus 1/2 cup water
1 cup whipping cream, whipped	=	2 cups whipped dessert topping
1 cup wine	=	1 cup apple juice or apple cider; or 1 cup chicken or beef broth
1 package active dry yeast	=	2 1/4 teaspoons dry or 1 package compressed yeast
1 cup yogurt	=	1 cup buttermilk or sour milk

British Cookery: Equivalents

This Conversion Chart* should be of assistance to you and a **quick reference** if you are cooking your favorite American dish or attempting to cook some new favorite British dishes, such as **scones** *(one of my and my daughters' favorite)* or some other local traditional dish.

Equivalents: U.S. vs. British Measurement Differences (Liquids)
This table gives the Equivalents with an Accuracy Slightly Greater than is Practical for Measuring *

U.S. Measure	U.S. Volume	British	Metric
1 teaspoon	1/6 fluid oz.	0.17 fluid oz.	5 ml
1 tablespoon	1/2 fluid oz.	.52 fluid oz.	15 ml
1 cup	8 fluid oz.	8.3 fluid oz.	250 ml

*See Source for more Conversions: *Science of Cooking Conversion Calculator:*
www.exploratorium.edu

1 Cup = 16 Tablespoons (Tsp) = 48 teaspoons (tsp)
1 Tablespoon = 3 teaspoons

Note*: These measurements in the table above work just fine for* **liquids; however, dry ingredients** *are also measured in* **cups and spoons,** *and this creates a further problem: British cooks are used to* **flour, sugar** *and other dry ingredients being measured by* **weight.**

Measuring Cups and Spoons
In America, a **cup is 8 US fluid ounces**, a **tablespoon is 1/2 US fluid ounce**, and a **teaspoon is 1/6 of US fluid ounce**. While you can use a British **teaspoon, which is 5ml**, and the British **tablespoon, which is measured as 15ml,** as used for medicines; they are very close to the US measures of a teaspoon and tablespoon.

However, don't make a mistake and use a British cup for cooking American recipes. The standard **British cup is half a pint, or 8.3 fluid ounces,** and it's about **a fifth greater** than the US cup equivalent.

It is certainly possible to convert U.S. cups and spoons to **a weight**, but it is not always a convenient thing to do as an exact equivalent weight because it will **depend on the type of ingredient used**. For example, **a cup of rice may weigh 8 ounces (about 225gm)**, but a **cup of plain flour may weigh only 4 ounces (about 115gm).**

British Cookery: Equivalents

An Important Assumption: It's important to realize that when an American Recipe calls for **"1 cup of flour"**, there is **an assumption** in how this is measured: Scooping out of a bag will compress the flour, and a cup can easily end up containing **an extra quarter** or **even half an ounce more**, and this could make a big difference to the recipe results. Instead, the USDA suggests the **"official" measuring technique** is to **stir the flour** with a spoon to **"aerate"** it first; then **pour** the flour into the **measuring cup** and **level it off with a straight edge.** **<u>DO NOT</u> pat it down, or tap the cup on the counter to level it off.** However, this only applies to very **powdery dry ingredients**, like flour. Other ingredients, **like rice, brown sugar or fats,** should be **packed** firmly in the measuring cup to avoid air gaps. The **<u>same</u> principle applies** when using **measuring spoons** for very **powdery dry ingredients**, like flour; and the "packing" technique for other ingredients, like rice, brown sugar or fats.

A Rough Guide: *If you don't feel comfortable to calculate and convert the ingredients to the American or British recipes, a rough guide to some key ingredients is given in the Table below. But, I recommend that you use the specific measuring "cup" (or "jug") to measure and go by the original recipe.*

But, to save you the thought process and for you to concentrate on your cooking of Hattie's southern cuisine "And Beyond" dishes, the Table below gives some approximate weights (in grams) for the most common dry ingredients that you will be using in my southern or British dishes—using whatever measuring utensils you already have. These equivalent weights should be taken as approximations; they are within 5 grams, as have been cross checked with the USDA approximations.

Approximate Equivalents: In British Grams (gm)

INGREDIENTS	1 CUP *	1 TABLESPOON *	1 TEASPOON *
Egg Noodles; dried	38 gm	2.4 gm	0.8 gm
White Flour	125 gm	7.8 gm	2.6 gm
Whole Wheat Flour	120 gm	7.5 gm	2.5 gm
Strong White Flour	140 gm	8.75 gm	2.9 gm
Rye Flour	100 gm	6.25 gm	2.1 gm
Brown Sugar	220 gm	13.75 gm	4.6 gm
Granulated Sugar	200 gm	12.5 gm	4.2 gm
Icing Sugar (Confectionery)	120 gm	7.5 gm	2.5 gm
Long-grain Rice	185 gm	11.5 gm	3.9 gm
Short-grain Rice	200 gm	12.5 gm	4.2 gm
Wild Rice	160 gm	10 gm	3.3 gm

*__*NOTE:__ These equivalents are based on official equivalent figures issued by the US Department of Agriculture (USDA) far back as 1996 and assume that ingredients like flour are "stirred" first before measuring, but that sugars, etc. are "packed" in the measuring utensil for use.*

British Cookery: Equivalents

British Oven Temperatures Conversion-- Experiences Encountered While Living & Cooking In Scotland: Another experience while **living in Scotland and cooking the British dishes**, and even the American dishes, I encountered a **difference in the Ovens temperature markings** used in Scotland and the conversion that I had to do—not to mention the difference in the electricity used for the American appliances shipped over by the military from America.

Nevertheless, the U.S. recipes always gave **oven temperatures** in **degrees Fahrenheit,** and the British stoves & ovens that came standard in the military housing in Scotland were in **degrees Celsius (centigrade).** Therefore, I had to convert the American recipes cooking temperature (given in Fahrenheit) to the Celsius (Centigrade) temperature when using the British oven (I reflected back to Mr. Tom Newby's eighth grade science class in Norfolk, VA for his formula for converting the Fahrenheit degrees to Celsius and vice versa. Rarely, would I tackle a British or an American recipe while in Scotland without a pen and pad, not only for the conversions in oven temperatures, but also, for the difference in the amounts of the British measurement utensils.

There are considerable variations in different references when it comes to the "gas mark" equivalents! However, for your convenience and having lived in Scotland for over two years, I wanted to mention these variations here just in case you travel abroad and encounter an UK oven or an UK recipe with such varied oven temperatures. Be sure to have access to my cookbook with this easy conversion chart ☺

Fahrenheit *	Centigrade * (Celsius)	Gas Mark
80	30	-
100	40	-
240	115	¼
265	130	½
290	140	1
300	150	-
310	155	2
325	160	-
335	170	3
350	175	-
355	180	4
375	190	-
380	195	5
400	200	6
425	220	7
450	230	8
470	245	9

The Table above gives the approximate equivalents of the Celsius (Centigrade) temperature to the Fahrenheit temperature as well as to the "Gas Mark" equivalents (The Gas Mark is another used equivalent that some UK appliances and/or UK recipes use, instead of the Celsius (Centigrade) temperature for the oven when cooking a particular recipe). <u>*Source:*</u> *Cooking Charts & Helps Index by Mike Todd at miketodd.net.*

Nutrient Counts for Various Food Servings

APPETIZERS

Food	Serv. Sz +	Calories +	Sugars	Carbohydrates	Protein	Fats
Bean Dip	½ cup	110	1 gram	18 grams	6 grams	1 gram
Buffalo Chicken Wings	3 pieces	233	0 grams	7 grams	13 grams	17 grams
Devil Eggs	3 eggs	184	1 grams	1 grams	11 grams	15 grams
Hush Puppies	3 pieces	195	3 grams	27 grams	4 grams	9 grams
Jalapeno Peppers	2 pieces	119	2 grams	8 grams	4 grams	8 grams
Meatballs (Beef)	4 balls 14 each	56	0 grams	2 grams	5 grams	3 grams
Meatballs (Turkey)	4 balls 10 each	40	0 grams	2 grams	5 grams	1.16 grams
Mozzarella Sticks	3 pieces	68	0 grams	5 grams	3 grams	4 grams
Onion Rings	4 pieces	79	1 gram	1 grams	8 grams	2 grams
Potato Skins with Cheese & Bacon	2 pieces	323	2 grams	36 grams	12 grams	15 grams
Shrimp Cocktail	4 pieces	111	4 grams	10 grams	14 grams	1 grams
Spinach & Artichoke Dip	½ cup	260	1 gram	8 grams	7 grams	23 grams

Nutrient Counts for Various Food Servings

BREADS: Biscuits, Pancakes, Rolls & Waffles

Food	Serv. Sz +	Calories +	Sugars	Carbohydrates	Protein	Fats
Bagel	1 regular	270	5.3 grams	53.02 grams	10-52 grams	1.7 grams
Baguette	I – 2 oz.	175	0.15 gram	33.22 grams	5.63 grams	1.92 grams
Biscuits*	1 - 2.5" dia.	212	1.31 grams	26.7 grams	4.2 grams	9.78 grams
Cornbread *	I cubic inch	183	4.42 grams	27.47 grams	4.39 grams	6.12 grams
Croissant	1 piece	231	6 grams	26 grams	4.7 grams	7 grams
Pancake **	1 Plain - 5" dia.	90	3.89 grams	15.72 grams	2.13 grams	2.07 grams
Roll *	1 small	77	1.4 grams	13 grams	2.7 grams	1.6 grams
Waffle **	1 plain (4" x 4")	121	3.72 grams	19.05 grams	2.85 grams	3.72 grams
Whole Wheat *	1 slice	67	1.43 grams	12.26 grams	2.37 grams	1.07 grams

* Add 102 calories for 1 tablespoon Butter

** Add 80 calories for 3 tablespoon Maple Syrup

+ Calories and other nutrients will vary according to the ingredients used in preparation, serving size & topping/s

Sources: fatsecret.com/calories-nutrition | usda.gov/food-and-nutrition | MyFitnessPal.com

Nutrient Counts for Various Food Servings

ENTRÉES

Food	Serv. Sz +	Calories +	Sugars	Carbohydrates	Protein	Fats
Barbeque Pork	1 cup	502	28 grams	35 grams	44 grams	19 grams
Beef Brisket	1 medium slice	121	0 grams	0 grams	11 grams	8 grams
Beef Stew	1 cup	264	0 grams	0 grams	48 grams	7 grams
Fried Catfish	1 fillet (5" x 2-1/2")	182	0 grams	5 grams	11 grams	13 grams
Chicken & Dumplings	1 ½ cup	151	1 grams	9 grams	9 grams	9 grams
Fried Chicken	1 medium leg	430	0 grams	14 grams	33 grams	26 grams
Crab Cake	2 ¾ inch portion	153	1 grams	5 grams	11 grams	9 grams
Jambalaya	1 cup	425	2 grams	21 grams	26 grams	31 grams
Lasagna	1 piece (2-1/2" x 4")	293	7 grams	33 grams	15 grams	11 grams
Braised Pork Tenderloin	(4 ounces)	161	0 grams	0 grams	31 grams	3 grams
Fried Jumbo Shrimp	6 pieces	432	2 grams	33 grams	26 grams	31 grams
Spaghetti & Meatballs	1 cup	332	6 grams	43 grams	14 grams	11 grams
Steak (Sirloin)	(5 ounces)	285	0 grams	0 grams	29 grams	18 grams

Nutrient Counts for Various Food Servings

SIDE DISHES

Food	Serv. Sz +	Calories +	Sugars	Carbohydrates	Protein	Fats
Baked Beans	½ cup	195	9 grams	28 grams	8 grams	6 grams
Black-Eyed Peas	½ cup	151	3 grams	17 grams	6 grams	7 grams
Brussels Sprouts	½ cup	45	0 grams	5 grams	2 grams	2 grams
Cabbage	½ cup	35	0 grams	4 grams	1 grams	2 grams
Cole slaw	½ cup	89	5 grams	10 grams	1 grams	5 grams
Collard Greens	½ cup	30	0 grams	4 grams	2 grams	1 grams
Corn	1 ear (7" long)	116	0 grams	21 grams	3 grams	4 grams
Fried Okra	½ cup	89	1 grams	11 grams	3 grams	4 grams
French Fries	1 portion (10 strips)	148	0 grams	17 grams	2 grams	8 grams
Green Beans	½ cup	40	0 grams	5 grams	1 grams	2 grams
Green Peas	½ cup	80	0 grams	12 grams	4 grams	2 grams
Grits	½ cup	150	0 grams	13 grams	6 grams	8 grams
Lima Beans	½ cup	112	1 grams	17 grams	6 grams	2 grams
Macaroni & Cheese	½ cup	246	2 grams	45 grams	10 grams	12 grams
Mashed Potatoes	½ cup	106	1 grams	18 grams	2 grams	3 grams
Pasta Salad	½ cup	157	2 grams	20 grams	4 grams	7 grams
Potato Salad	½ cup	162	1 grams	15 grams	1 grams	11 grams
Stuffing	½ cup	149	2 grams	17 grams	3 grams	7 grams
Sweet Potatoes	½ cup	92	6 grams	18 grams	1 grams	2 grams
Squash Casserole	½ cup	95	3 grams	9 grams	4 grams	5 grams

Nutrient Counts for Various Food Servings

DESSERTS: Cakes, Cobblers, Cookies, Pies & Puddings

Food	Serv. Size	Calories	Sugars	Carbohydrates	Protein	Fats
Angel Food Cake	(1/12 of tube cake)	268	30 grams	54 grams	6 grams	4 grams
Cheesecake w/Cherries	Slice (1/12 of 9" cake)	297	22 grams	26 grams	5 grams	20 grams
Chocolate Cake	Slice (1/12 of 2-layer cake)	408	52 grams	67 grams	4 grams	16 grams
Pineapple Upside Down Cake	Slice (1/8 of 9 "cake)	401	41 grams	53 grams	4 grams	20 grams
Pound Cake	1/10 of a loaf	496	57 grams	77 grams	4 grams	19 grams
Strawberry Shortcake	Slice (3" across)	286	35 grams	56 grams	5 grams	5 grams
Peach Cobbler	1 cup	432	51 grams	83 grams	5 grams	10 grams
Chocolate Chip Cookies	Large cookie	108	9 grams	13 grams	1 grams	6 grams
Peanut Butter Cookies	Large cookie	119	8 grams	15 grams	2 grams	6 grams
Peanut Brittle	1 piece	63	7 grams	9 grams	1 grams	2 grams
Jello w/ Whip Cream	1 cup	184	32 grams	34 grams	3 grams	4 grams
Blackberry Pie	Slice (1/8 of 9" pie)	393	24 grams	54 grams	4 grams	19 grams
Blueberry Pie	Slice (1/8 of 9" pie)	348	15 grams	52 grams	3 grams	15 grams
Cherry Pie	Slice (1/8 of 9" pie)	390	21 grams	60 grams	3 grams	17 grams
Pecan Pie	Slice (1/8 of 9" pie)	464	29 grams	68 grams	5 grams	19 grams
Sweet Potato Pie	Slice (1/8 of 9" pie)	403	26 grams	45 grams	5 grams	24 grams
Banana Pudding	1 cup	281	35 grams	49 grams	6 grams	7 grams

THIS 'N' THAT
Mama's Kitchen Southern Staples

Apple Butter

Churned Sweet Cream Butter

Buttermilk For the morning biscuits and/or cornbread or spoonbread.

Cracklin' Used as an ingredient in Mama' succulent cornbread or spoonbread.

Yeast for Rolls

Ham Hocks Used for seasoning greens, beans and other dishes.

Smoked Ham and/or Authentic Smithfield Ham—If Mama ran out of her own cured ham she only purchased Smithfield Hams—which she swore were the closest to her own ("Smithfield Hams" have a unique flavor and texture unchanged since colonial times).

Flour (Both Plain and Self-Rising)—Mama used for biscuits, rolls, pancakes, and for crusts for cobblers, casseroles, pies, turnovers, etc.

Fat Back Meat Used for frying and seasoning various foods or just eating the crunchy crisp skin and meat with breakfast foods or other dishes.

Lard Mama used for making biscuits, rolls, and frying everything, especially her fried chicken. She also used lard as a skin softener for our face, hands, legs and our feet and heels.

Pot Liquors Juice from cooked collards, kale, turnip greens, etc., fortified with vitamins and many nutrients.

Homemade Preserves Mama made preserves (strawberry, cherry, blackberry, raspberry, peach, pear, tomato, and apple) and all kinds of pickles (cucumbers, watermelon rinds, etc.)

Sassafras Root This root from our sassafras bushes was used for teas and as a remedy for colds, fever and other illnesses.

Mama's Homemade Sweet Wines (blackberry, cherry, grape, cherry & peach) Mama made her annual supply of sweet wines that she served to company, neighbors and visiting relatives.

Aunt Hattie's Cookbook
Essential Cooking Pans, Baking Dishes, Utensils, Etc.

Large Black Cast Iron Frying Pan Mainly used for frying the Southern Fried Chicken.

Medium Cast Iron Frying Pan Used for cooking a smaller amount of dishes or steps in another recipe; such as sautéed onions & vegetables, etc.

Large Pot Used for cooking big batches of various greens; for canning; plucking chickens; heating hot water for our Saturday night bathing ritual, etc,

Medium Sauce Pans Used for cooking side dishes as well as using as a deep fryer.

Large & Medium Rolling Pins Used for rolling out your biscuits, pies or cobbler crusts, etc.

Large Mixing Bowl or Pan Used for making biscuits, rolls or cakes, potato salad, etc.

Large Bread Pans Used for baking biscuits, roasted vegetable, meats, etc.

Large Roaster Used for turkeys, hens, beef, other meals in a roaster dishes.

Casserole Dishes For cobblers, mac & cheese, breakfast hash, and puddings, etc.

Sharp Knives (Various Sizes)

Cooking Spoons, Forks, Tongs, Spatula, Etc.

Set of Measuring Utensils with Markings (American Standard & British Metric):
Pint, Cup, Tablespoon, Teaspoon, Half Teaspoon

Plates & Platters Used for serving entrees or sides dishes as well as eating meals.

Old-Fashioned Ice Cream Maker w/Crank A time-consuming task, but, home-made ice cream was the best and freshest tasting ice cream ever. Mama would make it often in the summer all fruit flavors. We also made homemade ice cream every year at my two-room schoolhouse for May Day. Each of the children got a chance to turn the crank on the old-fashioned ice cream maker until the ice cream was firm and ready.

Butter Churner (Not practical today, but was a staple back in the day in the country where my stepmom churned and made her sweet cream butter from fresh cow's milk.)

AUNT HATTIE'S COOKBOOK
Additional Resources Pertaining to Health and Food

Paleo Diet

I am a fan of the Paleo Diet, and I am a website member. The Paleo Diet is an interesting lifestyle and it reminds me of eating closely to the way we ate in the country—with fresh ingredients. I suggest that you may want to visit their websites for great information on the topics below and many others: https//:www.thepaleodiet.com/what-to-eat-on-the-paleo-diet-paul-vandyken/

Ten Reasons Everyone Should Be Cooking With Lard (or Ghee)
Coconut Oils—The Importance of Coconut Oils and How To Pick The Best Coconut
Oils and Other Good Oils
Good Sugar Substitute
The Magic of Honey
The Benefits of Onions
What's the Difference between White Eggs and Brown Eggs

Good Fats

Believe it or not fats are a healthy part of your diet. The main thing to remember is to eat more good fats than bad fats. Good fats such as, lard, avocado, coconut, dark chocolate, nuts, whole eggs, Greek Yogurt, wild salmon, olive oil, and others.

Lard

Lard is making a comeback used by many nutritionists and top chefs as a healthy and pure form of cooking fat -it does not have all of the added impurities in other hydrogenated cooking oils-. See the Article in the *Huffington Post* entitled:

"10 Reasons You Should Be Cooking With Lard" By Julia B. Thomson
https://www.m.huffpost.com/us/entry/5212804

Aunt Hattie's Cookbook
Additional Resources Pertaining to Health and Food

Ten Reasons You Should Be Cooking with Lard
1) Lard makes the best fried chicken.
2) It's an extremely versatile fat.
3) Mexican tamales just wouldn't be the same without it.
4) It has less saturated fat than butter.
5) It makes for the flakiest of pie crusts.
6) Despite what you may think, it does not impart a pork flavor.
7) Vegetables roasted in lard come out crisper than you thought possible.
8) It's sustainable.
9) Biscuits turn out great with lard.
10) Lard is even good on a piece of bread, in place of butter.
Source: https//:www.m.huffpost.com/us/entry/5212804

Margarine vs. Lard vs. Butter and Why Lard is the Healthiest
https//:www.empoweredsustenance.com/lard-is-healthy/
https//:www.steadyhealth.com/articles/butter-margarine-or-lard-which-is-best

Coconut Oils—The Importance of Coconut Oils and How to Pick the Best Coconut
Coconut oil is high in natural saturated fat. Saturated fats not only increase the healthy cholesterol known as HDL cholesterol in your body, but also help convert the LDL "bad" cholesterol into good cholesterol.
Source, https//:www.draxe.com/coconut-oil-benefits/

Oils and Other Good Oils
A common mistake people make when they switch to the paleo lifestyle is not taking in enough healthy fats, which are important for satiety and getting through workouts. Typically, what comes to mind when we think of "healthy fats" are monounsaturated and polyunsaturated fats like avocado, olive oil, nuts and seeds, fish, and flax oil.

AUNT HATTIE'S COOKBOOK
Additional Resources Pertaining to Health and Food

Many of the fats consumed today are highly processed fats which are designed to be nonperishable. This allows them to have longer shelf lives, which is great for food manufacturers. These fats are trans-fats and hydrogenated fats (hydrogen is added to liquid fat to make it solid) like margarine, Crisco, Earth Balance, Smart Balance, and I Can't Believe It's Not Butter.

It can be easy to forget that our primitive ancestors' diets were mostly made up of fats of the saturated kind and from the organ meat of wild game, the blubber of sea animals, and plants. We didn't have access to olive oil or coconut oil. So which fats should you be eating more of and cooking with? When shopping for oils it is best to look for unrefined and cold pressed. These types of fats usually do well under heat and for cooking, such as animal fats (lard) and coconut oil.
Source: https//:ultimatepaleoguide.com/ultimate-guide-cooking-healthy-fats/

Good Sugar Substitute: Raw Honey; Dates; Coconut Sugar; Maple Syrup; Stevia; **and Hattie's personal favorite, Stevia Blend (Combination of Stevia & Xylitol).**
Source: https//:draxe.com/sugar-substitutes/

The Magic of Honey
It's been said that honey is the only food on earth that contains everything you need to sustain life, including carbohydrates (natural sugars), enzymes, vitamins, minerals, amino acids and water. All of these ingredients make the benefits of honey go far beyond its great taste. **It's a natural source of energy**: The natural sugars found in honey offer a wonderful source of energy. The glucose is quickly absorbed by the body and provides an immediate energy boost, while the fructose is slowly absorbed and thus provides sustained energy. Honey is also good at keeping blood sugar levels fairly constant in comparison with other sugars, so it's the ideal companion to an active lifestyle or exercise regime
Source: https//:www.yuppiechef.com/spatula/magic-honey/

Salt vs. Sea Salt
https://www.seasalt.avajaneskitchen.com/special/?AFFID=190039&customField
2=custom&subid=116http I https://www.healthline.com/nutrition/different-types-of-salt

AUNT HATTIE'S COOKBOOK
Additional Resources Pertaining to Health and Food

Facts About Sugar
https://www.wsro.org/aboutsugar/factsaboutsugar.aspx

Flour Types
https://www.whatscookingamerica.net/Bread/FlourTypes.htm

What's the Difference Between Sea Salt and Table Salt
https://www.mayoclinic.org/healthy-lifestyle/nutrition-and-healthy-eating/expert-answers/sea-salt/faq-20058512

Comparing Milks, Almond, Dairy, Soy, Rice, and Coconut
https://www.healthline.com/health/milk-almond-cow-soy-rice

The Benefits of Eating Chocolate
https://www.womenshealthmag.com/health/benefits-of-chocolate

Eggs as Food
https//:www.healthline.com/nutrition/6-reasons-why-eggs-are-the-healthiest-food-on-the-planet

What's the Difference between White Eggs and Brown Eggs
We've all noticed the difference in price at the grocery store as we stand scratching our heads, but have you ever stopped to wonder what the difference really is between white and brown eggs? Most of us inevitably choose whichever eggs are on sale, or we just buy the color egg we've always bought. Well, it turns out there actually is a difference between white and brown eggs.

It's all about the chicken
The answer is so simple that you may be surprised. White-feathered chickens with white ear lobes lay white eggs and red-feathered ones with red ear lobes lay brown eggs (this may not apply to all breeds). And besides that, there are certain chickens that even lay speckled eggs and blue eggs. But when you get down to the egg, nutritionally there is no difference — it's all just in the looks.
Source: https://www.huffingtonpost.com/2012/03/14/white-vs-brown-eggs_n_1342583.html

AUNT HATTIE'S COOKBOOK
Additional Resources Pertaining to Health and Food

The Benefits of Onions

When you think of foods containing vitamin C, onions may not come to your mind, but, as it happens, onions are a very good source of vitamin C, as well as B6, biotin, chromium, calcium and dietary fiber. In addition, they contain good amounts of folic acid and vitamin B1 and K. Like garlic, onions also have the enzyme, alliinase, which well-known for its health benefit, but causes your eyes to water. So as tears stream down your face as you cut your onions for the recipes in my Aunt Hattie's cookbook, just think of the amazing health benefits that you will experience as you enjoy the flavor of onions (My stepmother ate onions straight from the garden as if they were apples).

Source: https://www.foods-healing-power.com/health-benefits-of-onions.html

The Benefits of Drinking Water

https//:www.webmd.com/diet/features/6-reasons-to-drink-water#1

Healthy Eating Resources

https//:www.nutritionist-resource.org.uk/articles/healthy-eating.html

https//:www.helpguide.org/articles/healthy-eating/healthy-eating.htm

https//:www.cnn.com/2015/01/14/health/feat-healthy-eating-habits/

https//:familydoctor.org/nutrition-how-to-make-healthier-food-choices/

https//:time.com/4771515/cut-sugar-diet-nutrition/

Resources for Nutrition Tracking

https/:.www.supertracker.usda.gov

https//:medlineplus.gov/evaluatinghealthinformation.html

https//:www.nal.usda.gov/fnic/dietary-reference-intakes

https//:www.nutrition.gov/weight-management/strategies-success/interested-losing-weight

https//:www.heart.org/HEARTORG/HealthyLiving/HealthyEating/Nutrition/How-to-Track-Your-Sodium_ UCM_449547_Article.jsp#.WRljxmNlnow

https//:www.healthline.com/health/food-nutrition/top-iphone-android-apps#1

U.S. Department of Health and Human Services and U.S. Department of Agriculture. 2015 - 2020 Dietary Guidelines for Americans. 8th Edition.

https//:health.gov/dietaryguidelines/2015/guidelines/ | https//:www.choosemyplate.gov

Glossary of Cooking Terms & Definitions

I. **FOOD COOKING TERMS OF INGREDIENTS**

II. **COOKING HERBS, SEASONINGS, SPICES AND OTHER INGREDIENTS**

III. **COOKING ACTION TERMS**

I. FOOD COOKING TERMS OF INGREDIENTS

ALMOND EXTRACT
Flavoring derived by dissolving the essential oil of almonds in an alcohol base. Use only products labeled "pure" or "natural" almond extract (essence).

AMARETTO
Italian liqueur combining essences of apricot and almond.

ANCHOVIES
Tiny saltwater fish, related to sardines; most often found as canned filets that have been salted and preserved in oil. Imported anchovy filets packed in olive oil are the most commonly available; those packed in salt, available canned in some Italian delicatessens, are considered the finest.

APERITIF
A drink taken before a meal to stimulate the appetite.

APPLES
There are numerous kinds of apples, and they differ in color, size, flavor, texture and the shapes. The most common varieties of apples are Delicious, Golden Delicious, Granny Smith, McIntosh, and Rome Beauty.

Here are some varieties of apples my family grew and/or picked in Meherrin & Prince Edward County, VA.

Cortland - a dark red apple with red stripes, is large and has flat ends. It tastes sweet and is juicy and tender. It can be eaten fresh and is also used for cooking.

Delicious - has a solid dark red color or is dark red with darker stripes. It is medium-to-large and has an oval shape with five knobs on the bottom. This sweet-tasting apple is firm, crisp, and juicy and is usually eaten fresh.

Empire - is a dark red apple. It has crisp, juicy, slightly tart flesh and is eaten fresh.

Glossary of Cooking Terms & Definitions

Gala - is a yellowish-orange to red apple. Its yellow to cream-colored flesh is crisp and sweet.

Golden Delicious - has a golden-yellow skin and an oval shape. Its juicy, firm flesh has a sweet flavor. It ranges from medium-to-large and is a good all-purpose apple.

Granny Smith - is a bright green apple. It ranges from medium to large and has an almost round shape. Its firm flesh tastes tart and is eaten fresh and used for cooking, especially my fried apples recipe, apple pies, cobblers, tarts and other apple dishes.

Jonathan - is bright red, touched with yellow and green. This apple varies from small to medium and has a firm flesh, a tart flavor and is juicy. Its shape is round to oval and is eaten fresh and is also baked in pies.

McIntosh - a bright red apple, is medium sized and round or oval. It tastes mildly acid to sweet. It has tender flesh and is usually eaten fresh.

Rome Beauty - is red with yellow or green markings. It is large and has a round to oval shape. The crisp, firm flesh has a mildly acid flavor. This apple is used for cooking, baking, and processing.

Stayman - is dull red with darker stripes. This apple varies from medium to large and has a roundish shape. Its firm flesh has a mildly acid flavor and is eaten fresh and used for processing.

Winesap - is bright dark red and roundish. It ranges from small to medium and has a mildly acidic flavor. Its flesh is firm and juicy and is eaten fresh and used for processing.

ARROWROOT
A starch sold as a dried and milled white powder. Does not mask or alter natural flavors. Produces sauces and pastes and is used as a thickening agent in place of flour or cornstarch for fruit sauces, pie fillings, puddings, salad dressings, dessert sauces, vegetable sauces, and meat glazes; But, do not use to make gravy (Arrowroot reaches maximum thickening at lower temperatures than other thickeners, thus it is ideal for use with heat sensitive foods).

AU GRATIN
Topped with crumbs and/or cheese and browned in the oven or under the broiler.

AVOCADO
A fruit that grows in tropical and subtropical climates. The fruit may be round, oval or pear-shaped. Its skin color ranges from green to dark purple, depending on the variety. Avocados have a yellow-green pulp and contain one large seen. They are highly nutritious and rich in vitamins, minerals and oil. Eat fresh in dips, salads and desserts. Base ingredient for guacamole.

Glossary of Cooking Terms & Definitions

BABY BACK RIBS
Especially juicy and tender, small pork ribs cut from the top of a young animal's center loin section.

BAKING POWDER
Commercial baking product combining three ingredients, baking soda, the source of the carbon dioxide that causes quick batters and doughs to rise; an acid such as cream of tartar, which when the powder is combined with a liquid, causes the baking soda to release its gas; and a starch such as corn starch or flour, to keep the powder from absorbing moisture.

BAKING SODA
The active component of baking powder and the source of the carbon dioxide that leavens many baked goods. Also known as sodium bicarbonate or bicarbonate of soda.

BARBECUE SAUCE
Sweet, tart and spicy sauce used to baste foods or as a condiment for grilled foods. Although recipes vary widely, common elements include tomato, sugar or molasses, vinegar, and a hot spice such as a chili or mustard.

BECHAMEL (Béchamel), A sauce made from milk and a white roux (butter and flour paste)—also known as a white sauce--is one of the traditional sauces of the French cuisine. It is usually used as the base for other sauces and gravies (See Hattie's Brown Gravy recipe for Smothered Southern Fried Chicken).

BISQUE
A thick creamy soup.

CANAPE
Plain or toasted bread topped with a savory mixture, served as an appetizer or with cocktails.

CHUTNEY
A highly seasoned relish of fruits, herbs and spices.

CORN MEAL
Granular flour, ground from the dried kernels of yellow or white corn, with a sweet, robust flavor.

CORN STARCH
Fine, powdery flour ground from the endosperm of corn--the white heart of the kernel--and used as a neutral-flavored thickening agent in some desserts. Also known as corn flour.

Glossary of Cooking Terms & Definitions

CORN SYRUP
Light- or dark-colored neutral tasting syrup extracted from corn.

CORNED BEEF
Beef brisket, or sometimes other cuts, cured for about a month in a brine with large crystals (corns) of salt, sugar, spices, and other seasonings and preservatives to produce a meat that when slowly simmered in water, develops a moist, tender mixture, mildly spiced flavor, and bright purplish-red color.

CREAM
The terms light and heavy describe cream's butterfat content and related richness. Light cream has a butterfat level varying from 18-30 percent. It is sometimes called coffee cream or table cream. Heavy whipping cream, sometimes simply labeled heavy cream, has a butterfat content of at least 36 percent.

CREAM, SOUR,
Commercial dairy product made from pasteurized sweet cream, used as an enrichment in a wide range of savory and sweet recipes. Its extra acidity can boost the leavening action of baking soda in quick breads and rolls.

CREAM OF TARTAR
Acidic powder used as an additive to meringue to stabilize egg whites and for heat tolerance. Used as leavening agent most commonly with baking soda to make baking powder and an ingredient in syrups to prevent crystallization.

CREPE
A thin, delicate pancake.

CRUDITES
An assortment of raw vegetables, i.e., carrots, broccoli, mushrooms, served as an hors d'oeuvre often accompanied by a dip.

DRIPPINGS
The juices, fats, and browned bits that collect in the pan after meat or poultry has been roasted. Unless burned or very greasy, the drippings are valuable for a little sauce and for gravy.

EGGPLANT
A vegetable-fruit with tender, mildly earthy, and sweet flesh. The shiny skins of eggplants vary in color from purple to red and from yellow to white, and their shapes range from small and oval to long and slender to large and pear-shaped.

Glossary of Cooking Terms & Definitions

ENTREE
The main course.

FETA CHEESE
Crumbly textured Greek-style cheese made from goat's or sheep's milk. Notable for its salty, slightly sharp flavor (Since living in Greece, my family and I have acquired a taste for this pungent cheese and eat it often on most of our salads).

FILO (Phyllo)
Tissue-thin sheets of flour-and-water pastry used as crisp wrappers for savory or sweet fillings. Defrost thoroughly before use. Keep unused sheets covered with lightly damp towel to prevent them from drying out (A similar pastry is used for the Greek dessert Galaktoboureko).

FLANK STEAK
Large, thin, fairly lean, boneless cut of beef (In Scotland when we first arrived and were waiting for our military housing, we stayed at a lovely quaint Bed & Breakfast (B & B) in Dunoon, called The Ardfillan a favorite and frequent dish on the menu made of flank steak was called "Steak Diane").

FLOUR, ALL-PURPOSE
The most common form of commercial flour. This bleached and blended variety is widely available. Also called plain flour (a staple in my Mama's kitchen. I have added to my pantry staples, almond flour, coconut flour, wheat flour, gluten-free flour, etc.).

GELATIN
Unflavored commercial gelatin gives delicate body to mousses and desserts. Sold in envelopes holding about one tablespoon each of which is sufficient to gel about two cups.

HORS D'OEUVRES
Small portions of savory foods used as Appetizers

HORSERADISH
Pungent-hot-tasting root, a member of the mustard family. Sold fresh and whole or already grated and bottled as a prepared sauce. Now available in dehydrated form.

LARD
Good fat from various meats (Slices of fat can be placed on top of uncooked lean meat or fish for flavor or to prevent dryness).

Glossary of Cooking Terms & Definitions

LEEK
Sweet, moderately flavored member of the onion family, long and cylindrical in shape with a pale white root and dark green leaves. LENTILS, Small, disk-shaped dried legumes, prized for their rich, earthy flavor when cooked.

MERINGUE
Mixture of stiffly beaten egg whites and sugar. Also the cooked soft mixture on desserts or the cooked "hard" mixture as a dessert shell.

MOUSSE
A cold dessert made with whipped cream or beaten egg whites.

MOZZARELLA CHEESE
Rindless white, mild-tasting Italian variety of cheese, traditionally made from water buffalo's milk and sold fresh. Commercially produced and packaged, cow's milk mozzarella is now much more common, although it has less flavor.

NEW YORK STEAK
Beefsteak cut from sirloin; prized for its tenderness and flavor.

OIL, OLIVE
Extra-virgin olive oil, extracted from olives on the first pressing without use of heat or chemicals, is preferred for salads. Many brands, varying in color and strength of flavor, are now available. Store in an airtight container away from heat and light.

PARFAIT
A dessert made of layers of fruit, syrup, ice cream and whipped cream or beaten egg whites.

PARMESAN CHEESE
Hard, thick crusted Italian cheese with a sharp, salty full flavor resulting from at least two years of aging.

PEARS
Mildly sweet and aromatic and smooth to grainy in texture. A fine fruit for eating or cooking year-round.

Variety of Pears

Anjou pears - Rich in flavor with a hint of spice and a smooth texture; among the largest and plumpest of pears, they have short necks and thin yellow-green skins.

Glossary of Cooking Terms & Definitions

Bartlett pears - Medium sized and shaped roughly like bells with creamy yellow skin, sometimes tinged in red; fine-textured, juicy and mild tasting, they are equally good for cooking or eating.

Comas pears - Sweet and juicy, large, round and short-necked, with greenish yellow skins tinged with red.

Royal Riviera pears - Favored for eating or cooking, are among the most luxurious of all, large with red-tinged skins and juicy smooth sweet flesh.

PETIT FOUR
Small, decoratively iced cake.

PROSCIUTO
Italian-style cured and spiced ham, served sliced paper thin.

QUICHE
Savory one-crust egg-and-cream main dish pie (A variety of vegetables, cheeses and meats ingredients add a host of varieties to this breakfast or main dish—Can also be vegetarian with all vegetables & no meats. See my Quiche recipes—with and without a crust).

ROMAINE LETTUCE
Popular variety of lettuce with elongated, pale-green leaves characterized by their crisp texture and slightly pungent flavor.

ROMANO CHEESE
Italian variety of cheese traditionally made from sheep's milk, now made from goat and cow's milk as well. Sold either fresh or aged. Similar but tangier than Parmesan.

ROUX
A mixture of melted fat and flour (This is formed when making gravies, sauces and on other occasions when a thickening is needed--See Béchamel, the French term for a traditional white sauce made of flour, butter and milk).

STOCK
Flavorful liquid derived from slowly simmering chicken, meat, fish or vegetables in water, along with herbs and aromatic vegetables. Used as the primary cooking liquid or moistening and flavoring agent in many recipes (Mama referred to this flavorful liquid as "pot liquid" and had us children to drink about a half cup to prevent colds and other illnesses).

Glossary of Cooking Terms & Definitions

T-BONE STEAK
Tender, flavorful cut of beef from the center of the short loin containing a short t-shaped bone.

TAPIOCA, INSTANT
The finely ground flakes of the tropical manioc plant's dried, starchy root. Used as a thickener in pies, puddings and tarts.

TERIYAKI
Japanese style of grilling in which food is seasoned and basted with a marinade usually based on sweet rice wine and soy sauce to form a rich, shining glaze.

VINEGAR
An acid liquid used for flavoring and preserving. Among the types are cider vinegar (made from apple juice); distilled white vinegar (usually made from grain alcohol); herb vinegar (flavored with herbs); and red or white wine vinegars, which also may be flavored with garlic (My favorite is the Raw Apple Cider Vinegar--with The Mother).

II. COOKING HERBS, SEASONINGS, SPICES & OTHER INGREDIENTS

ALLSPICE
Sweet spice of Caribbean origin with a flavor suggesting a blend of cinnamon, cloves, and nutmeg, hence its name. May be purchased as whole, dried berries or ground. When using whole berries, they may be bruised--gently crushed with the bottom of a pan or other heavy instrument--to release more of their flavor.

ANISE
Green-gray fruit or seed of plan of parsley family; available whole and in extracts; unmistakable strong licorice flavor. Used extensively in confections, sweet pastries, and as a flavoring in liqueurs.

BASIL
Sweet, warm flavor with an aromatic odor, used whole or ground. Good with lamb, fish, roast, stews, ground beef, vegetables, dressing and omelets.

BAY LEAVES
A pungent flavor, use whole leaf but remove before serving. Good in vegetable dishes, fish and seafood, stews and pickles.

Glossary of Cooking Terms & Definitions

CAPERS

Capers are the small buds of a shrub grown in the Mediterranean. They are pickled in vinegar or dried and salted.

CARAWAY

A spicy smell and aromatic taste. Use in cakes, breads, soups, cheese and sauerkraut.

CARDAMON

Sweet spice native to India from ginger family. Used for coffee cake, sweet breads, fruit salad dressings, cookies, cakes, pickling spice.

CAYENNE PEPPER

Very hot ground spice derived from dried cayenne chili pepper.

CHIVES

Mild, sweet herb with a flavor reminiscent of the onion, to which it is related.

CILANTRO

Green, leafy herb resembling flat leaf (Italian) parsley with a sharp, aromatic, somewhat astringent flavor. Also called fresh coriander and commonly referred to as Chinese parsley.

CINNAMON

Popular sweet spice for flavoring baked goods. The aromatic bark of types of laurel trees, it is sold as sticks or ground.

CLOVES

Rich and aromatic East African spice used ground in baked goods and whole in pickling brines and as a seasoning for baked hams. Provides flavor to both sweet and savory recipes.

CONFECTIONERS SUGAR

A finely powdered sugar with exceptionally smooth texture. Ideal for making frostings, glazes, fudge, and candy-making. Contains cornstarch to prevent caking.

CORIANDER

Small spicy-sweet seeds of the coriander plant, which is also called cilantro or Chinese parsley. Used whole or ground as a seasoning. Particularly used for sausages and variety meats.

CUMIN

A Middle Eastern spice with a strong, dusky, aromatic flavor. Use in chili, marinades, and basting sauces, and add to Huevos Rancheros or other egg dishes.

Glossary of Cooking Terms & Definitions

CURRY POWDER
Generic term for a blend of spices commonly used to flavor East Indian-style dishes. Most curry powders will include coriander, cumin, chili powder, and turmeric.

DILL
Fine, feathery leaves with a sweet aromatic flavor sold fresh or dry.

FENNEL
Crisp, refreshing, mildly anise-flavored bulb vegetable. Seeds and leaves are both used as a spice. Has a sweet hot flavor. Wide variety of uses. Popular for seasoning pork roasts and fish dishes.

GARLIC
Member of the same group of plants as the onion. Robust flavoring, available as garlic powder, garlic salt, garlic chips, garlic seasoning powder, and garlic juice, in a huge variety of dishes.

GINGER
Ginger is a fresh, pungent root sold fresh, dried or ground. It is used as a confection or condiment. It may be found crystallized or candied, ground or as a syrup.

MACE
Produced from the same fruit of the nutmeg tree.

MINT
The most common commercial types of mint are spearmint and peppermint. Refreshing, sweet herbs used fresh or dry to flavor lamb, poultry, vegetables and fruits.

MUSTARD
Mustard is available in three forms, whole seeds, powdered (referred to as dried mustard), and prepared (which is made from powdered or coarsely ground mustard seed mixed with liquid such as vinegar or wine).

NUTMEG
Popular baking spice that is the hard pit of the fruit of the nutmeg tree. May be bought already ground or for fresher flavor, whole.

OREGANO
Aromatic, pungent and spicy Mediterranean herb. Use fresh or dried for all types of savory dishes. Especially popular with tomatoes and other vegetables.

Glossary of Cooking Terms & Definitions

PAPRIKA
The ground dried pod of a variety of capsicum. Paprika is more than a garnish. It is a seasoning that is a food enhancer for many dishes, including casseroles, baked potatoes, appetizers, rarebit, chicken, veal and salad dressings (I also use Smoked Paprika frequently in many of my recipes to add that hickory smoked flavor).

PARSLEY
A low growing member of the celery family. Available in two varieties, the curly leaf type, and the flat leaf, or Italian, type. Best when used fresh but can be used dry.

PINE NUTS
Small, ivory-colored seeds extracted from the cones of the species of pine tree, with a rich, slightly resinous flavor.

POPPYSEED
Used for fruit salads and salad dressings, sprinkled over yeast breads or rolls before baking, use in cottage cheese, cream cheese, scrambled eggs, pie crust, cheese sticks, fruit compotes, and noodles.

PUMPKIN PIE SPICE
A blend of cinnamon, ginger, allspice, nutmeg, and cloves in proper proportions. Used for pumpkin pie, gingerbread, cookies, fruits, squash, sweet potatoes, applesauce, and other apple dishes.

ROSEMARY
A perennial of the mint family. Use with partridge, duck, poultry, lamb, veal, seafood and vegetables. A strong, aromatic flavor.

SAFFRON
Orange yellow in color, this spice is used to flavor or color foods. Use in soup, chicken, rice and fancy bread.

SAGE
Pungent herb used either fresh or dried that goes particularly well with fresh or cured pork, poultry, lamb, veal or vegetables.

SAVORY
The dried brownish-green leaves of a plant of the mint family; has an aromatic piquant flavor. Blends well with other herbs. May be used alone or in combination with other herbs in stuffing for meat, fish or poultry; egg dishes; sauces; soups; meatloaf and hamburgers; stews; beans; and tomato juice.

Glossary of Cooking Terms & Definitions

SEASONING SALT

All-purpose seasoning with onion and celery and salt. Use with poultry dishes, Swiss steak and tomato-based sauces. May wish to use sea salt instead of the iodized salt (see article on sea salt in the Resource Directory).

SESAME SEEDS

Versatile annual with sweet, nutty flavor used in appetizers, breads, meats and vegetables.

SHALLOT

Small member of the onion family with brown skin, white-to-purple flesh, and a flavor resembling a cross between sweet onion and garlic.

SOY SAUCE

Asian seasoning and condiment usually made from soybeans, wheat or other grain, salt and water. Chinese brands tend to be saltier than Japanese (Persons who are gluten intolerant should use a substitute for soy sauce, that's made with wheat, and any other wheat-based ingredient--See the "Substitutions" Chart in the Resource Directory for possible ingredient substitutions).

TABASCO

Tabasco is a liquid pepper seasoning. It is extremely hot; therefore, use sparingly to suit your individual taste buds.

TARRAGON

Fragrant, distinctively sweet herb used fresh or dried as a seasoning for chicken, light colored meats, seafood, vegetables, salads, and eggs.

THYME

Fragrant, clean-tasting, small leafed herb, popular fresh or dried as a seasoning for poultry, light-colored meats, seafood or vegetables.

TURMERIC

Turmeric, also called Curcuma Longa, is the root of a plant belonging to the ginger family. Turmeric is somewhat medicinal in aroma and should be used with caution. However, more recently, Turmeric has been found to be beneficial to the body and effective at healing illnesses and certain diseases. Also, used in pickling (See article on "10 Benefits of Turmeric" at www.health facty.com).

Glossary of Cooking Terms & Definitions

WORCESTERSHIRE SAUCE
Traditional English seasoning or condiment; an intensely flavorful, savory and aromatic blend of many ingredients, including molasses, soy sauce, garlic, onion and anchovies. Popular as a marinade ingredient or table sauce for foods, especially red meats *(Persons who are gluten intolerant should use a substitute for Worcestershire® sauce, that's made with wheat, and any other wheat-based ingredient --See the "Substitutions" Chart in the Resource Directory for possible ingredient substitutions).*

ZEST
The thin brightly colored outermost layer of a citrus fruit's peel.

SHALLOT
Small member of the onion family with brown skin, white-to-purple flesh, and a flavor resembling a cross between sweet onion and garlic.

SOY SAUCE
Asian seasoning and condiment usually made from soybeans, wheat or other grain, salt and water. Chinese brands tend to be saltier than Japanese *(Persons who are gluten intolerant should use a substitute for soy sauce, that's made with wheat, and any other wheat-based ingredient--See the "Substitutions" Chart in the Resource Directory for possible ingredient substitutions).*

TABASCO
Tabasco is a liquid pepper seasoning. It is extremely hot; therefore, use sparingly to suit your individual taste buds.

TARRAGON
Fragrant, distinctively sweet herb used fresh or dried as a seasoning for chicken, light colored meats, seafood, vegetables, salads, and eggs.

THYME
Fragrant, clean-tasting, small leafed herb, popular fresh or dried as a seasoning for poultry, light-colored meats, seafood or vegetables.

TURMERIC
Turmeric, also called Curcuma Longa, is the root of a plant belonging to the ginger family. Turmeric is somewhat medicinal in aroma and should be used with caution. However, more recently, Turmeric has been found to be beneficial to the body and effective at healing illnesses and certain diseases. Also, used in pickling (See article on "10 Benefits of Turmeric" at www.health facty.com).

Glossary of Cooking Terms & Definitions

II. COOKING ACTION TERMS

AL DENTE
Italian term used to describe pasta that is cooked until it offers a slight resistance to the bite.

BAKE
To cook by dry heat, usually in the oven.

BARBECUE
Usually used generally to refer to grilling done outdoors or over an open charcoal or wood fire. More specifically, barbecue refers to long, slow direct- heat cooking, including liberal basting with a barbecue sauce.

BASTE
To moisten foods during cooking with pan drippings or special sauce to add flavor and prevent drying.

BATTER
A mixture containing flour and liquid, thin enough to pour.

BEAT
To mix rapidly in order to make a mixture smooth and light by incorporating as much air as possible.

BLANCH
To immerse in rapidly boiling water and allow to cool slightly.

BLEND
To incorporate two or more ingredients thoroughly.

BOIL
To heat a liquid until bubbles break continually on the surface.

BROIL
To cook on a grill under strong, direct heat.

CARAMELIZE
To heat sugar in order to turn it brown and give it a special taste (recipes use this term when they indicate to caramelize the onions, meaning sauté the onions until they break down and start to brown).

Glossary of Cooking Terms & Definitions

CHOP
To cut solids into pieces with a sharp knife or other chopping device.

CLARIFY
To separate and remove solids from a liquid, thus making it clear (For example, clarified butter has very little milk or water in the butter, which can be seen when butter is melted).

CREAM
To soften a fat, especially butter, by beating it at room temperature. Butter and sugar are often creamed together, making a smooth, soft paste.

CURE
To preserve meats by drying and salting and/or smoking (This was a common annual occurrence in the country during the fall when it was "Hog Killing" time).

DEGLAZE
To dissolve the thin glaze of juices and brown bits on the surface of a pan in which food has been fried, sautéed or roasted. To do this, add liquid and stir and scrape over high heat, thereby adding flavor to the liquid for use as a sauce.

DEGREASE
To remove fat from the surface of stews, soups, or stock. Usually cooled in the refrigerator so that fat hardens and is easily removed.

DICE
To cut food in small cubes of uniform size and shape.

DISSOLVE
To cause a dry substance to pass into solution in a liquid.

DREDGE
To sprinkle or coat with flour or other fine substance.

DRIZZLE
To sprinkle drops of liquid lightly over food in a casual manner.

Glossary of Cooking Terms & Definitions

DUST

To sprinkle food with dry ingredients. Use a strainer or a jar with a perforated cover, or try the good, old-fashioned way of shaking things together in a paper bag.

FILLET

As a verb, to remove the bones from meat or fish. A fillet (or filet) is the piece of flesh after it has been boned.

FLAKE

To break lightly into small pieces.

FLAMBE'

To flame foods by dousing in some form of potable alcohol and setting alight.

FOLD IN

To incorporate a delicate substance, such as whipped cream or beaten egg whites, into another substance without releasing air bubbles. Cut down through mixture with spoon, whisk, or fork; go across bottom of bowl, up and over, close to surface. The process is repeated, while slowing rotating the bowl, until the ingredients are thoroughly blended.

FRICASSEE

To cook by braising; usually applied to fowl or rabbit.

FRY

To cook in hot fat. To cook in a small amount of fat is called sautéing or pan-frying; to cook in a one-to-two-inch layer of hot fat is called shallow-fat frying; to cook in a deep layer of hot fat is called deep-fat frying.

GARNISH

To decorate a dish both to enhance its appearance and to provide a flavorful foil. Parsley, lemon slices, raw vegetables, chopped chives, and other herbs are all forms of garnishes.

GLAZE

To cook with a thin sugar syrup cooked to crack stage; mixture may be thickened slightly. Also, to cover with a thin, glossy icing.

Glossary of Cooking Terms & Definitions

GRATE
To rub on a grater that separates the food in various sizes of bits or shreds.

GRATIN
From the French word for "crust." Term used to describe any oven-baked dish--usually cooked in a shallow oval gratin dish--on which a golden-brown crust of bread crumbs, cheese or creamy sauce is form.

GRILL
To cook on a grill over intense heat.

GRIND
To process solids by hand or mechanically to reduce them to tiny particles.

JULIENNE
To cut vegetables, fruits, or cheeses into thin strips.

KNEAD
To work and press dough with the palms of the hands or mechanically, to develop the gluten in the flour.

LUKEWARM
Neither cool nor warm; approximately body temperature.

MARINATE
To flavor and moisturize pieces of meat, poultry, seafood or vegetable by soaking them in or brushing them with a liquid mixture of seasonings known as a marinade. Dry marinade mixtures composed of salt, pepper, herbs or spices may also be rubbed into meat, poultry or seafood.

MEUNIERE
Dredged with flour and sautéed in butter.

MINCE
To cut or chop food into extremely small pieces.

MIX
To combine ingredients usually by stirring.

Glossary of Cooking Terms & Definitions

PAN-BROIL
To cook uncovered in a hot fry pan, pouring off fat as it accumulates.

PAN-FRY
To cook in small amounts of fat.

PARBOIL
To boil until partially cooked; to blanch. Usually this procedure is followed by final cooking in a seasoned sauce.

PARE
To remove the outermost skin of a fruit or vegetable.

PEEL
To remove the peels from vegetables or fruits.

PICKLE
To preserve meats, vegetables, and fruits in brine.

PINCH
A pinch is the trifling amount you can hold between your thumb and forefinger.

PIT
To remove pits from fruits.

PLANKED
Cooked on a thick hardwood plank.

PLUMP
To soak dried fruits in liquid until they swell.

POACH
To cook very gently in hot liquid kept just below the boiling point.

PUREE
To mash foods until perfectly smooth by hand, by rubbing through a sieve or food mill, or by whirling in a blender or food processor.

Glossary of Cooking Terms & Definitions

REDUCE
To boil down to reduce the volume.

REFRESH
To run cold water over food that has been parboiled, to stop the cooking process quickly.

RENDER
To make solid fat into liquid by melting it slowly.

ROAST
To cook by dry heat in an oven.

SAUTE
To cook and/or brown food in a small amount of hot fat.

SCALD
To bring to a temperature just below the boiling point.

SCALLOP
To bake a food, usually in a casserole, with sauce or other liquid. Crumbs often are sprinkled over.

SCORE
To cut narrow grooves or gashes partway through the outer surface of food.

SEAR
To brown very quickly by intense heat. This method increases shrinkage but develops flavor and improves appearance.

SHRED
To cut or tear in small, long, narrow pieces.

SIFT
To put one or more dry ingredients through a sieve or sifter.

SIMMER
To cook slowly in liquid over low heat at a temperature of about 180°. The surface of the liquid should be barely moving, broken from time to time by slowly rising bubbles.

Glossary of Cooking Terms & Definitions

SKIM

To remove impurities, whether scum or fat, from the surface of a liquid during cooking, thereby resulting in a clear, cleaner-tasting final produce.

STEAM

To cook in steam in a pressure cooker, deep well cooker, double boiler, or a steamer made by fitting a rack in a kettle with a tight cover. A small amount of boiling water is used, more water being added during steaming process, if necessary.

STEEP

To extract color, flavor, or other qualities from a substance by leaving it in water just below the boiling point.

STERILIZE

To destroy micro-organisms by boiling, dry heat, or steam.

STEW

To simmer slowly in a small amount of liquid for a long time.

STIR

To mix ingredients with a circular motion until well blended or of uniform consistency.

TOSS

To combine ingredients with a lifting motion.

TRUSS

To secure poultry with string or skewers, to hold its shape while cooking.

WHIP

To beat rapidly to incorporate air and produce expansion, as in heavy cream or egg whites.

Aunt Hattie's
Southern Comfort
Food Favorites *Cookbook*

ABOUT THE AUTHOR

Dr. Hattie N. Washington's love for cooking started at an early age. Growing up in a family of cooks, she was taught by her stepmother and other relatives the key steps into making a dish. She wants her readers to enjoy these southern cuisine dishes of yesteryear when country southern comfort food meant "healthy eating"-as most all the veggies, fruits and meat were fresh from the fields, trees, bushes; grass-fed, organic, natural, preservatives-free and all the other terms people hear nowadays as society is challenged to eat healthy.

In addition to her stepmother, whom she still misses dearly, Aunt Hattie's two aunts in Norfolk were also great cooks. She would watch them cook, and they taught her their noted specialty recipes that people would come from miles around to eat their food. Aunt Hattie, an aunt after whom she was named, was known for her big pots of tasty kidney beans, big hot biscuits, crunchy corn cakes, hot flapjacks, chicken & dumplings, and her melt-in-your-mouth spoonbread. And, her Aunt Sadie owned three restaurants, called confectioneries back then, sold meals and sandwiches as well as products such as loaves of bread, canned goods and bags of potato chips. But, her restaurants were known for their complete breakfasts, and lunches and dinners.

A selected number of dishes in this cookbook were kitchen tested by a professional chef named Charles Warner, who cooked the dishes to verify the authenticity of the dishes and that each dish tasted the same as Aunt Hattie's traditional dishes that she has been cooking for years. After she tasted the prepared dishes, she felt satisfied that all of her recipes shared in this labor-of-lover cookbook will render the same results for her readers that her family and friends have enjoyed over the decades. Aunt Hattie's marketing consultant, Bruce Smallwood of Mt. Vernon Marketing, took photos of the kitchen tested dishes. The photos appear throughout the cookbook.

Book Cover Design: Bruce Smallwood I CookLook Publishing

CAREER HIGHLIGHTS

Dr. Washington's education includes a Bachelor of Science Degree in Elementary Education with a minor in Special Education from Norfolk State University; a Masters Degree in Counseling Psychology from Ball State University (Athens, Greece Overseas Program); and a Doctorate in Curriculum and Instruction from the University of Maryland College Park. She has engaged in further post-graduate study in Multicultural Education and Special Education at Glasgow University in Scotland, UK (on a Rotary International Scholarship); in Executive Management at Harvard University in Boston; and in Institutional Accountability in Higher Education at Oxford University in London, England. She taught for years in the United States, in Greece, and Scotland, UK.

Dr. Washington was the first female Vice President of Coppin State University (CSU). Prior to CSU, she was Assistant Superintendent of Baltimore City Public Schools (BCPS), where the Vision of Aunt Hattie's Place, a home for foster boys, originated. And, prior to BCPS, she was Program Specialist for the Maryland State Department of Education. She has received numerous awards, plaques, citations and other recognitions for her work with Aunt Hattie's Place, CSU, foster children, and community organizations. Just a few include: Top 100 Minority Business Entrepreneurial of the Year (2009 and 2012) and The Maryland Women's Commission 2018 Hall of Fame Award, honoring five outstanding women who exemplified a "Legacy of Leadership, Service and Excellence".

Dr. Hattie Washington is a devoted mother of two accomplished daughters (a physician and an attorney), proud grandmother of two precious granddaughters, and foster Mother to over 100 foster boys over a 20-year period. She resides in Maryland, where she enjoys spending her leisure time reading, writing, motivational speaking, community service ("giving back"), traveling, ballroom dancing, cooking southern cuisine, learning to play piano, and spending time with family and friends.

To learn more about Dr. Hattie N. Washington's book, *Aunt Hattie's Cookbook: Southern Comfort Food Favorites* and her previously published book *Driven To Succeed*, please contact the author directly:

Author, Dr. Hattie N. Washington
www.drhnwashington.com | info@drhnwashington.com

Recipe Index

Recipe Index

Recipe Index

Recipe Index

Recipe Index

Recipe Index

Aunt Hattie's New Recipe

RECIPE: _____

Ingredients:

1._____   7._____

2._____   8._____

3._____   9._____

4._____   10._____

5._____   11._____

6._____   12._____

Instructions:

_____

_____

_____

_____

_____

_____

_____

_____

_____

_____

_____

_____

_____

_____

_____

Aunt Hattie's New Recipe

RECIPE: _____

Ingredients:

1. _____
2. _____
3. _____
4. _____
5. _____
6. _____

7. _____
8. _____
9. _____
10. _____
11. _____
12. _____

Instructions:

_____
_____
_____
_____
_____
_____
_____
_____
_____
_____
_____
_____
_____
_____
_____
_____

Aunt Hattie's New Recipe

RECIPE: _____

Ingredients:

1._____   7._____

2._____   8._____

3._____   9._____

4._____   10._____

5._____   11._____

6._____   12._____

Instructions:

_____
_____
_____
_____
_____
_____
_____
_____
_____
_____
_____
_____
_____
_____
_____

Blank Ingredients/s & Substitution/s Chart

Ingredient/s		Substitution/s
	=	
	=	
	=	
	=	
	=	
	=	
	=	
	=	
	=	
	=	
	=	

RESOURCES

Blank Ingredients/s & Substitution/s Chart

Ingredient/s		Substitution/s
	=	
	=	
	=	
	=	
	=	
	=	
	=	
	=	
	=	
	=	

Grocery Shopping List

Lists the Groceries of Your Favorite Recipes For Quick Reference

1._____	1._____	1._____
2._____	2._____	2._____
3._____	3._____	3._____
4._____	4._____	4._____
5._____	5._____	5._____
6._____	6._____	6._____
7._____	7._____	7._____
8._____	8._____	8._____
9._____	9._____	9._____
10._____	10._____	10._____
11._____	11._____	11._____
12._____	12._____	12._____
13._____	13._____	13._____
14._____	14._____	14._____
15._____	15._____	15._____

A.	B.	C.
D.	E.	F.

Recipe Notes & Comments

Notes

1. _____
2. _____
3. _____
4. _____
5. _____
6. _____
7. _____
8. _____
9. _____
10. _____
11. _____
12. _____
13. _____
14. _____
15. _____

Comments: _____

_____

_____

_____

_____

Support & Networking

Alicia Perry, Mocha Ochoa Nana; Patricia Johnson-Harris; Monica Chestnut; Renee Starlynn Allen; Diane Smith; Jackie Turner; Debbie Ambush; Tony Ambush; Ruby Burrell; Clifford Burrell; Sharon McCullough; Charlotte Crutchfield; Rev. J. Samuel Williams, Jr.; Rev. Barbara Reid; Joy Cabarrus Speakes; Sherre Atkins; Mickie Carrington; Elizabeth Deza; Jackie Gaines; Rev. Dr. Haywood Robinson & The People's Community Baptist Church; Carolyn Moore-Lloyd & National Council of Negro Women-Potomac Valley Section Coppin State University Family; Peggy Morris & The Sisters4Sisters Network; Dr. Stephanie Myers & The Black Women For Positive Change Foundation; Sharon Parker & The American Mothers International, Inc.; Silvia Silverman & Altrusa International Association

Thank You for Reading!

Dear Reader,

Thank you for **reading AUNT HATTIE'S COOKBOOK: Southern Comfort Food Favorites.**
I trust that you enjoyed this labor-of-love cookbook.

As an author, I love feedback. Your comments about my first book, **DRIVEN TO SUCCEED:
An Inspirational Memoir of Lessons Learned Through Faith, Family, and Favor,** where I
mentioned my stepmom's down-home cooking and recipes straight from the garden,
orchard, barnyard, and pasture, generated numerous requests for me to write a cookbook
and share those mouth-watering recipes. Thus, that was the initiative and the birth of this
unintended beautiful award-winning cookbook. **YAY!**

This **"Aunt Hattie's Cookbook:"** and my **"DRIVEN TO SUCCEED:..."** memoir are available
in paperback, hardback, and in e-book formats. An audiobook of the **"DRIVEN TO
SUCCEED:"** book will be coming soon.

Also, the **"DRIVEN TO SUCCEED..."** book has been translated into Spanish
("DETERMINADA A TRIUNFAR:...") and is also available in the paperback, hardcopy, and
e-book. If you like what you read about this cookbook and my other books, I positively love
to hear from you; find out what you learned, or better yet, you can post a photo, or a video,
of you and my book on my Facebook page:

https://facebook.com/drhattienwashington.

However, if you find any mistake or error in my book/s and want to let me know or make a
suggestion, I welcome it; and ask you to send me an email at **info@drhnwashington.com.**

Lastly, if you are so inclined after reading one of my books, I would love it if you would
"Follow" me and write me a Review on my Author's Page on Amazon:
https://amazon.com/author/drhnwashington.

Thanks again for reading my books and for providing me with your helpful feedback.
In gratitude,

Aunt Hattie (Hattie N. Washington)

www.drhnwashington.com.

Printed in the USA
CPSIA information can be obtained
at www.ICGtesting.com
LVHW060206060124
768269LV00013B/1034

9 781950 707010